Fix the Pumps

Darcy S. O'Neil

Copyright

Written and Designed by Darcy S. O'Neil
Cover Art by Craig Mrusek

ISBN-13: 978-0-9811759-1-1

Designed with Corel Ventura

Table of Contents

Acknowledgements

Without the efforts of the following people this book would have never been completed. A special thanks to everyone who helped and especially:

Caroline O'Neil, my wife, for sacrificing a significant amount of her time to allow me to write this book. For helping edit the book while being the primary motivator, critic and realist during the writing process. And for watching our two young children, Fionn and Ciara, while I wrote in peace and tranquillity in my office.

My parents, Ted and Jane O'Neil, and my two sisters Kathleen and Megan. If I was the unchallenged ruler of the universe, they would still keep my ego in check.

Craig Mrusek (www.cm-id.com) for designing the book's cover art. Remember, a book is judged by its cover, so getting a great designer helps immensely.

Gabe Szaszko for assistance with editing and helping to focus the content.

Getting this far into the world of drinks would not have been possible without the backing of the core group of cocktail and spirits bloggers. Even though they didn't directly contribute to the book, they created the environment for it to flourish. There are too many names to list, but thanks to all.

Also, a thanks goes out to the traditional drink writers for creating the books that get people interested in this topic. Ted "Dr. Cocktail" Haigh, Jeff "Beachbum" Berry, Gary "Gaz" Regan, Dave Wondrich, Wayne Curtis, Dale DeGroff and Stephen Beaumont.

About the Author

Darcy S. O'Neil was born in Sarnia, Ontario and spent many of those years living near the beach. A cold Canadian beach, but a beach none-the-less. After high school, the decision of a career choice was whittled down to chemistry or the culinary arts. Chemistry was the winner. At the time it seemed logical that laboratory skills were more transferable to the kitchen than cooking skills to the lab. Four years later he received his diploma in chemistry.

After a six year stint working in a world class oil and gas research facility, the time for change arrived, via a downsizing notice. After a couple of false starts in the pharmaceutical and information technology worlds the possibility of going to chef school returned. During a period of quiet contemplation, and a few drinks, he was whacked with the epiphany stick and the marriage of chemistry and bartending dawned upon him.

With a little research into the world of mixology, and a completely stocked home bar, that rivalled many restaurants, and irritated his wife with all the clutter, the fusion of science and art began. As he rifled through the classic drinks and modern interpretations—plus the occasional vile concoction—the chemistry skills started to refine the art. A whole new world of experimental flavours opened up in a way that satisfied his experimental curiosity and his culinary cravings. A bartender was born.

With this new found knowledge Darcy set about looking for a place to apply these new skills. His optimism was soon dashed when he discovered that very few bars shared his passion for fine drinks. Darcy bided his time, learned the ropes, while trying to make the best of a poor situation. At every turn Darcy would try to make a poor cocktail slightly better, and eventually people started to notice. The bar managers lacked Darcy's vision, even though customers enjoyed the improvements. This would lead to a string of resignations, and on a couple of occasions, outright termination. Darcy tenaciously stuck to his principals, even in the face of pending unemployment.

To find a place of acceptance, Darcy turned to the Internet and started writing about tasteful cocktail on his website, Art of Drink. It started slowly with a few people taking notice. Then more people latched on when he transcribed a copy of Jerry Thomas' Bartenders Guide from the 1887, and placed it on his website. From there it has grown to over 3,000 unique readers per day.

As Darcy jumped from bar to bar, looking for a place where he could utilize his skills, and satiate his passion, he decided to take a part-time lab job, in a research centre at the University of Western Ontario. This was partially to ease the blow of future terminations, since his wife was never fond of those, and partially because he missed the scientific geekery.

Currently, Darcy works part-time as a research technologist at the University of Western Ontario, bartends occasionally and is developing a line of lost ingredients discovered while writing this book. He can also be found writing about original cocktail creations and other drink related topics at www.artofdrink.com.

Introduction

Mocktail, virgin cocktail, and Preggatini® are all terms for non-alcoholic beverages, and all are drinks men would never order. Mocktail screams out for taunting, guys don't like to be classified as a virgin in any endeavour and a guy ordering a Preggatini was obviously coerced by his pregnant wife.

Whether we like it or not, society has picked some regretful names for non-alcoholic beverages. However, there is one non-intoxicating drink that is an American institution. Millions of people fondly remember ordering this drink and having it served to them by a Jerk. No one chastises a person for ordering and enjoying one. The American soda was the alternative for abstainers. Unfortunately, Americans have passively allowed their unique culinary creation to fade into the past.

Carbonated beverages are a resounding success, with Americans drinking 13 billion gallons (58 billion litres) of soda-pop every year. That's about 3 quarts (3 L) per person, per week. Americans account for about ⅓ of the worldwide consumption. Considering that the US is only 5% of the world's population, it's safe to say Americans love their soda.

Drinks are one area of cuisine where Americans have been exceptionally creative. The cocktail and soda fountain are both American inventions. They reached their peak in periods where choice, quality and service were the battlegrounds. Today, brand, speed and price are considered premiums and quality is an afterthought.

The drive for efficiency, power and the almighty buck have decimated that creativity and turned carbonated beverages into industrial products of commerce served from a cold faceless machine.

The soda fountain was once an equivalent to the local saloon and the comparisons are obvious. Prior to prohibition, both cocktails and sodas were creative, well balanced drinks but evolved over the years to become synthetic mixtures laced with gads of sugar. Cocktails are only starting to recover after decades of abuse. The soda has shown no such signs of returning to its prior glory. The creative history of the soda fountain is quickly fading away.

There are meagre attempts at resurrecting the soda fountain, but the original recipes for drinks, like phosphates and lactarts, have been concealed in old, forgotten texts. Without this knowledge, imitative ingredients have been substituted into the recipes, but bear little resemblance to the original. The fountains of today are poor forgeries of their historical inspiration.

In 1919, there were 126,000 soda fountains in the United States alone. Today there are probably less than 100, and very few, if any, are as grand as they were at the peak of their popularity.

The only modern equivalent to the classic soda is the so-called "Italian soda". Browsing the Internet creates the belief that the combination of carbonated water and flavour syrup originated with two Italian immigrants, Rinaldo and Ezilda Torre. The story says they began making flavour syrups—with recipes from their hometown of Lucca, Italy—in their San Francisco grocery store in 1925. They mixed the syrups with soda and introduced America to the classic "Italian soda".

This is *definitely* not the case and is actually an instance of revisionist history created by the San Francisco syrup company Torani, whose founders just happened to be Rinaldo and Ezilda Torre. There is no doubt they created syrups, but it is apparent that the Torre's usurped the soda concept from the flourishing American soda fountain. Flavoured soda water is clearly an American invention.

Older generations may remember the last incarnations of the soda fountain, and occasionally some look to resuscitate their favourite drink to briefly reconnect with the past. However, information is limited on how these drinks were made. Most of the recipes were created by pharmacists and kept within the trade. Unlike cooking and cocktails, many of the recipes used pharmaceutical extracts, chemicals and tinctures whose access was limited to the profession.

Other issues, such as the system of measurements, caused confusion. Instead of ounces, grams and millilitres pharmacists would use scruples, grains, and minims written in a cabalistic apothecary script. Many of the recipes were kept secret, for competitive purposes, while others were published in pharmaceutical journals. These journals were rarely available to the public and, if they were, they came with a significant price tag and a jumble of cryptic terms. They did not want everyone to know their trade secrets—that was bad for profits.

Secrets could not be kept forever and many of the recipes were eventually made public, but a large number of them remained locked in the pharmacist's guides and books. Many of these pharmacy manuals saw limited distribution and can be hard to find, but not impossible. Older universities may have copies of these publications—probably unopened for decades.

One of the earliest soda fountain books available to the public was titled Saxe's Hint's to Soda Water Dispensers (1890). It was written by a man named De Forest Saxe as a recipe guide and soda dispensing manual. Prior to this, most guides on the subject were published by the fountain manufacturing companies. These were more like operating manuals with basic recipes.

Saxe published many of his own recipes and techniques for making drinks, a rare and charitable occurrence at the time. In a way, De Forest Saxe could be compared to pioneering bartender Jerry Thomas for his willingness to publicly document the methods most preferred to keep secret.

With the disappearance of the soda fountain, and effective market domination by a handful of multinational beverage manufacturers, drinks like lactarts and cherry phosphate vanished, leaving their stories consigned to the dusty old texts of history.

The vision most people have of the soda fountain is limited to the 1950s movie genre. However, the truly interesting history occurs at the turn of the 20th century and gives a surprisingly different impression of the soda fountain. It wasn't always the family-friendly drink we see today. In some cases, the local fizz counter was as bad, if not worse, than the neighbourhood ginmill.

To understand how the soda fountain raised the ire of the Temperance League and forced the government to draft drug interdiction laws, we need to look past the movie set constructs and explore the origins of the soda fountain.

How It All Got Started

Naturally carbonated waters, from volcanic springs, were well known throughout history and prized for their unique properties. The effervescing nature of the water was an attractive quality, and was thought to be a natural tonic. The problem was that capturing and transporting these mineral waters was costly. Only a few places stocked mineral waters, with pharmacies being the most common.

The stomach soothing nature of these effervescent waters made them a regularly prescribed treatment for dyspepsia or indigestion. The lack of side-effects from a glass of soda water, unlike many other medicines of the time, helped motivate researchers to discover, and recreate, how these gas bubbles dissolved in water.

The foundation for man-made carbonated water starts with Englishman, Joseph Priestley, in 1767. The first discovery was infusing water with carbon dioxide by placing water over a fermenting mash. The carbon dioxide given off by the yeast dissolved in the pure water suspended over top. This would have been very weakly carbonated, but sufficient to realize that it was possible. His research led him to publish the book "*Impregnating Water with Fixed Air*" in 1772.

In 1783, German born Johann Jacob Schweppe used this information to invent a device to create artificially carbonated water. He sold his company in 1799, but his name is still prevalent today as the Schweppes Company.

Artificially carbonated waters quickly caught the attention of the public. Given the medicinal properties ascribed to mineral water, the idea of being able to recreate mineral waters was compelling. Making these waters available to everyone—by adding formulated salt mixtures that mimicked mineral waters from around the world—was desirable for businessmen and physicians alike. These artificial waters eventually transformed into flavoured soda when businesses started adding flavours and sugar to the soda compositions.

Before devices were created to artificially carbonate water, people realized they could duplicate the tingling sensation, though poorly, by combining sodium bicarbonate and tartaric acid in water. This resulted in a glass of fizzy saltwater similar to Alka-Seltzer. To make the drink more palatable, fruit juices and artificial flavours were added. To make the effervescence convenient, the tartaric acid went in the flavouring and the sodium bicarbonate in the water. When the two liquids were combined, it would fizz. This was the precursor to modern soda-pop.

At the turn of the 19th century, chemists continued experimenting with methods of impregnating carbon dioxide gas in water. It still hadn't achieved a level of efficiency that made wide distribution possible. However, it was becoming fashionable to have soda water at home.

Improvements continued until Charles Plinth invented the soda syphon in 1813. This syphon allowed portions of water to be dispensed, while retaining carbonation in the unused portion. This was a major advancement over corked bottles.

These improvements helped, but the syphon bottles still had to be filled at a manufacturing facility, delivered and the empty syphons then collected for refilling. This method was tedious and inefficient, but better than glass bottles.

Aside from yeast or mixing sodium bicarbonate with an acid in a sealed bottle, there was no cheap and efficient method for the end user to artificially carbonate water. This problem wouldn't be solved until 1832 when a British born inventor, named John Mathews, created an apparatus to artificially carbonate water in quantities suitable for a drugstore or street vendor.

Mathews' fountain designs were spartan but functional. They consisted of a lead lined chamber where sulphuric acid and powdered marble (calcium carbonate) were mixed to produce carbon dioxide. The generated gas was purified and then sent to a tank of cool water. The tank was manually sloshed around, for thirty minutes or more, to help the gas dissolve, and then piped to the dispensing tap. These units were sold as bottling systems and fountains. Used as a fountain it was revolutionary in terms of efficiency.

! It is estimated that New York City had over 670 soda draught fountains in 1836.

With the inefficiencies of the syphon bottle removed and self-contained units being sold at a lower price, the barriers to entry were now reasonable. The improved soda water capacity also helped increase the number of sodas being served from a couple dozen per day to a couple hundred and, in some cases, thousands. The lower start-up costs spurred the growth of soda fountains across America, giving it legs and booming sales.

It wasn't uncommon, in the early years, for soda fountains to explode. The process for making carbonated water not particularly safe. The biggest threat was when the pressure vessel holding the carbonated water failed. When this happened, metal, glass and people were sent flying about the store.

These explosions were caused by improper mixing of sulphuric acid with calcium carbonate. Because this was the least desirable job, it usually fell upon "green hand" employees to do the mixing. When done properly the components would be mixed at a controlled rate, producing a steady stream of carbon dioxide. When mixed by an inept neophyte, excess gas would be produced eventually rupturing the tank.

There were also cases of soda jerks falling into the vats of sulphuric acid and improper mixing of the acid and lime resulting in the mixture "bumping" which contaminate the carbonated water with sulphuric acid. A painful drink for sure.

Over time the systems became safer, and in larger cities CO_2 cylinders were being supplied by enterprising companies, so fountains no longer needed to produce it.

John Mathews made the soda fountain efficient, but G.D. Dows made it an eye pleasing apparatus. With the combination of functionality and style, it was now a vital investment for every pharmacy.

This new breed of fountain was decked out in marble, onyx and brass with large mirrors and elegant decorative elements. The best fountains had gold trim with Tiffany lamps and Favril glasswork. They were not the kitsch designs of the 1950s diner, with wild colours and over-the-top branding. Classic fountains were more akin to the greatest hotel bars in the world with classy, dignified decor.

By 1875, there was a soda fountain in almost every city across America. It was now becoming part of the American culture. In the peak of summer, sales were reaching 1200 glasses of soda per day. This was a period where soda fountains gained critical mass and started to compete with the local taproom.

The soda fountain started to gain international attention as early as the 1890s, with cities around the world partaking in this new flavoured beverage. The first European cities to adopt these flavoured seltzers were London and Paris. Even though natural mineral waters were extremely popular in Europe, it was America's lust for sugar that made the combination a success.

The feverish growth of the soda fountain created a highly competitive environment. Not only were pharmacies competing amongst each other, they were vying for customers from the local saloon and confectionary shops. This rivalry meant that to compete they needed to create the perfect drink, at the lowest possible price.

Public houses commanded the drink business for years, even with significantly higher prices, because of the inebriating effects of alcohol. In an effort to compete, druggists conjure up pharmaceutical concoctions that easily trounced the saloons best offerings. Once these drinks were unleashed on the public, the bracer and pick-me-up would never be the same again.

Zaharako's Soda Fountain - Columbus, Indiana circa 1933

People's Drug Store - Washington, D.C. circa 1921

Halliday Drug Store - Salt Lake City, Utah circa 1905

Soda Controversy

The rapid growth of the industry wasn't always based on the wholesome image portrayed by pharmacists and temperance zealots. Many of the temperance groups ignorantly promoted soda fountains as the healthful alternative to bars. They wrongly believed that pharmacists and doctors were altruistic and above profiteering. That idealism was short lived. Beneath the marble counter tops, with the gilded gold trim, there were significant problems. These issues caused the soda fountain to suffer the same backlash that saloons received, and for good reason.

The belief that carbonated water was medicinal put it squarely in the hands of the medical profession and their whims. If served straight, naturally carbonated water was a wholesome, hydrating beverage with no downside. It was even helpful at easing an upset stomach. But the medical community of the time decided that wasn't good enough and began using it as a vector for other medicines. At first, they used the sweetened soda water to conceal the taste of bitter drugs like quinine and iron. Then they started to add more exotic substances.

Prior to the Pure Food & Drug Act of 1906, almost anything could be used as an ingredient in a drink. This "wild west" scenario meant that many chemicals and drugs were used to make soda, often putting the consumer's health at risk.

www.artofdrink.com

Pharmacists, who were actually chemists, had access to a wide array of compounds, and created chemical based products that could mimick natural flavours. This was done because the natural flavour in fruit tended to degrade quickly or was exceedingly expensive to make in the winter months. Competition was also a factor, and lower prices helped drive business.

The most common adulterated flavours were strawberry, raspberry and pineapple. This was especially prevalent in bottled drinks. These adulterated flavours were called essences and were made from a variety of chemicals. For example, pineapple essence was made from butyric ether, acetic aldehyde, chloroform, amyl butyrate, glycerin and ethanol. This mixture created a flavour very much like pineapple. Many people thought it tasted better than the real thing.

Druggists didn't stop with artificial flavours, they also used soda water as a vehicle for the prescription side of their business. A key reason for this was that medicines in the 19th century were provided in liquid form. Pills were not in vogue yet, and pharmacists used standardized liquid extracts and tinctures as a rudimentary dosing system. Since alcohol was a consumable solvent, that readily dissolved many of these organic compounds, pharmacists and patent medicine manufacturers used a good deal of it to make their elixirs, tinctures and extracts. Drinking these medicines straight-up was probably a nasty experience, but diluted with sweetened soda, these patent medicines were probably quite acceptable, even pleasurable. Tonic medicines were well known at the time to contain a significant amount of alcohol. In dry counties it was often the salvation of the drunk.

Pharmacists were well aware of alcohol's intoxicating properties. Many of the elixirs and tonics contained as much alcohol as a shot of whisky. This was popular with both the imbiber and pharmacy. The imbiber could get an alcoholic drink at a fraction of the bar's price because there were no taxes on alcohol-based "medicine".

After alcoholic medicine, the most popular choices were narcotics. These were often called "nervines" and usually contained cocaine, strychnine, cannabis, morphine, opium, heroin, and other neurochemicals. This may sound frightening today, but this was a period in time when tobacco injections, cocaine lozenges, arsenic, and explosives were prescribed by doctors. Morphine was thought to be a reasonable medication for a baby with colic.

It was a common practice for a person to call for a "dope" at the soda counter. Dope was a colloquial term, believed to come from the Dutch "doop", meaning sauce. The English word "sauce" was often used to describe an alcoholic drink, but at the soda counter it usually referred to a bracer or pick-me-up style drink.

In the last quarter of the 19th century, people who drank soda habitually were said to have the "soda habit". This was a derogatory term that implied some form of addiction. In most cases it was true—they were unknowingly addicted to the powerful narcotics present in the soda.

Unlike the raucous behaviour of drunks, persons with the "soda habit" were fairly well behaved. It was only after the withdrawal symptoms kicked-in that irritable and irrational behaviour became obvious. A quick fix at the fountain usually did the trick, but a casual one or two sodas daily eventually became a habitual dozen.

One of the reasons for this excess consumption was the quantity of drug contained in a drink. Narcotics like strychnine and morphine were common, but cocaine was the preferred drug of the soda fiend. The most popular drinks contained coca wine, which contributed 5mg to 10mg of cocaine per glass.

Cocaine is a potent stimulant that increases dopamine in the brain, resulting in euphoria and hyperactivity. At the dosage used in a single soda drink it was sufficient to get mildly energized. It's also enough for the body to crave more, almost like the morning coffee (caffeine) fix, but significantly more powerful.

The combination of narcotic stimulants and alcohol synergistically increased the addictive powers. Once hooked, a person with the "soda habit" would be compelled to get their daily fix.

Today, we know these drugs are lethal but at the time they were believed to be harmless. The actions of the drugs seemed beneficial—compared to alcohol which dulled the mind and made a man sloppy and lazy—with the stimulants sharpening the mind and increasing productivity. Cocaine was a true pick-me-up. For that reason, it's not hard to see why the morning cocktail went out of fashion.

www.artofdrink.com

Soda Replaces the Cocktail

The cocktail was the traditional morning bracer for almost a century, but a significant shift happened in the 1880s. The soda fountain was now the place to get a morning pick-me-up and alcohol consumption shifted to later in the day.

The reasons for the shift are theoretical, but the fact that a person could get a drink containing cocaine would be a compelling reason to switch intoxicants.

A single cocaine loaded soda in the morning was a quick brain boosting beverage, but five to six per day—which was more common—could get a person really "jacked up". This most likely led to chronic cases of insomnia. Cocaine withdrawal also causes tremors, nausea and stomach cramps.

The solution to this problem was the cocktail nightcap. Alcohol, being a depressant, would help the soda fiend come down from the cocaine high and ease them into a night of unproductive sleep. The cocktail was also the preferred method for curing gastrointestinal distress, like dyspepsia, making it a logical choice to settle the stomach after a day of cocaine abuse.

The cycling of stimulant drugs in the morning and depressants in the evening was a better fit for the "brain" workers like accountants, politicians and lawyers. Cocaine was a heaven-sent hangover remedy as well. Once trapped in the cycle it would have been extremely difficult to extract oneself from addiction.

The change in the drinking habits was noticed by a number of newspapers, which reported on the decline in bar-room patrons. The Boston Daily Globe (July 21, 1885) had an article that almost celebrated the decline of men in saloons. The success is credited to the "temperance beverages" that "robs bar-rooms of a great many customers". The Knoxville Journal (August 21, 1894) reports on the Passing of the Saloon where the drink habit change was noted by bartenders. The switch was credited to the maturing or evolution of the American drinker to the more civilized habits of the European imbiber.

The most likely cause was not an evolutionary step, nor the will of man, but the direct result of powerful narcotics being sold at a much lower price than alcohol. These "temperance beverages" were far more powerful than anything at the local saloon. The drunk had now become a druggie.

Price was another factor working against cocktails. In June 1885, the price of a cocktail in New York was 15¢ for a basic drink and 50¢ for the fanciest. A typical soda, like Coca-Cola, could be had for 5¢ or less—cocaine included. The main price difference was tax. Alcohol was taxed heavily whereas sodas were not.

It soon became obvious that soda "narc-tails" were not the answer for teetotallers. But, pharmacists had a solid business model—and university degrees—so bowing to the will of the less educated, sober minority was not a consideration.

With pharmacies earning significant income from the beverage side of their business, and the government complacent about the use of narcotics, a new battle front opened up for the abstainers in their ceaseless, puritanical crusade.

The Temperance League regularly declared war upon soda fountains and the medical fraternity for their evil nostrums and drug laced preparations. Druggists used a wide variety of substances in their sodas, many harmless and many medically effective, but the temperance movement considered anything they didn't understand as evil. Some of them believed that plain soda water was intoxicating.

They went to great lengths to shut down these establishments, including the invocation of long forgotten "Blue Laws" and publishing soda fountain "black lists". These actions were only mildly effective, and it wasn't until the first decade of the 20th century when the government began to regulate the sale of narcotics, that soda fountains became the temperance oasis abstainers once dreamt about.

The 1900s were a tumultuous time for the soda fountain. The Pure Food and Drug Act was implemented in 1906, which restricted the use of many ingredients in soda formulations. This put a serious dent in the pharmacist's business and took away their medical monopoly on many tonic sodas.

After the invocation of the Pure Food and Drug Act, the medical community began straightening themselves out. There was a concerted effort between doctors and pharmacists to weed out those who peddled and prescribed all manner of miracle cures. This banished many of the "patent medicines" from the shelves of the pharmacy, along with the alcohol most of them contained. This trimmed the sales of medicinal sodas as it was no longer professional to sell Calisaya cordial as a medicine, since it was more akin to what the local saloon was dispensing.

Soda Health & Hygiene

As people became aware of the chemical dangers present in a glass of soda, the medical community began pointing out other dangers, like communicable diseases and bacteria contamination. Most people were ignorant of the detrimental health effects of sharing their drinkware with one thousand strangers. Health inspections were non-existent until the 20th century and fountain operators rarely cared.

The cleanliness of early soda fountains would be considered revolting by most people today. The soda syrups were usually made in a dirty basement or barn, where conditions were deplorable. Spillage from syrup bottles created thick layers of bacterial growth medium under the counters. Glasses were typically washed by rinsing them in a bucket of cold water, and then dried with a well soiled cloth. Detergents were rarely used in the 1800s, and the water wasn't changed until—as the Dallas Morning News described in 1922—it was "syrupy". The glassware in these places was often referred to as "railway drinking cups" for obvious reasons.

The best stores used running water. They would plug the sink and allow the water to run continuously into the overflow, ensuring fresh water was used to rinse every glass. This had been advocated for decades, but not everyone had access to a city water supply nor the motivation to invest in proper sinks.

The increased production of bottled soda presented further problems. The bottles were reused as many times as possible, but were rarely given a thorough cleaning. Once used, the bottles were stacked behind the shop for days, being exposed to all manner of contamination and "growth". At best, the bottles may have been rinsed with a cleaning solution, but many times they were just refilled.

It didn't go unrecognized in the communities that the bottles and glassware were not of pristine cleanliness. There was even a movement in the 1910's to abolish the soda glass and pop bottle because of the hygiene issues. It was suggested that paper cups replace all manner of glassware and, as we see today, it happened.

Even the soda jerks were under scrutiny from the health department. In the 1920s it was proposed that all soda jerks should undergo a medical check-up to ensure they were disease free. This idea didn't pass, but the medical officers were fixated on improving the hygiene of soda fountains.

The Great War, a luxury tax, refrigeration, bottles, disease and the battle against medical quackery were the final nails in the traditional soda fountain's coffin.

The war created strains on sugar supplies making it hard for syrup makers to negotiate a reasonable price, thus increasing the cost of a soda.

> ! In 1911 there were 100,000+ soda fountains in America, serving 8 billion drinks yearly.

After the war, there was no relief. The government implemented a luxury tax on May 1, 1919 to pay for the war effort. The tax directly targeted the soda fountain. A soda that cost 5¢ was now 6¢. A milkshake that was 10¢ was now 11¢, and a drink that cost 15¢ now had an additional 2¢ tacked onto the price.

The tax was not applicable to bottled beverages, as there was another tax applied at the manufacturing level. Most manufactures absorbed the costs and refused to increase their prices. This created a huge demand for bottled soda.

The combination of lower bottle prices and rapidly improving refrigeration units made every corner store capable of competing with the soda fountain.

These factors forced soda fountains to rethink their business model. It became obvious that serving just soda and ice cream was only marginally profitable. Many of the owners began adding additional services, including food. This eventually evolved into the diners many wrongly envision as a traditional soda fountain.

> ! In 1926 it was estimated that over 20 billion bottled drinks were consumed yearly in America

The soda fountain's death writ was delayed by prohibition. Once prohibition was repealed in the 1930s, adults abandoned the soda fountain and went back to the bar. The new breed of soda fountain / corner store / diner was now the domain of school kids and a dwindling number of abstainers.

The fountains demise was once again forestalled with the second World War. Alcohol was harder to access because of the war effort, so people returned to soda fountains to bide their time until the war ended. This was the final reprieve and within 20 years the soda fountain was on the critically endangered list.

www.artofdrink.com

The 1950s saw soda move into the mainstream business world. It was now a basic necessity at restaurants, theatres and bars. The drive thru diner was dishing out the malted milkshakes and banana splits as well as, or better than, the local drugstore. This happened because soda was no longer a vehicle for medicine, and technological advances made it easy for any business to install a soda fountain. With the increased competition, convenience of bottles and the invention of the aluminium can in 1957, pharmacists began jettisoning their fountains.

> ! In 1892, the average person drank 12 bottles of soda per year, by the 1960s it was over 400.

By the 1960s, many pharmacies had closed their soda fountains and were focussing solely on the professional side of the business. A Los Angeles Times article (Vanishing Soda Fountain Marks Decline of American Institution, August 15, 1967) reported that many felt the fountains were a "dangerous distraction" that interfered with the prescription business. The increased potency of the drugs and the advancement of pharmacy services were seen as requiring the pharmacist's full attention. Other cited reasons for the closures included "creating hangouts for youths who could pilfer or disturb operations", finding reliable waitresses and maintenance costs of the fountain.

In 1965, pop bottles were being dispensed from vending machines making soda available everywhere. The convenience of a self-serve soda dispenser made the ramshackle soda fountain look utterly antiquated.

With that, the vibrant story of the soda fountain was relegated to the history books.

Radioactive Beverages

In 1911, Herbert Hewitt, of London, England was granted a patent from the United States Patent Office for a method "rendering mineral or aerated artificial saline waters, cordials, quinine concoctions, bitters and similar preparations radio-active" using radium.

In the early 1900's, the effects of radioactivity were not well understood. However, it was known that natural mineral springs had background levels of radiation, which many physicians thought were responsible for the associated healing properties. Incorporating radium and other radioactive elements into beverages and patent medicines wasn't uncommon during this period. The use of these elements was labelled as "radioactive quackery" once people became aware of the deadly reality of radiation exposure.

Frederick Patton, President,
Edward A. Warne, Vice-President,

H. H. Reed, Treasurer,
Wm. D. Frismuth, Jr., Secretary.

Philadelphia Soda Fountain Company,

[Successors of E. C. THOMPSON,]

140 S. Fourth Street, Philadelphia, Pa.,

MANUFACTURERS OF

PORTABLE SODA FOUNTAINS,

LONG'S PATENT, GREATLY IMPROVED.

Triple Silver-Plated. Price, $150.

In presenting LONG'S PORTABLE SODA FOUNTAIN, *for 1875, we are putting upon the market the most perfect Fountain for* Beauty of Finish, Style, Durability, Labor-saving, Economy, and Safety, *ever manufactured.*

These Fountains are Triple Silver-Plated, *inside and out, highly finished, and are an ornament to any counter. They are about one foot in diameter, and over two feet in height.*

The Soda Water is manufactured in this Fountain without the aid of any cumbersome or expensive machinery, *the entire apparatus being confined to the space occupied by the Fountain, as represented in the cut.*

They hold about three gallons of water, with sufficient quantity of ice to cool it, and can be replenished at any time by simply taking off the cover and filling up with water, in which the ingredients for making soda water have been dissolved, and which it takes but a moment to prepare. Thus a pure article of soda water can be made and dispensed at a less cost of time and money than by any other process.

The Fountain is charged by means of a lever projecting from the side next the operator, a few strokes of which will charge the Fountain sufficiently to draw fifteen or twenty glasses of soda, and the Fountain contains sufficient water to draw about two hundred glasses.

This apparatus is designed to supply a want long felt by dealers in Soda Water, viz.: **An Apparatus that can be easily moved from place to place, and at the same time, Capable of Dispensing as much Soda Water, and of as good quality, as the high-priced and cumbersome Machines now in use.**

These Fountains, being strictly portable, can be used for FAIRS, RACES, PICNICS, EXCURSIONS, BALLS AND PARTIES, *as they can be carried in a common traveling-trunk, and set in full operation in five minutes.*

Colder Soda Water can be drawn from this than any other apparatus, by using but one-half the quantity of ice.

As no acids come in contact with any metallic substance whatever, PURER soda water cannot be made by any other apparatus. **The Fountain has no superior as a draught apparatus for natural Mineral Waters.**

These Fountains are sold at the uniform price of $150, *bringing them within the reach of all.*

We also keep, for the convenience of our customers, **Labeled Glass Syrup-Bottles, Tumblers, Silver-Plated Tumbler-Holders, Flavors and Coloring, for Syrups.** For Price List of same see next page.

Send in your orders as early in the season as possible, stating about when you want your Fountain shipped. Address all orders to

PHILADELPHIA SODA FOUNTAIN COMPANY,

N. B.—Responsible Agents wanted.
140 South Fourth Street, Philadelphia, Pa.

The Soda Jerk

When the soda fountain's popularity erupted, the pharmacists could no longer dedicate the time required to serve drinks. However, the fountain portion of the business was a significant source of income, especially in the summer. This meant that an assistant was required, and since pouring soda was thought to be an easy job, it often meant that teenage boys were employed to perform the task.

These young associates came with an abundance of enthusiasm, but lacked the social and analytical skills that comes with age. The image of the soda jerk was quickly cast as an awkward young man, who appeared to find new ways to make mistakes, but made up for it with his creativity, blunt honesty and boyish charm.

The nickname "squirt" evolved from soda jerks whose job it was to "squirt" syrups into soda.

This exuberance made the young men do things a stodgy old druggist would never do, like toss glassware into the air and throw liquids from one glass to another. This element of flair started with bartenders, but was quickly mimicked by the young soda jerks. From there, the teenage dispensers took the entertainment to another level. At the best fountain, it was expected that soda was to be made with a splash of flash.

The parallels between pre-prohibition soda jerks and bartenders is obvious, but the skill sets diverge once past the serving of drinks. A bartender was usually older and many times the owner. The bar's clientele were mostly men, who spent a lot of time socializing at the bar late into the night. The bartender needed to be informed about politics, sports and local events while drinks needed to be prepared precisely as the guest requested, and spillage was frowned upon. There was also the issue of intoxicated guests. Bartenders had a special set of skills for those situations.

A young soda jerk circa 1936

The soda jerk's job was to be fast. Most sodas were consumed within 5 minutes, usually less, and on a hot summer day there would most likely be a long line of customers waiting for a drink. The fountain was generally not a place to "hang out". Once narcotics were removed, women and kids became the regular patrons of the soda fountain. Men might stop by for a quick drink but rarely stuck around. Late nights were unheard of and intoxicated patrons were rare.

Soda Clerk Union

The rapid growth of the soda business created a new category of pharmacy employee that outnumbered pharmacists and earned nearly as much. The soda jerks were such an important part of the pharmacy business that they formed a union to protect their "business" and rights as early as the 1890s.

A first grade soda clerk, working in New York in 1919, commanded a salary of $40 per week. A licensed pharmacist working at a chain drug store was paid $50 a week. The fact that a full-time soda jerk earned 80% of a pharmacists salary, is a clear indication of their importance to the drugstores.

From Bartender to Soda Jerk

In 1919, the *Volstead Act* was passed banning alcohol and bringing the saloon to the brink of extinction. Many people were unhappy with the law, barmen being particularly dysphoric. The Temperance League saw it as a victory and lionized it. The *San Jose Evening News (July 1918)* asked readers to submit new names for ex-barkeeps and saloons. Some of the suggestions were: *Pussybooters, Has-Beens, Camouflagers, Bevo-Carbonatantoriums, Near-Beerists and Fizz Parlours*

People across America realized that bartenders were not the sole blame for the troubles with alcohol, even though the Temperance people were extremely harsh on them. Bartenders only existed to supply the demand. Many were upstanding individuals with families. It wasn't uncommon for bartenders to be teetotallers, because it would have been impossible to do the job long-term in an inebriated state. The enactment of prohibition created uncertainty for thousands of bartenders whose skills were not thought to be easily transferable to other careers.

When prohibition began, there were few places that bartenders could take their skills. Newspapers reported on how bartenders were coping with the change (Bartenders Get to Become Soda Dispensers, The Inquirer (October 23, 1920) and Ex-Barkeeps Shines as Soda Dispenser, Morning Oregonian (July 9, 1921)). Some abandoned the continent and went to Europe, others took jobs as insurance and real-estate agents. Bartenders were actively recruited by these industries because of their large social networks and their natural ability to interact with people. The vast majority ended up working at soda fountains, at least for the first few years. Most of the bartender holdouts believed that people would not tolerate prohibition for very long, and that the Volstead Act would be repealed within the year.

At the same time, drugstores realized that bartenders made exceptional employees. Unlike teenage boys, bartenders were adept at making drinks, versed in the skills of socializing, reliable and took pride in their job. Those traits complimented the professional image of the pharmacy.

A major difference for bartenders was the clientele. The saloon was, for the most part, the domain of men, and any self-respecting dame avoided them. Once the barmen assumed their new positions behind the soda counter the change was obvious—there were ladies sitting at the counter looking for a drink.

One of the characteristics of a good barman was cleanliness. When he wasn't making drinks, he was usually polishing the bar or glassware, with his ever present bar towel. Teenage soda jerks had the opposite inclination, which meant sticky surfaces and less than perfect glassware.

Refined women appreciated the well kept soda counters, and enjoyed the company of a courteous, middle aged, well-groomed, charming, knowledgeable bartender. It was impossible for the squeaky voiced, zit faced, nerds to compete. This was likely the inception of the "new order" bartender whose interest in girls was the main reason for being employed behind a bar.

Hiring bartenders was a boon for the drugstores, even at the higher wages they commanded. Not only did it help sell more drinks to the female demographic, it reduced costs. Having worked with heavily taxed spirits, careful mixing and spillage were always considerations for the bartender. Behind the soda counter these habits continued, efficiency increased and fewer drinks went down the sink.

Bartenders also had the skills that allowed them to serve many people and maintain control. Green-hand soda jerks lacked these skills and were lucky if they could serve two people at a time. A skilled barman could handle the whole room.

Lastly, a teenage soda clerk would often get hung-up with girls who couldn't decide on a drink. As the line of customers grew behind the holdups, the young man behind the counter would get flustered and worsen the state of affairs. An experienced bartender would take control of the situation using his years of experience, human insight and charm to direct the girls to a drink, all the while making them feel like they were making their own decision.

The change wasn't easy, but for many old-time bartenders, who spent their lives behind the bar, it was the only option. The change would have been like going from a Black Sabbath concert, to listening to Celine Dion in an elevator. The lively, unpredictable saloon gave way to the orderly, family friendly drugstore.

Once it became clear that prohibition was going to be around for a long time, many former bartenders began to accept their quandary. Some even admitted that things were better.

A column by Edith Daley (*Whipped Cream for Whiskey is Betterment Says Ex-Bartender, San Jose Evening News, July 10, 1920*) highlights some of the changes bartenders and their customers were going through.

www.artofdrink.com

Morris Jensen, a bartender at a former South First Street saloon, had this to say about becoming a soda jerk. *"I liked the old days best—and sometimes I miss 'em; but I have to admit that things are better the way they are now."* He had observed that customers, who were at times heavy drinkers, now had clear heads, more money in their pocket and spent more time with their family. Instead of going for a drink before dinner, they waited until after dinner and brought the family along. Girls were now coming to the converted bars, changing the whole social dynamic. To Mr. Jensen, these ex-drinker's lives seemed easier and more secure.

The nature of the non-alcoholic drink changed many things. A few too many milkshakes could make a person feel uncomfortable, but they were still sober. Any biliousness was quenched by the sugar and fat content. Over indulgence was more likely to induce a nap, rather than instigate a fight. Drinking with acquaintances became less of a social past-time.

With bartenders accepting the inevitable, they slowly faded away. The former Bartender Unions were renamed the Drink Dispenser Unions and soda jerks were admitted as equals.

It's not that alcohol had disappeared, it was as popular as ever at speakeasies and through the local bootlegger and there were still many bartenders working underground. But the time of the professional, union bartender was gone. For a long period of time, they were dispensers of malted milkshakes and banana splits.

Once prohibition was repealed in 1933, soda jerks exchanged their ice cream scoops for jiggers, but the old bartenders, with their encyclopaedic knowledge, had moved on to new careers. Very few places could duplicate the bar experience prior to prohibition, and many of the classic drinks were no longer popular. America's taste for strong liquor had been replaced by a desire for anything sweet. Ironically, these new bartenders, who originally served sodas, probably played a significant role in this change of taste.

EXTINCT

ACID PHOSPHATE

"Rediscovering Lost Ingredients"

www.extinctchemical.com

DAWNS BREAK COCKTAIL
1½ oz G'Vine Nouaison
½ oz Lillet Blanc
Dash of Bitters
Egg White
Stir and strain with ice then
add 3 drops Acid Phosphate.

Talk Like a Soda Jerk

The soda fountain became such an important part of American culture that the soda jerks developed their own language. This was as much youthful rebellion, as it was entertaining and cryptic for the customers.

A paper titled *Linguistic Concoctions of the Soda Jerker* (*Harold W. Bentley, Columbia University*) published in the journal American Speech in 1936, documented the *slanguistic* language of the soda jerks.

Soda jerks worked in a unique environment where codes or new words were helpful. For example, many people go to drugstores with embarrassing problems that they'd like to keep private. To avoid aggravating the customer's embarrassment, a code word would be used to conceal the issue.

Other words or phrases were developed for entertainment value, while some were internal codes shared only between soda jerks. For example, the number "95" was the code for someone leaving without paying and "13" meant that one of the big bosses was drifting around.

Other phrases were used to make daily banter more colourful, like "*hold the hail*" for a drink without ice or "*shake one in the hay*", a double entendre that got you a strawberry milkshake. The title of this book was a soda jerk code to let each other know they were going to "*check out the girl with the large breasts*", as in "*I'm going to fix the pumps*".

For a period of time, creating unique names for everything was considered part of the job. Today, a few of the terms, coined by soda jerks, have found their way into the lexicon, but the majority have fallen by the wayside.

Adam & Eve on a Raft
Two poached eggs on toast

Adam's Ale
glass of water

Bib
napkin

Break It and Shake It
Put an egg in a milkshake

Axle Grease
butter

Blood
Ketchup

Black Cow
Root Beer

Bar Mop
towel

Baby
Glass of fresh milk

Bronx Vanilla
Garlic

Bird Seed
cereal

Burn It and Let It Swim
Ice Cream Float

Bessy in Bowl
Beef Stew

Bellywash
soup

Belch Water
Glass of Seltzer

Burn One
Glass of beer; or malted milk

Black & White
Chocolate Malted Milk

Choke One
Hamburger

Chemist of Salt Beverages
counter person or soda jerk

Cow Feed
salad

Canned Cow
Condensed milk

Chopper
Knife

Cowboy
western sandwich

Cackle Berries
eggs

C.J. White
Cream cheese and jelly sandwich

Cup of Mud
Coffee

Chase
pass

Cowcumber
pickle

Chicago
pineapple soda

Cream de Goo
Milk Toast

Clinker
Biscuit

Dining Room Lumber
toothpick

Dream
reference to Coca-Cola with cocaine

Dough Well Done With Cow to Cover
Bread and butter

Draw One Black
black coffee

Echo
Repeat Order

English Highball
cup of tea

Eighty-Six
Item on menu, currently not available

Eighty-One
Glass of Water

Eighty-Seven and a Half
Girl at table with legs conspicuously crossed or otherwise attractive

Eve with the Lid On
Apple pie

Freeze One
Chocolate frosted

Fly Cake
Raisin cake

Fifty-Five
Root Beer

Fix the Pumps
See the girl with the large breasts

Five
large glass of milk

Fourteen
Special Order

Forty-One
Lemonade

Fish Eggs
Tapioca

First Lady
spare ribs

Fly Pie
Huckleberry pie

Haemorrhage
ketchup

Fifty-One
Hot Chocolate

Hen Fruit
eggs

Hebrew Enemies
pork chops

Gravel Train
sugar bowl

Glob
plain Sunday

Go For a Walk
take-out

Grand on a Plate
baked beans

Ground Hog
Frankfurter sandwich

Gorp
eat greedily

George Eddy
man who leaves no tips

Graveyard Stew
Milk toast

Grass
lettuce

House Boat
Banana split

Hot Sauce
Mustard

H2O Cocktail
water

Hops
malted milk extract

Hasher
counter person

High Yellow Black and White
Chocolate soda with vanilla ice cream

Hot Dog
Frankfurter sandwich

23

Hold the Hail
soda without ice

Hudson River Ale
water

Ice the Rice
Rice pudding with ice cream

Inhale
drink

In
any soda

Italian Hurricane
Spaghetti with garlic

Hot Cha
hot chocolate

Hoboken Special
Pineapple soda with chocolate cream

Loooseners
prunes

Lumber
toothpicks

Irish Turkey
corned beef and cabbage

Irish Cherries
carrots

Load of
plate of anything

Let the Sun Shine
Fried egg, unbroken yolk

In the Weeds
counter is swamped with customers

Mug of Murk
coffee, no cream

Mike and Ike
Salt and Pepper shakers

Java
coffee

Mystery
chocolate vanilla sundae

Make it Virtuous
Cherry Coca-Cola

Manhattan Cocktail
Castor oil

Midnight
coffee without cream

Ninety-Eight
the manager

Ninety-Five
customer walking out without paying

Nervous Pudding
Jello

Maiden's Delight
Cherries

One In All the Way
Chocolate soda with chocolate ice cream

Noah's Boy with Murphy Carrying a Wreath
Ham and potatoes on cabbage

One on the City
Glass of Water

One on the Country
Buttermilk

One on the House
glass of water

One Up
glass of beer

Potomac Phosphate
water

One Down
order of toast

One On
Hamburger on bun; or order of toast

Pair
two items

Pest
Assistant manager

Pin a Rose
Onion on a sandwich

Pop Boy
Soda man who doesn't know his business

Pink Stick
Strawberry ice cream cone

Perk
Percolated coffee

Plain Vanilla
Soda man once manager now behind the counter

Pig Between Two Sheets
Ham sandwich

Pittsburgh
toast is burning

Red Lead
Catsup

Repeaters
Order of baked beans

Root Beer Special
Castor oil drink

Radio Sandwich
tuna fish sandwich

Roach Cake
Raisin cake

Red Ball
Orangeade

Sand
sugar

Saturday Night Special
This girl can be dated for Saturday nights

Shake One in the Hay
Strawberry milk shake

Scoop
spoon

Salt Horse
corned beef

Shoot a Grade 'A'
Glass of milk

Salt Water Man
ice cream mixer

Shoot a Pair and Spike It
Two Coca-Colas with lemon

Set Up
table utensils

Sinkers and Suds
doughnuts and coffee

Spoil'em
scrambled eggs

Shoot One
Glass of Coca-Cola

Shoot One from the South
Strong Coca-Cola

Souvenir
stale egg

Shake One
Milk Shake

Shimmy
jelly or jello

Salve
Butter

Shoot One in the Red
Cherry Coke

Spiker
lemon phosphate

Soda Clerk
soda man in first rate shop

Slab of Moo-Let Him Chew
rare rump steak

Slice of Squeal
ham

Splash
soup

Snow Shoe
cup of hot chocolate

Squeeze One
orange juice

Scandal Soup
tea

Soup
gravy

Skid Grease
butter

Spla
whipped cream

Stretch On
Large Coca-Cola

Slab of
Piece of

Spike One
lemon as flavour on phosphate

Squirt
soda dispenser

Stiff
customer gives no tip

Stack
wheat cakes

Sunny Side Up
eggs fried on one side only

Spear
fork

Sweet Beverage Man
Old time soda man

Snappers
baked beans

Sprinkle
Spirits of Ammonia

Thirty One
lemonade or orangeade

Sea Dust
salt

Trilby
ham sandwich with onion

Thirteen
one of the big bosses is drifting around

Toast Two on a slice of Squeal
ham and eggs

Team of Grays
Two crullers

Twins
Salt and Pepper shakers

Twist It, Choke It, Make it Cackle
chocolate malted milk with egg

Twenty-One
Limeade

Triple Threat
Three scoops of ice cream

Tin Roof
water

Tools
fork, knife, spoon

Vanilla
There's a nice looking girl out front

Twelve Alive in a Shell
a dozen raw oysters

Vermont
maple syrup

Vichy Water
carbonated water

Van
vanilla ice cream

White Stick
Vanilla cone

White Cow
vanilla milk shake

Wreck 'Em
Scrambled eggs

Wart
Olive

Virgin Coke
Coca-Cola with a cherry

Western
Coca-Cola strong with chocolate flavour

Yum Yum
sugar

White Bread
manager or boss

Whistle Berries
order of beans

Yesterday, Today and Forever
an order of hash

Zeppelin
hot dog

1063

I NEVER DRINK

BEHIND THE BAR.

Words by Edward Harrigan.   Music by Dave Braham.

I used to own a fine saloon,
  With mirrors on the wall,
The finest class would never pass,
  But just drop in and call.
" Good morning, Pete," they'd say to me
  " You're looking slick—ta-ta!
Will you jine?' " I must decline
  While I'm behind the bar."

CHORUS.

I never drink behind the bar,
But I will take a fine cigar,
Or a sip of Polinar,
I never drink behind the bar.

Like a pink I'll mix a drink
  And toss the glass in style,
"The round on you, a dollar due,"
  I'd whisper with a smile.
" Don,t go home, I'm quite alone.
  You've time to call a car;
Try one with me, oh, don't you see
  That I'm behind the bar!"—*Chorus.*

Oh, I could mix a lemonade,
  A cocktail or gin fizz;
'Twas given out that none about
  Could beat me at the biz.
" You're a lally cooler, Pete—
  A regular lardy-da,"
They'll wink at me and bet a V
  I'd drink behind the bar.—*Chorus.*

H. J. Wehman, Song Publisher, 130 Park Row, N. Y.

I never drink behind the bar. Copyright, 1882, by Wm. A. Pond & Co. Words by Edward Harrigan.

Types of Soda

Carbonated beverages have been around for a long time, with beer and champagne being the most common historical references. Soda water was the freshman of the fizzy drink category and perceived as a tonic. The health factor was very important and one of the key reason that pharmacists opened fountains.

Beyond plain soda water, flavoured sodas were the true driving force behind the fountain. With carbonated beverages, there was an endless array of flavours, unlike beer and sparkling wine. The idea of adding flavours to carbonated water is trivial today, but in its infancy it was a sensation.

Creating new soda flavours was a regular occurrence. They were quite often labelled as fad drinks, but occasionally one would hit the mark and stay popular for a few years. These flavour creations were an experimental outlet for a lot of pharmacists, who liked to dabble with new flavours. More importantly, it was a significant source of income for the pharmacists. If they were lucky enough to become the fad flavour of the month, they would reap significant financial rewards. Plain soda water quickly transformed into a blank canvas for an infinite number of flavour combinations.

Ice Drinks

Today, ice is something we take for granted. Businesses use it to pack extra large glasses to give the impression of value, while chilling the drink to the point of flavourlessness. This wasn't always the case.

In the first half of the 19th century, ice was simply used to cool soda, and rarely used in the drink. The medical minds of the time believed that drinking ice cold water caused serious injury and possibly death. Swallowing a large ice cube was thought to cause spasms of the stomach and fatal inflammation of the bowels. Single pea sized ice pieces were considered safe. If ice water was the only drink available in the winter, small sips 30 seconds apart were recommended. Because of this many people avoided drinking anything frigid, and ice in a drink was strictly for those insane wildmen who threw caution to the wind.

These wildmen were usually found in the local saloon drinking Mint Juleps, Knickerbockers and Gin Slings. Alcoholic drinks were unique, they tasted better chilled, and even better when served with ice, like the Mint Julep. This was contrary to every recommendation of the medical community at the time.

Mark Twain, being one of those wildmen, wrote about drinking ice cold glacier water "until his teeth hurt" in *The Tramp Abroad* (1880) while mentioning America's ice water addiction.

Former General Surgeon of the US Army, Dr. Hammond, was still recommending the avoidance of ice water in 1889. He laid the blame for the chronic levels of dyspepsia and other stomach ailments effecting Americans on their extravagant indulgence in ice water. In 1894, the *Chicago Herald* called ice water drinkers equal to morphine eaters in their addiction, and recommended that no-one should drink it.

To counter much of the misinformation, the *American Association for the Advancement of Science* had to take out ads stating that ice water, consumed in moderate quantities, was healthful. It would still take many years for people to truly accept ice cold drinks, but things were changing.

The real health issue, with ice, was its contents. In northern regions, enterprising entrepreneurs would harvest the ice from lakes and store it in underground cellars. Much of the harvested ice came from contaminated water sources, and people were well aware of the consequences of its consumption. Cholera, dysentery, e. coli and many other types of waterborne diseases were all too common.

The harvesting and storing of ice made it an expensive luxury. Even more so in the South, where ice had to be imported by boat. If a Mint Julep arrived at the table, packed with ice, it could be construed as a grand gesture—or attempted murder—depending on what side of the ice water debate the guest was aligned.

Even though Americans consumed a lot of ice, most of it was used to chill the tanks containing the soda water and to keep the ice cream frozen.

The process for making ice was known, but the efficiency of the equipment was limited. The refrigerants were also toxic because they contained ammonia and sulphur dioxide. However, the benefits of clean ice and the growing disbelief in the injurious properties of ice water helped propel refrigeration into the mainstream. As the 20th century arrived, ice produced by refrigeration became more common in major cities creating demand for even colder beverages.

Lemon Soda

As soda fountains propagated throughout the US, trends emerged and lemon became the most requested flavour of soda. Lemonade was a common drink, so adding carbonated water must have been an easy way to create something unique.

Part of the demand for lemon syrups was due to its use as a base flavour for many medicines. These medicines were served in liquid form and contained bitter compounds. Masking these with a fruit flavour would have been good for business.

Citrus was likely prominent in sodas because the majority of citrus fruits' flavours come from oils. Once these oils were extracted, they could easily be stored year round. Other fruits, like apples, cherries, grapes, etc. perish quickly and lack easily extractable oils. Most of the early recipes for citrus syrups used the fruit's oil, a sugar and an acid.

These citrus flavours remained popular, especially with gentlemen, until the late 1800s. The incorporation of additional "medicinal" ingredients was the key to expanding the flavour range beyond citrus.

Ginger Ale

Ginger was a very common ingredient in drinks and was referenced in brewed beverages for centuries prior to the soda fountains popularity. The medicinal properties of this root made it valuable, but the pungent flavour made it tasty.

Many sources state that ginger ale was created in Ireland in the 1850's, but that information appears to be false. Ginger ale was advertised in Baltimore, Maryland as early as 1818, by J. De Gruchy. The advertisement highlighted a list of artificial mineral waters and only one flavoured soda, labelled ginger ale. A simple homemade version was promoted in the 1820's in an article titled "Ginger Ale" from the Providence Patriot (1821). It described using the sodium carbonate and tartaric acid method of making an effervescent drink. Advertisements for Ginger Ale abruptly stopped in 1826 and didn't reappear for a couple of decades.

Ginger beer was still found in newsprint and the process for making it was very similar to ginger ale. In the Middlesex Gazette (1828) an article (Pacumatic Punch and Ginger Beer) describes the same process for making Ginger Beer as the early version of Ginger Ale. However, most ginger beers called for fermentation. The use of the term "ale" was likely used to differentiate brewed vs unbrewed.

The first bottlers of ginger ale realized, but didn't understand, that the ginger flavour degraded quickly. This resulted in a beverage that tasted like sweetened soda water with a hint of ginger. It lacked the pungent ginger spiciness found in the fresh product. To compensate for the flavour loss, bottlers added capsicum and other flavouring agents in an attempt to duplicate the spiciness of fresh ginger.

 See Page 88 for more information on how to stabilize the pungent components in ginger.

The real growth of ginger ale started in the 1850s. Belfast Ginger Ale was considered the epitome of ginger ales, and other manufacturers strived to duplicate their success. The original Belfast recipe(s) were trade secrets, but many attempts were made at reverse-engineering the formula.

There were a number of flavours detected in the Belfast version, and most written accounts included lemon, rose, vanilla and a hint of cinnamon. A small amount of capsicum was also used to give the ginger ale its characteristic bite. Some synthetic adulterants were probably added, like oenanthic ether (cognac oil), which gives fruity, brandy wine like aroma.

American manufacturers had a difficult time trying to reproduce the Irish version, and many written accounts speak of the failure. Through scientific research it was discover why ginger degraded and left a tepid beverage. The production methods were tweaked and domestic ginger ale quickly caught on.

John McLaughlin, a graduate of the University of Toronto pharmacy program, was responsible for the modern version of ginger ale. It was patented in 1907 and marketed as Canada Dry Pale Ginger Ale.

The inclusion of "ale" in the name caused some issues with the temperance groups who believed it was a genuine intoxicant. Many of the ginger beers and ales were fermented, but the Belfast and pale versions were not. Facts didn't deter the attacks from the teetotallers.

While most ginger ale sold today is of the Canada Dry pale type, stores still carry some brands of ginger beer which has a spicier character due to the use of capsicum and is closer in flavour to the original Belfast versions.

Crush

Some modern soda-pop varieties are labelled "crush", like Orange and Grape Crush, but where did the name come from? It seems to have originated in the late 1880's when soda fountains began using real crushed fruit in fountain drinks.

Prior to the real fruit revolution, the domain of the soda fountain belonged to artificial flavours. Pharmacists were quite adept at working with chemicals, extracts, and synthetic flavourings, like acetic ether, chloroform and amyl alcohol. In the beginning, soda fountains were unique enough that people were happy to just try something new, but as rivalries developed, good flavour became a competitive edge.

We still see this today with good restaurants and bars using fresh fruit, at a higher cost, while large chain restaurants and fast food outlets use prepackaged, artificially flavoured products that decrease operating costs.

It is doubtful that modern versions of soda-pop labelled Crush use real fruit. Like the early days of the soda fountain, artificial and extractive flavourings are the preferred method of manufacturing soda today.

Mead & Root Beer

In its original context, mead is usually thought of as a fermented honey beverage. That changed over time and came to mean a sweetened beverage flavoured with herbs and spices. Unlike traditional meads, these American meads were made by boiling bark, berries, leaves and roots. The key ingredients were sassafras, sarsparilla, and wintergreen (checkerberry / pipsissewa). A quantity of sugar was added, usually molasses, but sometimes maple or birch syrup. After boiling and skimming, it was cooled, filtered and then the yeast was pitched. The mead was bottled while the fermentation continued, resulting in a carbonated beverage.

A recipe from the *Newport Mercury* (1842) takes the basic sarsparilla mead recipe and adds tartaric acid to the mix. Readers are then instructed to add a spoon of sodium bicarbonate to a glass and drink while fizzy.

The alcohol content of the fermented mead was fairly light, in the 1% to 3% range, but it was carbonated. Since the bottle corks were held on with wire, the carbon dioxide pressure increased to the point where it dissolved in the liquid.

There are hundreds of recipes for meads and root beers, and most recipes contain at least one ingredient that helped define the "root beer" flavour. Almost every root beer recipe, prior to the 1960s, used sassafras. Because of the health issues with safrole, the FDA no-longer considers sassafras a safe flavouring ingredient. Today, wintergreen is the primary flavour in root beer.

> New Orleans mead and Otaki were names for root beer before they were just called root beer.

The temperance movement was a very vocal supporter of "soft drinks" like root beer. There was one problem—most root beers were made using fermentation. Once the temperance leagues realized that fermentation with yeast created alcohol they began to demonize root beer much like ardent spirits.

Some companies, like Hires Root Beer, always made their product with extracts and were never fermented. The original Hires product was sold as "powder packs" that were mixed with carbonated water to make an alcohol free root beer.

Cream Soda

The original meaning of cream soda had nothing to do with dairy products, other than the implied quality of cream. Like the idiom "cream of the crop", the term "cream" was used to imply the best, or a quality product. If you walked into an old-school soda fountain and asked for a cream soda, you would get whatever the soda clerk thought was the best. This changed when people realized that sweet cream in a soda tasted exceptional.

Adding sweet cream was usually a competitive proposition between pharmacists playing the one-upmanship game. If a pharmacy offered a basic soda with real vanilla for 5¢, another pharmacy down the street might add milk, or an egg, for the same price. The pharmacy across town would add sweet cream and charge 5¢ to get the business. By all accounts it was a very competitive business and having the best drink in town guaranteed people walking through the door.

The use of cream eventually led to a new category of cream based drinks called ice cream sodas. Originally this meant a float of sweet cream in the drink, but would evolve to mean a scoop of unflavoured frozen cream. The transition happened somewhere in the 1870s with a number of people taking credit for its creation. By the late 1880s, it was the number one selling soda fountain drink and, like any fad, quickly fell out of fashion by the mid-1890s, being replaced by "phosphates".

The other reason for the decline in ice cream soda was profitability. Using real ice cream was expensive, but storing the ice cream, washing the glasses and the time it took for people to drink one, made it doubly so.

Ice cream presented a particular problem when it came to cleanliness because the oils in the cream were hard to wash off using just water. Most soda fountains only had a couple dozen glasses, so having toilsome glassware was not favourable for business. Once the ice cream soda fad was in decline, soda fountains happily accelerated its demise by not serving them, or charging significantly more for one.

The modern version of Cream Soda is a limp blend of artificial vanilla flavour, sugar, carbonated water and sometimes "Red Dye #40". Some independent bottlers produce a better version, but nothing like the original cream soda.

Chocolate Soda

Of all the sodas, chocolate may have been the most important in the Soda Jerk's inventory. Historically, it was the preferred choice of the ladies and young men.

The quality of the chocolate syrup was an important factor. Sure, chocolate syrup is common and every grocery store will stock at least one brand today, but soda fountain syrup was made in-house to compete with the business down the road. Making chocolate syrup was fairly easy, and adding flavours like vanilla and cinnamon gave fountains a unique recipe, and therefore, a competitive edge.

Recipes typically called for either cocoa powder or confectioners chocolate. Using cocoa powder produces better results with soda water, and confectioners chocolate works better in dairy products, like milkshakes, because of its oil content.

High quality chocolate was the first step to a successful chocolate syrup. Since every chocolate syrup includes sugar, sweetened or milk chocolate wasn't used. Unsweetened or bittersweet chocolate were the most common confectioners varieties used, but cocoa powder was still the most frequently used. Cocoa powder could be used in smaller quantities but made more syrup, at a lower cost. The only problem with cocoa powder was it formed a visually unappealing sediment in the bottom of a glass.

A method for suspending the cocoa solids in solution was described in a patent in 1935. The research was conducted to help avoid the not so pleasant pool of chocolate debris forming at the bottom of a glass. This sediment isn't noticeable in chocolate syrup today, because of modern manufacturing processes.

The 1935 patent used pectin to prevent the chocolate sediment. The two keys to the method were to use cocoa powder that wasn't made using the Dutch process and to add pectin at about 10% of the quantity of cocoa powder used. The reason for avoiding Dutch processed cocoa powder was due to the high alkalinity, and for the pectin to work, it needs to be in a slightly acidic environment, with a pH of 5.5 or lower. Pectin also worked with confectioners chocolate, but require the addition of a small quantity of acid—citric or malic acid.

Phosphates

Some of the most popular sodas were those tangy concoctions made with acids. A soda consisting of just sugar and carbonated water was rather ho-hum, so adding an acid caused the drink to brighten up and gave it character.

Originally, soda fountains used only natural acids, from citrus fruit, in their drinks. Lemon soda was the king of the fountain for a couple of decades and its success was partially due to its thirst quenching properties from the lemon's citric acid content. Fountain operators looked to duplicate this refreshing quality by increasing the acid content of their drinks and using other acids. The problem for the northern climates was that natural acids, from lemons and limes, were expensive and had a limited self-life. The solution to that problem was to use a mineral acid, like phosphoric acid, that wasn't prone to spoilage.

Phosphoric acid was considered a general tonic, aphrodisiac and stimulant of the nervous and cardiovascular system. Pharmacists regularly provided it as an over-the-counter pick-me-up or bracer. It was most commonly prescribed as acid phosphate—a mixture of phosphate mineral salts and phosphoric acid. The acid phosphate was served by diluting it with water and adding sugar to improve palatability. It wasn't long before people acquired a predilection for this acid mixture and it quickly found its way into sodas. The belief that phosphoric acid, and the phosphate salts, helped all manner of ailments only encouraged its adoption.

These drinks that used acid phosphates were tagged "phosphates". A number of companies manufactured this product with Horsford's Acid Phosphate being the most common. The mineral salts gave phosphates their unique flavour and the phosphoric acid gave the drink its renowned dry, acidic bite.

Today, cola drinks still use phosphoric acid in their formulation, but most other sodas now use citric acid. It is difficult to find a properly made phosphate, like the cherry, chocolate and lemon phosphates of a century ago, but not impossible.

CADALOQUIAN COCKTAIL
1 1/2 oz Irish Whiskey
A dash of Bitters
A few dashes Grenadine
A few drops Vermouth
Stir and strain with ice then
add 3 drops Acid Phosphate.
Served at the Hotel Cadillac (Detroit, Michigan)

EXTINCT
ACID PHOSPHATE
www.extinctchemical.com

Cola

One of the principle ingredients in early colas was the African kola nut. This nut was a significant cultural, monetary, and culinary item to the African people. Kola nuts come in red or white varieties, and they were used as a stimulant, because of their high caffeine content, but also as cultural signs. When two tribes joined forces, they exchanged the white nut, and if one declared war, they'd send a red nut. Marriage, judicial proceedings and religious rituals all involved the kola nut in some manner. Much like tobacco amongst native North Americans the kola nut was a valuable commodity, with cultural significance.

It seems fitting that the kola nut was regarded with such high esteem, since North Americans quickly became enamoured with this stimulating nut, usually in the form of soda. The kola nut was known among Africans and Europeans, but wasn't widely available in North America until the early 1880's, when transplanted trees in the West Indies and Brazil became a viable crop.

Early newspaper articles described the high caffeine content of this nut, and its unique performance enhancing characteristics. They believed it would become the "beverage of the future" replacing both coffee and tea. Medical Journals recommended it for digestion prior to a meal, and to sprinkle the powdered nut on cuts and wounds to help healing. Even the military looked into the value of the kola nut as a way to improve the fighting spirit of soldiers. A headline in the *Chicago Daily Tribune* (1895) boasted that a kola nut—four actually—enabled a sick soldier to beat a healthy man in a 25 mile tramp.

Cuba Libre

Coca-Cola was a very important component in the Cuba Libre or "Rum and Coke". The recipe is very specific about using Coca-Cola, and the most likely reason was cocaine.

Historians says the Cuba Libre was first mixed in 1900. At this time cocaine was still fully employed in Coca-Cola. Mixing cocaine and alcohol is synergistic, creating a more intense and longer lasting high. It also increases the chance of sudden death by 18 times.

Rum may give the Cuba Libre kick, but cocaine loaded Coca-Cola was the booster rocket that put you into orbit.

Los Angeles Times February 25, 1902

THEY THIRST FOR COCAINE
Soda Fountain Fiends Multiplying

Slaves to the "Coca Cola" Habit. Los Angeles Physician Says it is as Dangerous as Any "Dope."

Soda-fountain proprietors struck a bonanza when the drink known as coca cola was introduced, for of all the beverages sprung on a public desiring variety and change it stands first in favour, and its popularity, instead of waning, is on the increase.

That is what the men behind the marble counters in Los Angeles say. They even go farther and claim for the brown beverage qualities peculiar to those potions which make habitues or "fiends" of their drinkers.

YESTERDAY'S ILLUSTRATION

A well-dressed business man yesterday dropped into a Spring street ice cream parlour, where soda water may be had in all its alluring variety of concoctions. As soon as he had entered the door, one of the white-coated attendants said to another, "There comes one of our coca cola fiends."

After the gentleman had quaffed the coffee-coloured draught in evident appreciation, one of the drink-dispensers volunteered some interesting information regarding coca cola "victims."

According to his statement and those of several others who are in a position to observe, a great many people in Los Angeles have contracted the coca cola habit.

It is advertised to cure you of "that tired feeling" and is said by its habitues to have medicinal virtues that sooth the over-worked mind and nerves. Stimulating qualities are also claimed for it.

It is perhaps not statistical, but the statement is made that three-fourths of the men who drink soda-fountain concoctions call for coca cola. Also, that of these, a large percentage are brain workers.

A young politician of this city, who occupies a responsible position, drinks his coca cola twice a day regularly. He declares that it has become

37

very attractive to him and almost necessary on account of the relief it gives his nervous system. He admits that he has the "habit" but thinks it a very good one, both because of its essential virtues and its cheapness.

THE COCAINE DOES IT

Two or three of the largest sellers of soft drinks in the city were interviewed on the subject yesterday and they stated that a great many of their patrons call regularly and often for the drink and it is conceded by those who understand its nature that coca cola contains a small percentage of cocaine. This accounts, they say, for the hold it has upon its drinkers. It is also claimed that very few women indulge to any great extent.

To determine, if possible, whether the small amount of cocaine in the beverage may be injurious or not, and if so, to what extent, an interview was had with a prominent physician of this city, who is considered by his professional brethren as an expert on questions relating to kindred drugs used as anaesthetics.

WHAT A DOCTOR SAYS

He claims that the coca cola "habit" is a dangerous one to contract. "If coca cola contains even the smallest percentage of cocaine," said he, "no one should allow himself to become a victim of it, for its effect will be similar in nature, though in a lesser degree, perhaps, to that noticed in confirmed cocaine and morphine users."

"If I am not misinformed, the beverage contains extracts from the kola nut and the cocoa leaf, and must therefore contain cocaine or caffeine, which is an alkaloid of cocaine. It is a dangerous drink."

It was also observed that chewing and holding a small piece of kola nut in the mouth would make bitter and stagnant water sweet and agreeable. This led many to believe that the kola nut had purifying properties. Basically, the kola nut seemed to have almost magical properties, which caused a huge increase in its use. The main product was cola beverages, like Coca-Cola.

It wasn't just the caffeine content of the kola nut that helped drive the sale of cola products, the addition of cocaine had a substantial positive effect on its popularity.

Many of the sodas served at pharmacies were called "nervines", which are described as "*medicines that have a soothing influence, and quiet the nerves without destroying their sensibility*".

Coca-Cola was the company that used cocaine most effectively in its early years. The company went from zero market share to the number one soda syrup, and most popular drink ever sold in Atlanta, in the period of one year. People in Atlanta were drinking 12 or more glasses a day—everyday—to get their cocaine fix. Newspapers from that period are peppered with articles talking about the dangers of Coca-Cola and speculated what made it so popular.

The growth of Coca-Cola in the early years was substantial, and the company dominated the south-eastern United States. The addition of cocaine continued to be an issue through the first decade of the 20th century. By this time, many other companies had started adding cocaine to their beverages. In an effort to curb cocaine's use, the government pressured companies that included cocaine in their products to stop.

Companies went from purveyor of narcotics, to distributor of caffeinated soda-pop in 1906. The formulas quietly changed to be cocaine free, to comply with the *Pure Foods Act*. It must have been a very grumpy period in American history.

By this point, the Coca-Cola company was already well established with overflowing coffers. They began—what should be noted as the first signs of decline in the soda fountain business—a series of lawsuits targeting every company with a name remotely close to Coca-Cola. Some of the victims included: Roxa Cola, Ko-Kola, Cherri-Cola, Gay-Ola and Toca-Cola.

The only serious competition to Coca-Cola was Pepsi Cola and even they went bankrupt in 1923. Small regional cola brands still exist, but only account for a small percentage of the overall market share. Coca-Cola is still the dominant company and has been ranked as the #1 soft-drink manufacturer for decades.

Lactarts

This is a unique, and mostly forgotten, fountain drink. Phosphates, with their intriguing acidity, were the dominant beverage for a long period of time. Creating a new product to compete with this universally accepted acidulent was a challenge, but one enterprising company decided to try.

The Avery Chemical Company created a formula using dilute lactic acid around 1881. This product called Lactart—a brown liquid that had aromas similar to yogurt—was recommended as a substitute for acid phosphates. Due to manufacturing problems it would take 20 years before Lactart would see widespread use. The category of drink, called lactarts, quickly attained popularity in the early 1900s.

Lactart was a moderate success, partially because of its advertising as the wholesome "acid of milk". Its use increased during the Great War and World War II. During the wars many of the regularly available acids became scarce because of the war effort. Lactic acid was substituted in many foods and drinks because phosphoric and citric acid had industrial uses valuable to the war effort, while lactic acid had limited application.

Lactic acid was also used in low alcohol beers during prohibition because the acid has the unique property of masking the yeasty bread odours created during the alcohol removal process.

Today, lactic acid is used in many foods as a flavour enhancer.

Hot Soda

Cool drinks were the primary choice for summer, but hot soda was preferred in the winter. These drinks did not have any soda water in them, but most proprietors didn't make this distinction because everything at a soda fountain was considered soda. Most of these "hot sodas" were just hot water mixed with a soda syrup. Some of them were coffee with vanilla syrup, or bouillon with a dash of celery bitters. Hot chocolate was a another popular choice.

EXTINCT
ACID PHOSPHATE
"Rediscovering Lost Ingredients"
www.extinctchemical.com

DAWNS BREAK COCKTAIL
1½ oz G'Vine Nouaison
½ oz Lillet Blanc
Dash of Bitters
Egg White
Stir and strain with ice then
add 3 drops Acid Phosphate.

Egg Drinks

Eggs have been used in beverages for centuries. In China they had Egg Tea and at the saloon there were egg nogs, flips, fizzes and sours, among others. The soda fountain was no different, and since the egg was considered the perfect food, incorporating one into a soda was medicinally sound, and a boon for business.

The other benefit of the egg, especially the white, was how it changed the texture of a drink. Instead of being a thick, heavy egg nog style drink, the egg soda was light and frothy, giving it a unique appeal.

The whites of eggs were commonly used as a fining agent to remove haze from liquids like wine and beer. Pharmacists employed the same technique to clarify their tinctures, tonics and syrups. Inevitably, some egg white would remain in the liquid and when added to soda water it was that syrups clarified with egg white produced a frothier head. By the 1860's, many soda syrup recipes called for egg whites to help create foam.

Egg whites also increased profits because the drink had a significant proportion of air incorporated, which meant they could use less ingredients in a drink.

In 1890, De Forest Saxe, a man who had been in the soda business for over 14 years, wrote *"A Complete and Modern Formulae for the Manufacture and Dispensing of all Carbonated Drinks"*. He detailed many aspects of the soda business and the recipes that made him successful in the book. The most useful information from it was a detailed tutorial on how egg drinks should be mixed. This information is invaluable to anyone making frothy egg drinks.

In 1888, a drink called the Ramos Gin Fizz was created in the city of New Orleans. This singular drink incorporated egg white, citrus juice, soda water and cream. This combination wasn't common in the world of ardent drink until Henry C. Ramos debuted it at the Imperial Cabinet saloon. However, it was all the rage at soda fountains. Soda clerks had been whipping egg-cream styled sodas well before Henry C. Ramos. This likely means that the Ramos Gin Fizz was based on a soda fountain drink like the Egg Fizz.

New York Egg Cream

One of the few places you can order an "egg cream", and not get a perplexed look, is New York. However, this is not the original egg cream found at 19th century soda fountains, even though native New Yorkers may vehemently oppose such as statement.

Prior to the New York version, egg creams were an evolution of the ice cream and egg sodas served at fountains throughout America. The unresolved question of who invented the ice cream soda was a hotly debated topic in the early 20th century, but the cities of Detroit and New Orleans are frequently cited. A similar debate rages about the egg cream.

In the March 8th, 1971 edition of New York magazine, Daniel Bell puts the creation of the egg cream in a candy store a few doors down from the corner of Second Avenue and Eighth Street in Brooklyn. It was supposedly created by his Uncle Hymie in the 1920s and the original recipe did include eggs and cream, just like the milk shakes from the 1880s.

There are others who claim ownership of this fountain creation, but the reality is the New York Egg Cream is a simplified version of the original Chocolate Milk Shake (*Standard Manual of Soda by A. Emil Hiss, 1897*).

The transition from the original recipe to the "adulterated" product—and the one New Yorkers drink today—made with chocolate syrup, milk and seltzer happened because of competition and economic decline.

We know that competition between soda fountains was fierce and price was always a serious consideration. Soda sippers had a psychological barrier at 5¢, so most operators did everything they could to keep their basic drinks at that price point. As economic times grew more difficult, removing the egg, and then switching the cream to milk, was probably quite common. However, it is doubtful that these operators would change the name of the drink, and signage, every time they modified a recipe.

Logical answers are the least entertaining, but attrition probably accounts for the egg cream version New Yorkers love today.

Milkshakes

The phrase "milk shake" was used as early as the 1870s and the word "milkshake" entered the lexicon around 1885. The milkshake may have been a new word, but the drink goes back to at least the 1600s, when it was called syllabub. The only difference being the syllabub was whipped with a fork, not in a shaker. There was also the alcoholic milk punch, eggnog and sack posset. The milkshake was just another evolutionary step for egg and cream drinks.

Modern milkshakes are generally blended milk and ice cream. Others are just soft serve ice cream in a cup. These milkshakes usually come in two flavours, chocolate or vanilla, and are loaded with sugar. There is also the smoothie or the "breakfast to go", which is a combination of yogurt, berries, low fat milk, granola, various protein powders and vitamin supplements.

Speed and efficiency rear their ugly heads once again, turning a once wildly popular drink into a high-speed sustenance delivery device, like the smoothie. This hasn't always been the case, and it was once possible to order a milkshake made with sweet cream, eggs and any flavour you wanted, just for pure enjoyment.

The original milkshake was not a form of soft serve ice cream, nor was it a blender drink. They were made by a soda jerk using a cocktail shaker. The consistency was thinner and lighter, which can be attributed to the use of eggs in many of the recipes. Like the egg drinks, milkshakes were shaken with small lumps of ice to help aerate and emulsify the mixture. After shaking, it was served cold, but never frozen. Early recipes often called for the addition of soda water, which helped to lighten the texture further.

The Cream Puff was another type of milkshake served at fountains. It was a combination of flavoured soda and whipped cream. The drink was made by filling one shaker glass half-full with syrup and soda, and another glass half-full with whipped cream. The contents of the two glasses were poured rapidly back and forth between the two mixing glasses creating a very light, frothy drink.

The milkshake is a survivor of the soda fountain extinction, but what most people think is a milkshake is simply soft serve ice cream.

Malts

Some milkshake recipes included malted milk powder, which would eventually become known as "malteds". The only difference was the addition of the malted milk which was an early food supplement manufactured by Horlicks.

According to the manufacturer, malted milk was created using a special cooking and dehydrating process designed to make the milk, barley and wheat in its composition "easily digestible for children, babies, invalids and the sick". The wheat component lightens the malt flavour, but adds a grittiness to malted drinks.

Malted milk powder can be purchased at most grocery stores, but it's not as popular as it once was. If it is not available, it is possible to make a similar malt flavoured powder with dry malt extract and powdered milk.

Malt extract is the primary flavour in malted milk and is widely available in the homebrew business. Malt extracts vary in the intensity of malt flavour with extra light malt having the strongest malt flavour, since the barley is only lightly roasted. This is best choice for making a malted milk powder.

Mixing one part malt extract with two or three parts of milk powder will give a close flavour approximation. Wheat extract can be added, but doesn't add much to the flavour. This mixture can be used to make a milkshake "malted".

Frappé, Splits and Sundaes

With the fear of dying from an ice cold drink foregone and refrigeration making strides in efficiency, new drinks were being introduced at an accelerated pace in the early 1900s. Part of this trend was the introduction of frozen drinks.

The milkshake went from milk, shaken with an egg and ice, to milk and ice cream blended with whatever flavour one desired with chocolate remaining the favourite. The soda fountain was no longer a place to just get a quick pick-me-up, it was now a place to go with the family or take a date and to nosh some ice cream.

Ice cream became the new favourite at soda fountains, whether it was in the form of a milkshake, banana split, sundae or coupe. Dispensed soda was quickly taking a back seat. Bottled pop was becoming more common and the standard soda no longer had the dopamine boosting narcotic kick they once had. To fill the void, copious quantities of sugar became the drug of a new generation.

The frappé became popular around 1910. They were usually a simple mixture of shaved ice, a flavour syrup and soda water. Other frappés were similar to a snow cone and served in sherbert cups without soda water.

The sundae was the result of laws that prohibited the selling of intoxicating drinks on Sundays. Saloons were required to be closed, as were drug store soda fountains, since the soda was considered a nervine or pick-me-up.

The *Los Angeles Times*, in 1905, puts the origin of the sundae in New Orleans. A druggist, unable to get his supply of soda water, had a moment of creativity when he sold ice cream with the soda syrups poured over top. It was a huge success and he started promoting it as "Sunday drinks".

The story combines two facts; selling soda on Sunday was forbidden, but ice cream would have been fine, and these ice cream concoctions were served only on Sunday. The idea of a shop serving "Sunday drinks" throughout the week would have been typical marketing. As for the spelling, it was probably a spelling error.

The Banana Split came after the Sundae. The inventor of the Banana Split isn't known, but a recipe for a prototype banana split was published in the *Wilkes-Barre Times* (*June 19, 1908*) and was called the Merry Widow.

The Merry Widow was a light opera / play that came to America in 1908. It was tremendously popular and people began naming things in it's honour. The idea to name the ice cream dainty after it originated in Grand Rapids, Michigan.

One of the earliest published recipes, under the title "Banana Split" comes from the *Chicago Defender* (July 22, 1911). The recipe is as follows:

First have your bananas thoroughly chilled in a refrigerator for several hours if possible. Remove the skin from the banana. leaving the skin whole, fill it with ice cream, pour some kind of fruit syrup or maple sugar sauce over the Ice cream. Lay two or three maraschino cherries on top of this if it is fruit syrup, or sprinkle nuts if it is maple syrup. Lay the peeled banana on same plate beside the ice cream if it is served in an oblong plate, or slice and place the fruit around if served on a round plate.

After its introduction, the banana split became one of the most popular items served at a soda shop. Even today most people can easily identify a banana split.

Fancy Drinks

The term "fancy drink" was lifted from saloons, but it has the same context. A fancy drink is something that is more complicated than mixing a couple of ingredients. It could also be used to identify drinks containing special, more expensive ingredients. The main difference between a fancy drink and regular drink was usually the price.

Medicinal Drinks

Seeing as most soda fountains were run by pharmacists, no menu would be complete without a list of panaceas. Many similar drinks could be found at local bars, in the form of intoxicating liqueurs and bitters. However, under the watchful gaze of a pharmacist they were considered medicine.

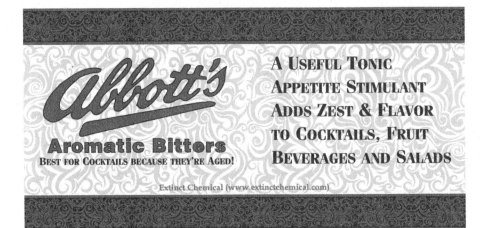

Carbonated Water

The emergence of soda, from a natural curiosity to the dominant drink category, owes everything to carbon dioxide's ability to dissolve in water. Without this carbonation, soda-pop falls flat and is hardly different than a glass of juice.

Carbonation was once the sole reason to order a glass of soda. The lively, tingling sensation of the carbonic acid tickling the tongue was fascinating to the early drinker. Today, people still order unflavoured carbonated water, but rarely ever contemplate or understand what makes carbonated beverages so appealing.

The replacement of the soda fountain with bottles and soda guns created a huge information void. Soda was once the domain of the pharmacist who manually prepared the water for carbonation. One hundred years later, soda is almost exclusively controlled within the sphere of industrial manufactures and bottlers. Even with soda syphons, the instructions never go beyond water and carbon dioxide. Most people think soda water is nothing more than water and carbon dioxide.

The reality is that soda water was developed by dispensers who attempted to duplicate the natural salt content of famous mineral springs. These natural mineral waters are a complex combination of sodium, potassium, calcium, magnesium, strontium and other minerals. These salts are what gives soda its distinctive taste.

Modern transportation has made these "house" mineral waters a thing of the past. Artificially prepared soda water has been replaced by bottles of the genuine article shipped from all corners of the globe. Aside from the environmental concerns, the bottled product is significantly more expensive. House seltzer waters can be made for pennies a glass, and the quality is as good as, or better than, the imported product.

Producing a house seltzer is relatively easy with modern equipment and there are benefits beyond cost savings. The added mineral salts can enhance the flavour of most drinks, much like salt does for food. These salts can improve the fizziness of a soda, especially with the addition of carbonate and bicarbonate minerals.

The carbonates in the mineral water reacts with the soda syrups, which are exclusively acidic, to enhance the effervescence. The chemical reaction between the acid and salts tends to produce smaller bubbles, creating a different taste sensation than bottled sodas. The carbon dioxide production also lasts longer since the solution is sufficiently dilute, which reduces the reaction time of the alkaline and acidic components.

Club Soda or Seltzer Water?

The term Club Soda originated in 1877 as a brand name for carbonated water, manufactured by Cantrell & Cochrane (C&C), of Dublin Ireland. It was promoted as a wholesome beverage that neutralized lactic acid in the blood. In reality it was just carbonated water. The Club Soda trademark is still owned by C&C.

Seltzer water was a brand of naturally carbonated water from Niederselters, Germany, which was bottled and sold as early as 1728. The name was brought to the US by European immigrants in the 1800s, and was applied as a generic name for any form of carbonated water.

There are no specifications for seltzer or club soda and both can contain mineral salts or be plain carbonated water. The terms are interchangeable, but Club Soda is still a trademarked term, where seltzer is not.

Vichy is another term that was tossed about as a generic name for carbonated water. The origin of the name is similar to that of seltzer, but comes from the French town of Vichy, which hosts a very famous mineral spring.

www.artofdrink.com

Modern Soda Water

Access to carbonated water is easier than ever. Plain soda water can be found every-where, and is fine for most applications. The creation of house seltzer may be advantageous because it is significantly cheaper to produce and the physical charac-teristics of the water can be controlled.

The first factor to consider is the size of the bubbles. Taste perception is critically linked to aroma and smaller bubbles pick up more aroma molecules than larger bubbles. However, soda aromas are garish compared to the nuances of champagne, so small bubbles shouldn't be the sole focus. Traditionally, fountains used highly pressurized water that violently discharged from the draft arm. The vigorous soda stream helped to mix the thick soda syrups and even froth egg mixtures.

There are a number of factors that affect bubble formation. The three most impor-tant ones are carbon dioxide pressure (quantity of CO_2 dissolved in water), temper-ature and nucleation points (glassware surface and particles in the water).

Excess pressure in a carbonated water system will result in much larger bubbles. When the carbonated water is exposed to atmospheric pressure (e.g. opening the bottle), the excess carbon dioxide quickly comes out of solution. As the bubbles turbulently rise through the glass, they grow by merging with their neighbours.

Lower pressure produces a finer bubble, but the seltzer water may lack the biting sensation found in heavily carbonated water. Carbonated water can be unruly if over pressurized but the general recommendation is to use a higher pressure, and adjust drinks and equipment accordingly.

Many soda syrups contain foaming agents formulated to produce a head on the drink. Highly carbonated soda water will often lead to excess foaming and the dreaded overflow. One of the methods employed by pharmacists to manage foam control was to add a small amount of alcohol to the water before pressurizing. A teaspoon of vodka per litre is sufficient. This helps to produce a thick, stable foam, similar to that of beer. The alcohol interferes with the proteins responsible for the foam, resulting in a reduced bubble size. The down side of the alcohol addition is that egg based drinks are harder to froth.

Soda fountains with higher pressure can cause rapid degassing by the turbulent action of the CO_2 gas which results in a flat glass of seltzer. However, if tempera-ture and nucleation points are controlled this degassing can be controlled.

Water at 0°C (32°F) can dissolve twice as much CO_2 than water at 20°C (68°F). If the carbonated water is warm, and the CO_2 pressure is high, this will result in very large bubbles. However, if the water is chilled, more CO_2 will dissolve in the water resulting in a slower release and smaller bubbles.

Bubbles can be controlled by using good glassware. New glassware has fewer nucleation points on the glass surface than heavily used and scratched glasses. Every nick and flaw will be a point where a new bubble can form. Excessive nucleation points will cause your soda water to quickly go flat.

 Experiment: Pour a tall glass of soda and add a sprinkle of salt. Each grain of salt is a new point where bubbles can form. The salt will cause a significant release of gas.

Clean water is also very important. Many water sources, even though safe to drink, may contain a high number of very small particles. These contaminants are usually fine sand, insoluble salts and other flotsam. When a glass is rinsed with this turbid water the particles will adhere to the glass creating undesirable nucleation points. If the water source is also used to make the seltzer, these particles will act as additional nucleation points, creating more places where bubbles can form. Filtering is highly recommended for turbid water.

Soap residue can cause havoc for carbonated beverages. Rinsing glassware with filtered water is the most effective solution to the problem. Also, using a lint free cloth to dry glasses and occasionally dusting the bar will help to improve the longevity of the carbonation in all sparkling beverages.

Large Scale Soda Water Preparations

A simple method for producing large batches of seltzer is to use a Cornelius soda keg or Sankey draught keg. New Cornelius 20 litre (5 gallon) kegs can be purchased for about $100 and used ones for less. The Cornelius system was designed for soda and are easy to maintain. The Sankey keg has the benefit of a larger capacity.

In addition to a keg, a regulator, CO_2 cylinder, a few fittings, some tubing and a dispensing tap will be required. A two stage regulator is best because it registers the pressure inside the keg and the CO_2 cylinder. This helps indicate when it's time to get a refill, before the gas runs out. The CO_2 tanks are available through most compressed gas companies. Any restaurant that serves beer, or homebrew shop, should have a list of suppliers.

Original soda fountains pressurized their tanks between 120 psi and 170 psi, which is a bit excessive today. The high pressure was due to the serving temperature of the water, which was about 7°C (45°F). The higher temperature meant less CO_2 could be dissolved, so soda fountains compensated with higher pressure. Water at 0°C (32°F) can dissolve 25% more CO_2 than water at 7°C (45°F). Therefore, excessive pressure is not necessary in refrigerated systems. As a reference point, a chilled champagne bottle has an internal pressure of 75-90 psi at 10°C (50°F). A continuously pressurized system at 80-100 psi and 4°C (39°F) is sufficient to reproduce seltzer water from the original soda counters.

Once the system is pressurized the CO_2 gas will start to dissolve in the water, reducing the internal pressure. This effect is found in soda syphons where a specific amount of CO_2 gas—usually 8 grams per litre—is added to the water. In a continuously pressurized system, like draught kegs, the internal pressure will remain at the regulators setting because the supply of CO_2 allows the water to absorb CO_2 until it achieves saturation.

Carbonating water takes time since the CO_2 needs to dissolve. The process can be helped by keeping the keg refrigerated and occasionally sloshing the keg around. A few hours may be needed to charge large Sankey keg systems.

Removing the air from the keg and water, prior to charging the system with CO_2, is *very* beneficial. Atmospheric air displaces carbon dioxide in the water, which results in a weak seltzer. When the air is put under pressure it is mechanically forced into the water, but when the pressure is released the air immediately comes out of solution because air does not react with water like CO_2. This violent degassing of air causes more CO_2 to be released, resulting in a rapidly deflating beverage. Air is part of the reason soda syphons, charged with cartridges, never achieve the same level of fizziness as bottled seltzer. Removing the air from any carbonation system will vastly improve the quality of the seltzer.

To remove the air, charge the keg system with 65-75 psi of CO_2, turn off the CO_2 supply and allow the CO_2 to dissolve with agitation. After 10 minutes the pressure can be released (pressure release valve) and the keg is charged again. These steps are repeated 2 or 3 times, after which the water can be charged as normal.

It is important to avoid over pressurizing the keg. A standard Cornelius keg is designed to handle a maximum pressure of 135 psi. Even though the keg can handle that much pressure, the tubing and fittings may not. A ruptured in any part of the system will create an appreciable mess.

> ⚡ Boiling the water to remove dissolved air will produce an even better seltzer, especially in syphons

Before filling any keg with water, it should be cleaned with a detergent and thoroughly rinsed. Even if the keg is new, it's still a good idea to give it a good scrub.

When opening a previously filled keg, it is imperative that you *depressurize it first*. To do this, simply depress the ball lock with a long screw driver and wait until all of the gas has been released. Once that is done, you can open and refill the keg.

Choosing a proper dispensing tap is important. The best choice is a soda fountain draft arm. They accurately reproduce the "coarse" and "fine" streams originally used in soda making. Brand new, they range in price from $250 to $400.

There are some less expensive soda faucets available, but they lack the dual control mechanism for stream control. It is worth the extra investment to get a proper fountain arm since the results will be much better.

Beer faucets are an option, and can be found at very reasonable prices. The type to look for are faucets that have a dual stream control found in stout or "creamer" faucets which are vaguely similar to a soda draft arm.

The Wunder Bar style soda guns are the least desirable since they lack the ability to control the soda stream and were designed to deliver the syrup and soda water together. The nozzle velocity of the soda is much lower than a true soda arm or syphon. With soda syrup, the soda gun may not be forceful enough to mix the syrup properly. Extra stirring may be necessary, which can cause the soda to become flat. These gun type systems also lack the ability to add soda salts and other additives to the water, which severely limits flexibility.

Mineral Water

The basic difference between carbonated water and mineral water is the inclusion of mineral salts. Most mineral waters are from natural sources, but they can also be produced by adding the proper proportion of mineral salts to the water, before carbonation. This was the primary practice in the early days of soda fountains.

Many famous mineral waters have been analyzed for their mineral content and recipes published in old pharmaceutical journals. These salt recipes will produce mineral waters similar in composition to these famous springs and they will also enhance the flavour of drinks. The flavour enhancing properties of salts are well known in the food world, but these properties are also applicable beverages. Using mineral water can make a drink taste better.

Compounding the more complicated formulas can be a delicate task. If mixed improperly the mineral salts can precipitate out, creating a hazy solution. The primary offenders are calcium and magnesium carbonate, along with calcium sulphate. The mineral carbonates are soluble in carbonated water, and calcium sulphate will dissolve slowly in large quantities of water.

The process for making the mineral mixtures requires very small quantities of the salts. With basic kitchen equipment, it is almost impossible to do accurately for a soda syphon. Making large batches of the mineral salts and then using a measure, like a ¼ or ½ teaspoon per litre, is the best method for syphons. Small changes in the salt quantities will not be perceptible in the final product.

The majority of the salts used to make artificial mineral water are available at grocery, health food and homebrew stores. Some of the rare salts like strontium and manganese are only available through chemical supply companies and should be avoided. Some compounds called for in old formulas, like barium and borax, are toxic and are not safe for use. They cause gastrointestinal distress, which is definitely not the desired result for a house seltzer. For almost every application the salts of sodium, potassium, calcium and magnesium are sufficient to produce a wide variety of high quality seltzer waters.

....

In the 1930s, 7-Up contained lithium and was called "7-Up Lithiated Lemon-Lime Soda"

....

Mineral waters from Lithia springs contain the element lithium. Historically, chemists and pharmacists formulated artificial mineral waters with lithium before it became a regulated medicine due to its mood altering properties.

There are tens of thousands of natural springs in the world, but only a handful are regarded as table water calibre. The qualities that make a good sparkling table water are a moderate amount of mineral salts, with low levels of sodium chloride and higher levels of carbonates and bicarbonates.

Waters from Badoit, Carlsbad, Apollinaris, Vichy, and Selters all have high levels of sodium carbonate / bicarbonate and lower levels of sodium chloride. In mineral waters like Perrier, calcium carbonate is the main mineral salt.

Creating simple artificial mineral waters can be done with basic grocery store items. Sodium bicarbonate (baking soda) is cheap and abundant, as is sodium chloride (table salt). Magnesium sulphate is Epsom salt, potassium bicarbonate is available at wine making stores and calcium carbonate is lime stone/marble. Calcium carbonate needs to be finely powdered and won't dissolve until the water is charged with carbon dioxide. Other salts may be harder to find but pharmacies and health food stores are good places to start.

Many recipes call for mineral carbonates or bicarbonates. In the case of sodium carbonate you can substitute sodium bicarbonate at a ratio of 3:2. For example, if a recipe asks for 90 g (3 ounces) of sodium carbonate, substitute 135 g (4.5 ounces) of sodium bicarbonate instead.

 Sodium carbonate can be made by heating sodium bicarbonate to 175°C (350°F) in an oven for one hour. Avoid using aluminium pans because they react with the salt.

Using sodium chloride in a mineral water recipe will suffice, however substituting a gourmet sea salt will help to introduce a variety of trace minerals that may improve the taste of the mineral water. Avoid flavoured or smoked salts and look for natural products like Alaea Hawaiian Sea Salt, which contains traces of iron, or Kala Namak which is a volcanic salt with sulphur compounds. Most mineral waters come from volcanic springs, so using volcanic salts is an authentic choice. Remember that high sodium chloride levels makes poor seltzer.

A typical house seltzer should contain sodium carbonate—or bicarbonate—and sodium chloride as the base ingredients. A ratio of 4 parts carbonate to 1 part chloride is a good starting point. Many natural waters have higher ratios of 10:1 and 20:1 and may be a better starting point.

The addition of calcium or magnesium is dependant on the hardness of the water source. For distilled or soft water, calcium and magnesium can be added. For hard water, they should be used sparingly as these minerals are already present, and the addition of more magnesium or calcium can cause a precipitate to form.

Other salts, like sulphates and phosphates, are discretionary but may add to the flavour of the water. They could also be insignificant or negative additions and may cause the mineral water to form a precipitate.

 A simple visual test can give you an estimate of water hardness. Take a bowl of tap water and a bowl of distilled water (bottled), add a small amount of pure soap to each and mix. The distilled water should lather easily. The harder the tap water, the less lather is formed.

Colloidal gold and silver can be added to mineral water for an interesting marketing effect, but little else. They are moderately expensive to purchase, but a teaspoon or two is all that is needed. The gold and silver are not salts, but merely very small particles suspended in solution. Purchase from reputable vendors only.

For practical reasons mineral water recipes usually call for salts that are soluble in water. When the salts are mixed they react to form the proper insoluble salt found in the natural spring. If the solution were left as is, without being charged with CO_2, the insoluble salts would come out of solution, forming a haze. This is done to avoid the hassle of dissolving salts like calcium carbonate.

The reason sparkling waters from volcanic springs can dissolve normally insoluble salts is due to the CO_2 gas already present in the water, which creates carbonic acid. The action of this acid helps to dissolve these salts, but if the CO_2 was removed the insoluble salts would precipitate out.

The artificial mineral water recipes work in reverse to the natural process, with the salts being added first and then the CO_2. Adding salts after charging the fountain is almost impossible. Once the water is charged with CO_2 the insoluble salts dissolve, resulting in a clear mineral water.

When preparing artificial mineral waters, it is important to remember that dumping all of the salts in at once can result in a hazy solution, even after charging with carbon dioxide. Add the salts according to Table 1 below, by dissolving each group of salts used in the recipe in a portion of water first and then add the solutions in order from 1 to 5 to the remaining water.

Table 1: Addition Order of Mineral Salts

Group 1	Group 2	Group 3	Group 4
Ammonium carbonate	Aluminum chloride	Alum Salts	Calcium carbonate
Potassium carbonate	Calcium bromide	Zinc Sulphate	Calcium sulphate
Potassium chloride	Calcium chloride		Magnesium carbonate
Potassium nitrate	Calcium nitrate		
Potassium sulphate	Magnesium chloride		Manganese sulphate
Sodium bicarbonate	Magnesium nitrate		(Epson Salt)
Sodium carbonate	Strontium chloride		
Sodium chloride			Gold Colloid
Sodium borate			Silver Colloid
Sodium iodide			
Sodium nitrate			
Sodium sulphate			
Sodium phosphate			
Sodium silicate			

As an example, Cosmos Table Water was the standard water of the German Mineral Water Manufacturers' Union. This recipe used a two solution system to generate the proper salts of calcium and magnesium carbonate.

Cosmos Table Water

Solution I		Solution II	
Sodium Chloride	1 lb	Calcium Chloride	8 oz
Sodium Sulphate	½ oz	Magnesium Chloride	13 oz
Sodium Carbonate	2 lbs		

Make two separate one gallon solutions using the salt mixtures. To make 10 gallons of mineral water, mix 1 pint of Solution I with 1 qt of Solution II, add to the water and charge with carbon dioxide.

By using the two solution method, the precipitation of calcium sulphate and calcium / magnesium carbonate is avoided.

EXTINCT
SODA SALTS
www.extinctchemical.com

Formulated to match the natural mineral content of springs from around the world.

Badoit - Source Nouvelle

Kissingen and Apollinaris

Health

The increased consumption of salt has led some people to believe that mineral water is a significant source of sodium in the diet. In some cases this can be true, but in many cases it is not. The Cosmos water recipe above is high in sodium (350 mg per 240 ml serving), but others like the artificial Badoit water contain only 50 mg of sodium per serving. That is 15 mg less sodium than the commercially available Schweppes Club Soda. Even though the sodium content is less, the Badoit water has a higher content of healthy minerals (calcium, magnesium and potassium) than commercial soda water.

Making tasteful, healthy house seltzer doesn't require anything special, just some trial and error experimentation. It is possible to create a mineral water without using any sodium at all. Even though sodium free mineral water is possible, that doesn't mean it should be a standard. Most people are fine with some sodium, plus sodium is a natural flavour enhancer. A balanced approach is always recommended and having more than one house seltzer water doesn't cost much more and may pay dividends over the long term.

Tasting Carbonation

It was originally thought that carbonation was a tactile experience. The theory was that an expanding bubble of CO_2 made physical contact with a mechanoreceptor on a taste bud and the physical force from thousands of expanding bubbles was enough to create the sensation. But that is not the case.

On the highest mountain peaks in the world mountaineers gather to challenge their human endurance and conquer some of the most difficult terrain in the world. In the early days, only the most capable people could ascend these peaks, but as we learned about the difficulties we adapted and improved our technological prowess so others could experience the grand sense of accomplishment of summiting a mountain peak.

Many of the inventions included physical improvements, such as better rope, lightweight gear, synthetic fabrics and compressed oxygen. At higher elevations the atmospheric pressure is lower, which makes it harder for our lungs to absorb oxygen, resulting in "mountain sickness" or hypoxia. The early solution was to breath pure oxygen from a cylinder, but this wasn't always practical, considering the extra weight wasn't helpful during the ascent.

For mountaineers who developed signs of mountain sickness, there were medicinal treatments that could keep them climbing. One of the drugs prescribed was Diamox (acetazolamide), a carbonic anhydrase inhibitor, which blocks the enzyme responsible for converting CO_2 in the blood to carbonic acid. An unexpected side effect of Diamox was referred to as the "Champagne Blues".

The obvious thing to do when summiting a mountain is to celebrate. Some people do this by reflecting quietly while others break out a bottle of champagne, the traditional celebratory drink. A fine glass of champagne is a palate pleasing combination of flavour and carbonated tingle, and something we recognize and enjoy. For climbers who had taken Diamox the champagne lacked the characteristic sparkle. Over time people began to realize that the Diamox was the problem. The original theory that carbonation was a mechanical sensation began to descend and the revelation that it was a chemical sensation began to ascend.

Early researchers realized that high concentrations of carbon dioxide gas (>50%), applied to the eyes caused a lingering irritation. They discovered that the CO_2 gas combined with water created carbonic acid. This acid excited the nociceptors in the eye which were reacting to the noxious acid, and not the mechanical action.

The sensation of carbonated water can be considered a response to a noxious substance. Because it is mild in its action, we do not perceive it as dangerous, but embrace it as an enjoyable experience. Carbonated water can be more aggressive and some people find it mildly irritating to drink. However, the perception is similar to that of spicy food which causes the body to release natural pain killers (endorphins). These neurochemicals create a sense of well-being and contribute to the addictive consumption of painful stimuli like spicy food. This same effect can be found in heavily carbonated water.

There are many other factors that influence human perception of carbonated beverages. Research has shown that auditory cues, such as the fizzing sound of soda and the visual appearance, increase the enjoyment of carbonated drinks. But, the primary enjoyment comes from water that is sufficiently carbonated.

Art of Soda Making

The fact that pharmacies were run by chemists doesn't mean the soda fountain was a purely technical profession. Many of the concepts, inventions and mixtures relied heavily on science, but the actual making of the soda was considered an art.

Pouring Soda

Presentation was an important part of the soda experience so a proper pour was essential. Different drinks required a different style of pour.

Some common terms that described the style of pour were "fine stream" and "course stream". These are terms used to describe the rate at which the soda is discharged from the fountain (or soda syphon). The fine stream is a fast jet of soda that is used to mix the syrup and create foam. The course stream produces a higher volume of soda to quickly fill a glass.

Serving "Still"

If a recipe calls for the drink to be served "still", it means to draw a glass of soda without any foaming. The basic method is to fill a 240 ml (8 ounce) glass ⅞ with soda, add 30 ml (1 oz) of syrup, and stir gently with a spoon. The idea is to mix the drink, without releasing all of the carbonation.

Serving "Solid"

To serve a drink "solid" is the reverse of serving one "still". The syrup is added to the glass first, and then soda is added to fill. Most recipes state to fill ¾ full with the coarse stream and finish off with a fine stream. This coarse stream simply fills glass while mixing the syrup and the fine stream helps to release some of excess gas. A quick burst from the fine stream at the start can help mix the syrup.

Nobody likes their drink to be mostly foam, or as they said in the 1800s "too windy". When serving a "solid" there should only be a very thin head of foam, or preferably none at all.

Deciding which method to use will depend on your equipment. Modern systems, like soda guns and syphons don't have a proper mechanism to vary the stream. In these instances you will need to adjust your pouring method to get the results or use the "still" method.

One simple method for mimicking the coarse stream with modern equipment is to point the carbonated water at the side of the glass, to help reduce the turbulence. This will reduce agitation of the liquid in the glass. This is a commonly used method to avoid excess foam.

Equipment

Soda fountains had a lot in common with the local bar and tools and techniques were regularly passed back and forth. The saloon gave the soda fountain the cocktail shaker and bar spoon, with the seltzer bottle being reciprocated in favour.

Soda Syphon

The workhorse of the early carbonated beverage world was the soda syphon. It is still a valuable tool used to make house soda. The benefit of a good soda syphon is convenience and the ability to add mineral salts and other additives.

The downside of the standard soda syphons is they can't replicate the pressures found in commercial soda or syphons filled at a manufacturing facility. Commercially filled syphons usually have the air removed and the pressure is about 120 psi in the bottle, after the water has been saturated with CO_2.

Vintage soda syphon

Shaker

Every soda jerk was familiar with the shaker. When the soda fountain was at its peak, electricity was still in its infancy. This meant that any drink that needed to be blended was done with a shaker. Stand mixers started showing up around 1910. The *Bellingham Harold* (May 31, 1911) published an article, titled *Mixing Drinks Made Easier for the Soda Fountain Man*, which takes a look at how this avant-garde piece of equipment, and its 7000 RPM spindle, are employed to make milkshakes.

The article continues with a comparison of the new mixing method and how long it would take a soda clerk to duplicate using a cocktail shaker. They figured 30 minutes would suffice. The reporter concluded that the new equipment eliminated the hardest part of the soda jerk's job. Bartenders took a different view of the mixer and stated *"they are not mixing cocktails that way yet. What is more, they don't much expect that they ever will."* How times have changed.

The cocktail shaker is still the workhorse behind the bar. Most professionals use a two piece Boston shaker, with a Hawthorn strainer. The technique is easy to learn and with a little practice anyone can become proficient. The three piece shaker, with a built in strainer and might be more convenient for home use.

Long Handled Spoon

The humble spoon is an invaluable piece of equipment for the aspiring soda jerk. The extra reach helps to properly stir a drink—while keeping fingers out—get the last cherry out of a gallon jar, or to scoop sugar without leaning over.

Long handled, or bar spoons are more important today than 100 years ago. The modern concept of serving gargantuan portions has caused glassware capacity to increase from a typical 8 oz (240 ml) glass to the 16 oz (480 ml)—or larger—monstrosities we see today. A normal spoon would be sufficient in an 8 oz glass, but the generous glassware of modern times requires an extended reach.

EXTINCT
ACID PHOSPHATE
www.extinctchemical.com

CALUMET COCKTAIL
½ Jigger Bourbon
½ Jigger Italian Vermouth
Three dashes Acid Phosphate
One dash Angostura
Stir with ice and strain into
a cocktail glass..
Served at the Calumet Club in Chicago

Mortar & Pestle

The most valuable piece of equipment used by druggists was the mortar and pestle. Its use was so common it became synonymous with medicine dispensaries and is stilled used in the logos of various medical organizations.

The primary purpose of the mortar and pestle is to pulverize course substances into powders or pastes. Pharmacists often dealt with the medicinal raw materials and it wasn't uncommon for them to start with chunks of bark, resins and seeds when preparing a prescription. Getting these ingredients into a suitable form required brute force.

A mortar and pestle is essential for making tinctures, elixirs and extracts. Starting with whole raw materials is important for consistency and to extract the best flavour. Using the mortar to crush and grind the coarse components into smaller pieces or powders helps to release the oils and maximize the extraction.

Stone, ceramic and metal mortars are the best for working with herbs and spices. Wooden versions will absorb some of the oils released during the process, making flavour transfer a possibility. Stainless steel and cast iron versions can be bought for as little as $20 to $30, while ceramic variants cost only $5. The benefit of metal is that they resist staining, don't absorb oils and the heavy pestle makes crushing much easier and faster. A large, deep mortar also helps to keep the contents where they need to be, and not scattered all over the work space.

Modern spice and coffee grinders are also a great choice. They are compact and many of them can easily pulverize tough ingredients, like cinnamon quills. Coffee grinders will breakdown faster if barks and resin are ground too frequently because hard ingredients dull the blades and strain the motor. A proper spice mill, or burr mill, uses gears made of metal or ceramic to crush the material and are more durable than coffee mills. The old fashioned, hand cranked burr mill is a very durable piece of equipment and perfect for pulverizing spices.

For longevity a cast iron mortar can't be beat. Not only will it furnish years of reliable service, it will most likely outlast its owner.

Percolator

The percolator is a piece of laboratory glassware vaguely resembling a tall, cylindrical funnel. It was used to extract compounds from herbs, spices, barks and resin using a solvent. The original percolators are no longer manufactured, but there are similar pieces of equipment used in the laboratory and beverage industry. Any large funnel will work if the outlet can be plugged with a cork and the stem fitted with cotton or sand, to act as a filter.

The method for percolation requires the herbs and spices, called "drugs", to be moistened and firmly packed into the percolator. If the drugs are too loose the solvent will run through quickly and the extract will be weak. Once packed, the solvent is added until the drugs are completely covered. As the solvent works its way through the mixture, it extracts the oils and flavours. The speed of the process varies and is usually specified in the formula. Many extracts require a maceration period before percolation, and this can be done in a large percolator or a separate vessel if necessary.

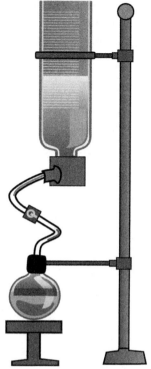

A typical pharmacist's percolator

Percolation is useful for making extracts of a specific strength, or to express certain compounds and not others, based on their solubility in the solvent.

The percolation concept is similar to brewing coffee—the longer the water is in contact with the ground coffee beans the stronger the coffee. Extended contact time has its downside, like the extraction of excess bitter compounds. To rectify this, more coffee beans are used, with a shorter percolation time. This gives a strong flavour but avoids the bitterness. This coffee brewing principal can be applied to almost any extraction process.

Macerating and filtering various materials will produce similar results. However, percolators are preferred when a consistent extract is desired or for finely powdered or dense materials that require long filtration times.

Soda Fountain Admixtures

After carbonated water and flavouring agents, the other ingredients used in a basic soda are simple syrup, foaming agents and an acid. These components can be considered the highlights of the drink. If they are made improperly, the quality of the soda will suffer.

One important consideration about classic soda is that many of the components listed as ingredients were created according to the USP Pharmacopoeia, which is the official standard and authority for pharmaceutical products manufactured and sold in the US. The ingredients did not follow standard culinary recipes.

This is an important fact to consider before substituting a standard cooking or drink making ingredient. Old copies of the Pharmacopoeia can be found on the Internet or local library if the proper formula for an ingredient is required.

Simple Syrup

Sugar in soda was ubiquitous. It was the base solution for flavour syrups and the primary preservative. Syrups high in sugar resisted yeast fermentation and bacteria growth by creating an unfavourable environment. Through the process of osmosis, sugar pulls water from these single cell creatures and effectively dehydrates them, halting any potential contamination.

To make a proper simple syrup, the sugar content needs to be high enough to inhibit microbe growth, but not so sweet that it makes a cloying drink. The viscosity of the syrup is another important factor to consider. Thick syrup is more likely to adhere to the wall of the glass and less likely to mix when the carbonated water is added.

Luckily, more than a century of fountain experience has concluded that a thinner syrup, in the range of 3 parts sugar to 2 parts water (3:2), was most useful. It should be noted that this ratio is less sweet than a typical 2:1 syrup used in cocktails.

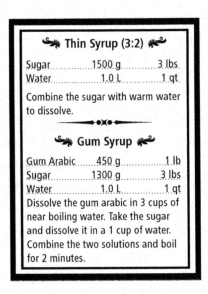

Thin Syrup (3:2)

Sugar	1500 g	3 lbs.
Water	1.0 L	1 qt.

Combine the sugar with warm water to dissolve.

Gum Syrup

Gum Arabic	450 g	1 lb
Sugar	1300 g	3 lbs
Water	1.0 L	1 qt

Dissolve the gum arabic in 3 cups of near boiling water. Take the sugar and dissolve it in a 1 cup of water. Combine the two solutions and boil for 2 minutes.

Gum Syrup

This is a common variation of simple syrup that adds gum arabic, a resinous material from the acacia tree. Its primary purpose was to help produce a stable foam on a soda and improve mouth feel and texture. The addition of gum arabic makes a significantly more viscous syrup, which can cause problems with mixing. The cost of gum arabic is $10 per pound, or higher, making gum syrup expensive. When used in a soda, the results are excellent.

Cream Syrup

When the combination of cream and syrup became the fad drink of the period, the two components were combined to improve efficiency. Cream Syrup a simply a mixture of equal parts simple syrup and sweet cream.

Fresh, unpasteurized cream was originally used and was prone to sour, usually within a day or two. Early recipes called for the addition of sodium bicarbonate to retard the souring. This didn't prevent bacterial growth, it just neutralized the lactic acid being created and covered up the sour flavour. Pasturized cream stored in a refrigerator made the addition of sodium bicarbonate obsolete.

Making Fruit Syrups

Fruit syrups are the basis of many soda drinks. Preservation of the fruit's character is extremely important since quality ingredients make the best drinks. Using the following method, the fruit syrup will retain its character for months.

Standard Fruit Syrup Procedure

1. Select the best quality fruit that is at the peak of ripeness.
2. Remove stems and stickers then wash other extraneous material off.
3. Juice the fruit by whatever method is convenient.
4. Filter the juice through a fine mesh strainer.
5. Place the juice in a pot (copper preferred, but stainless will work).
6. Carefully bring to a boil and remove the scummings.
7. While hot, filter through a felt strainer and place the juice back in the pot.
8. Add 125 grams (½ cup) of white sugar for every litre (quart) of liquid.
9. Once the sugar has dissolved, taste and adjust sweetness as required.
10. Bring the syrup back up to a boil for 30 seconds.
11. Pour into clean bottles and refrigerate.

Soda Foam

The combination of carbonated water and plain flavour syrup creates an unstable, short lived head of foam. Since a foamy head was visually appealing and known to increase sales, many fountain operators looked for methods of creating a stable foam, similar to beer, to improve customer satisfaction.

An additional benefit of a stable foam head is improved sensory perception. The foam helps to create an aerosol of aromatic compounds close to the drinker's nose, which increases the aroma. This has been scientifically proven to improve the perception of taste.

There are a number of food ingredients that have the ability to make a thick, stable foam. Gum arabic and egg whites had culinary uses for centuries and were obvious choices. Other ingredients started off as medicines, like cough syrup, but their foaming and thickening properties made them a perfect ingredient for soda.

Irish Moss, a type of seaweed found in the Atlantic, that contains a gelatinous compound called carrageenan was commonly used. It was also used as a fining agent in beer and it may have been noticed that beers that were clarified with it produced a more stable head.

ᔈ Tincture Of Soap Bark ᔇ

Quillaya Bark	120 g	4 oz
Glycerine	120 ml	4 oz
Water	360 ml	12 oz

Moisten the quillaya with a mixture of glycerine and water. Allow to stand one hour. Pack it loosely in a percolator. Cover with the liquids and cork the percolator exit. Allow the mixture to macerate for 24 hours. Then continue the percolation until all the liquid has passed.

This tincture is an opalescent colour and is likely to precipitate with age. Keep in a cool place.
30ml (1 oz) is sufficient for 4 L (gallon) of syrup.

ᔈ Compound Soda Foam ᔇ

Sarsaparilla Root	60 g	2 oz
Quillaya Bark	60 g	2 oz
Alcohol 20%	480 ml	1 pints

Prepare by percolation. For every litre (40 oz) of syrup use 30-60 ml (1-2 oz) of this compound.

ᔈ Irish Moss Foam ᔇ

Irish Moss	30 g	1 oz
Water	480 ml	16 oz

Thoroughly wash the Irish Moss to clean the salt off. Combine with water and boil for five minutes. Strain and bottle. Use at a concentration of 1-2 tablespoons per litre (40 oz) of syrup.

ᔈ Solution of Gum Arabic ᔇ

Gum Arabic	240 g	8 oz
Water	480 ml	1 pint

Combine the gum arabic with the water, stirring occasionally until dissolved. Use 30 ml (1 oz) of solution per litre (40 oz) of syrup.

Quillaya

Quillaya or soap bark was found in early cough syrups but soon became a soda fountain requirement. It had the benefit of being less susceptible to bacteria growth than egg whites and doesn't impart any off or bitter flavours.

To extract the foaming compounds, a solvent other than water is needed. Alcohol was commonly used, but it reduces quillaya's frothing power. The alternative is to use a mixture of glycerine and water, which produces a better soda foam.

Albumen Foam

The best foaming agent is still egg whites, however some people fear raw eggs because of the rare chance of being infected with salmonella. The reality is that most cases of salmonella come from improper handling of foods. A person is as likely to get salmonella from an organic tossed salad as they are from a raw egg. For those that refuse to use raw eggs there are other options like powdered egg white.

To make egg foam, the white of 1 egg or 2 tablespoons of egg white powder, should be added to 480 ml (16 ounces) of water. Stir until dissolved, and strain if necessary. Do not use heat, otherwise the egg protein will coagulate, creating a lumpy mess while hampering the egg whites ability to produce foam.

Egg solutions deteriorate quickly and they are best made fresh, with very clean utensils and bottles. It should be stored in the fridge. Leftover egg solution should be dispose of at the end of the day.

Serving Egg Drinks

In the book *Saxe's Hint's to Soda Water Dispensers* there is an excellent dissertation on how to make a proper egg drink, which can be a difficult task if you've never tried it before. When made correctly the drink should be light and frothy, not thick and sloppy.

The proper way to mix an egg drink is to take an egg and crack it on the rim of a 16 ounce shaker glass, with the egg falling unbroken into the glass and the shell staying out. Next, add the syrup, acid solutions and other flavouring agents. Traditionally, one or two walnut sized lumps of ice were used during shaking to add mechanical action to help emulsify the contents, without excess dilution. Shaking should be a vigorous action that whips the egg into a froth. It can take a minute or two of shaking to develop the proper frothiness.

After shaking, bring the shaker into a vertical orientation, with the metal part down, collecting the liquids. Open the shaker and turn in a fine stream of soda water, to about two-thirds full (about 10 ounces) and with the following steps this should create enough foam to fit perfectly into a 12 ounce glass.

Rapidly pour the liquid back and forth between the glass and shaker, repeating three or four times, ending in the glass. This helps to mix the ingredients and creates a smooth foam. The two glasses should be close together. Excess showmanship at this stage will also cause the drink to loose its carbonation.

To create a little extra foam, on the last pour hold the metal shaker high, and at a distance, and pour the last quarter of the drink into the glass, slowly. This should only be done on the final pour into the glass, otherwise the drink will foam excessively, and distribute the contents beyond the confines of the glassware.

One of the biggest mistakes is using too much ice. One or two walnut sized cubes is sufficient, otherwise there will be an excess of water which makes frothing difficult. The second error is slowly pouring the drink between the shaker and glass. This action should be preformed post-haste. It should almost be like throwing the contents from one part of the shaker to the other. If done correctly, it should look like a smooth deliberate motion.

Post Hoc Fallacy

The problem with raw eggs is that if a person who eats one gets sick, for any reason within 24 hours, the egg will get the blame. People get sick everyday for thousands of other reasons, but because they ate a raw egg, and they heard raw eggs were bad, it must have been the egg.

This sequence of events is called post hoc ergo propter hoc (after this therefore because of this) fallacy which is based upon the misguided belief that because one thing happens after another, the first event caused the second event. Post hoc reasoning is the basis for many superstitions and erroneous beliefs.

For example, a drought occurs so you sacrifice a goat daily until the rain comes back. Eventually it rains, proving to you that goat sacrifices bring rain. Coincidences do happen.

The Art of Mixing.

The growth of the soda business during the past five years is simply wonderful, and it is fast becoming the principal part of the retailers' business, instead of a simple side issue. The time has passed (and very fortunately, too, for the customer) for a ten-year-old boy to draw soda, and it now requires, to do any business, a first class man in every respect, one who has not only learned to make the syrups properly, but also, what is even of greater importance, one who knows how to mix and serve the drink in the most artistic style, proportioning the. different flavors in such a way that they will not only tickle the palate and please the eye of the customer, but when drank will leave such a pleasant after-taste that the party drinking will surely call again.

I think I can safely say that nine-tenths of the proprietors of soda stands give much more attention to making fine syrups, and a big display of crushed fruits and preserves on their counters, than they do to the proper mixing of the drinks. I do not mean to say that too much care is observed in making pure, wholesome syrups, for one can not be too careful in that respect, but I do say that from close observation I find only occasionally (even at some of the finest soda stands in the country) soda men who are competent to mix drinks properly. The comparison between a good soda man and the ordinary run of them is about the same as that of a fine mixer at a high-toned bar and a common beer-slinger in a second rate saloon. Very few soda men who have worked for me (and I have had a great many of them in the past ten years) knew how to draw correctly even a plain glass of soda with sweet cream, at first, even though they had been in the business before, and some of them for years, and as for mixing fancy drinks to make them palatable, and to suit the taste of the customer, I have found very few who could do it properly.

It is the little points in mixing drinks that are most important, and are overlooked by the ordinary dispenser: for instance, such as too much ice in making an egg drink, pouring from glass to shaker and from shaker to glass too long, making the drink too dead and solid, or in other cases the reverse, making the drink all wind, which will not do. To mix properly requires not only good judgment, but practice under an experienced teacher. I have taken young men to work for me who never had drawn a glass of soda in their lives, and taught them in one season enough about the business so they were able the next to command good wages, and often more than men who had been drawing soda for years for some one else. In giving formulas for my fancy drinks, I have tried as best I could to explain just how they should be mixed, giving the exact proportion of each ingredient used, and telling also how to serve them, etc., etc. Any one with a fair knowledge of the soda business, and a desire to improve all the time, ought to be able, after studying carefully my formulas, to produce the same results as I do, and make as fine drinks as can be made.

Egg Drinks.

Why is it, in calling for an Egg Phosphate or Egg Lemonade, that at about half the soda fountains they will serve you what we call a sloppy drink dead and tasteless? One reason is, the dispenser uses too much ice in shaking up the egg with the syrup ; the other is, he takes too much time in pouring from glass to shaker and from shaker to glass. Often you will see two men at the same fountain mixing drinks, and using the same material, and while one will make a first-class Egg Drink, that will be relished by the customer, the other will produce such a poor, sloppy mixture that it can hardly be drank. The reason of this is simple enough. The first dispenser has learned the art of mixing properly, while the second has not, and, while they both use the same material in mixing, and from the same apparatus, the results obtained are widely different.

How An Egg Drink Should Be Mixed.

First take your mixing-glass in the left hand, and, with the right, put into the glass a lump of ice about the size of a chestnut. Set the glass on the counter; take an egg in right hand between the forefinger and thumb, give it one tap lightly on edge of glass, just enough to crack the shell nicely, but not hard enough to break the yolk of the egg (learn by practice to be able to crack the egg the first tap you make); then open the shell quickly, using both hands (see cut), and allow the inside to drop in the glass. At once drop the shell into a bucket under the counter, and don't allow the white to drip on to the counter.

Next add about 1½ oz. of Lemon Syrup, or whatever syrup you wish (depends, of course, on which Egg Drink you are making) ; then put on shaker and shake thoroughly, in the manner shown in cut on another page of this book. When thoroughly shaken, take out the glass (empty) and leave on the counter, egg and syrup being in the shaker; hold the shaker, with contents, under draught arm (soda), and, using the fine stream, fill the shaker about two-thirds full; then use the coarse stream till the shaker is full. Now pour from

First three positions in mixing Egg Drinks.

71

shaker to glass, repeating the operation three times only. When pouring the last time from shaker to glass, just before serving, while shaker is nearly full, pour fast, holding shaker near the glass, but when the glass is nearly full hold the shaker higher and pour slowly, making a fine stream, which will top off the glass nicely. Next shake a very little nutmeg on top, and the drink is ready to serve.

Many dispensers think they must use lots of ice, which in itself deadens the drink, all being necessary is enough to break the yolk of the egg. Then they often pour the drink too many times from glass to shaker and back again, and, to show off, hold the shaker too high above their head, and too far from the glass, which results in forcing all the gas out, and making the drink flat and tasteless. A first-class soda man throws the drink from shaker to glass, but does not pour it like pouring water from a tumbler into a basin.

It is unnecessary, after shaking the egg, ice and syrup together, to use a strainer, as the ice is nearly all melted by that time, and if you are rushed and time is any object, you will find by dispensing with the strainer, and making your Egg Drink according to my rule, you will save much valuable time.

Second three positions in mixing Egg Drinks.

An Egg Drink should be light and creamy, not heavy and sloppy, and the only way to make the drink properly is to remember: first, don't use too much ice; 2nd, don't pour too long; 3rd, do not use a strainer.

Egg Drinks are quite popular, and very profitable, when properly made and served, but from the fact that there are so many would-be soda men in the business, who know scarcely anything about mixing, and think they know it all, the trade is a little skeptical about trying Egg Drinks, unless they are acquainted with the dispenser.

I have always made a great specialty of Egg Drinks, because they are profitable to me, and I consider them very healthful to the customer. Customers often ask me why it is my Egg Drinks taste so much nicer than at other places. The reason is, I always insist on my new dispensers (whether experts or not) learning my way of mixing and serving, and then I feel pretty sure of giving satisfaction.

One very essential feature of success in running a soda fountain is to be able to mix a drink daintily, correctly and quickly, and the soda men who can do this are worth a good salary every time, but they are very scarce, and hard to get.

Last three positions in mixing Egg Drinks.

HIRES' COUGH CURE

will be found to be one of the most reliable remedies that a family can keep in the house. It gives relief in all cases of coughs, colds, hoarseness. For croup or whooping-cough there is nothing discovered so valuable. Mothers should always have it handy where children are. It contains no opium, morphine, or other deleterious drugs, being prepared from white pine balsam, and pure gum arabic. It soothes and heals the membrane of the lungs, prevents night sweats and tightness across the chest, at the same time it is pleasant and agreeable to take. Can always be depended upon when directions are followed.

Ask your Druggist or Storekeeper for it. Take no substitute.

Hire's Root Beer THE GREAT HEALTH DRINK
864 BOTTLES SOLD IN 1878.
1,941,319 BOTTLES SOLD IN 1891.

0068

Soda Acidulants

Acid Phosphates

In the 1800s, a wide variety of tonics were believed to help the human condition, with phosphates being a highly regarded substance for biological development. It worked wonders as a plant fertilizer, so why not as nutritional tonic for humans?

Parrish's Chemical Food was one of the first phosphate based tonics created in the 1800s. It was an iron and phosphate mixture that was believed to help a random assortment of conditions associated with the nerves and skeletal system. The early formulas were not stable, and tasted rather vile. Eventually Parrish's tonic fell out of favour when more refined products entered the market.

One of these new products, and the real driving force behind acid phosphates in soda, was called Horsford's Acid Phosphate. It was created by Professor Eben N. Horsford of Cambridge, Massachusetts. He taught at Harvard for 16 years and during that time invented a new form of baking powder (1856), using calcium biphosphate, and another product called "solution of acid phosphates"(1857). With these, he started the Rumford Chemical Works of Providence, Rhode Island.

The early method for making acid phosphate was to treat bone ash (mostly calcium and magnesium phosphate) with sulphuric acid. Mixing these two compounds would produce calcium sulphate and phosphoric acid. Calcium sulphate is practically insoluble in water, so it would precipitate out. Filtering out the calcium sulphate would leave a liquid composed of phosphoric acid and leftover phosphate salts of calcium, magnesium, potassium and sodium. This acid mixture would be called by a variety of names, but eventually "acid phosphate" would become ubiquitous.

The method was patented by Professor Horsford in 1867, and then bottled and sold as a medicine, condiment (vinegar substitute) and beverage. Like many products of the time, it was named after the inventor, and was henceforth known as Horsford's Acid Phosphate.

The product was indicated in all manner of illness, including: exhaustion, dyspepsia, sea sickness, anxiety, indigestion, loss of appetite, headache, sunstroke, hysteria, depression, alcoholism, fevers, sexual exhaustion and many more. Surprisingly, it worked for exhausted people as an energizer and also helped with sleeplessness. If it wasn't for the support of the medical community and soda fountains, Horsford's Acid Phosphate might have been considered "snake oil".

Acid phosphates didn't require a prescription, so pharmacists could sell it in an over-the-counter fashion. It quickly found its way into the soda fountain and was served as a nervine or pick-me-up. The perceived medicinal qualities of acid phosphate was useful when competing against the Brain Dusters, Eye Openers and Corpse Revivers served at the local saloons.

www.artofdrink.com

The method and quantity of acid phosphate in a drink varied. In 1868, it was recommended to use one teaspoon in a glass of water, sweetened with some sugar. At soda fountains it was one or two teaspoons per 8 ounce glass.

By the 1880s, carbonated beverage sales were booming. Quality was becoming an important sales factor, and finding shelf stable products was a new priority. Acidulants like citric acid and tartaric acid were hard to obtain lead free, were not shelf-stable and often contained adulterants. Because fruit acids were organic, they would develop mould when diluted with water. Pharmacists considered other types of acid, and many turned to mineral acids, like phosphoric acid, that were not susceptible to mould or bacteria.

Since Horsford's was making a product that already met this criteria, soda fountains began employing it. This was a key reason for Horsford's exceptional growth through the 1870s and into the 1880s. It came to a point where "acid phosphate" was synonymous with Horsford's Acid Phosphate.

Problems began when Horsford's patent expired and high prices made it hard for soda fountains to use it in 5¢ sodas, and maintain a reasonable profit. The solution was competition, and the Park, Davis & Company of Detroit, Michigan responded in 1881 with a similar product called "Liquor Acidi Phosphorici". The name didn't help move product quickly, so Park Davis renamed the product "Liquid Acid Phosphate".

This new name competed directly with Horsford's monopoly on "acid phosphate". Like most competitive companies Rumford Chemical Works launched a lawsuit claiming trademark infringement of their brand.

The court case was decided in 1888 with the judgement favouring Park, Davis & Company. The term "acid phosphate" could not be trademarked because those words were descriptive and indicated product composition.

The loss of the lawsuit opened the doors for manufacturers to create products using those two important words. Rumford Chemical continued to promote and sell Horsford's Acid Phosphate, but they were no longer king.

Acid phosphate had become so common that every pharmacist was expected to know it and be able to make it. Independent soda syrup producers were also including acid phosphate in their products, further straining Horsford's margins.

By the 1950s, soda fountains were backsliding into oblivion and so was the phosphate'd soda. Horsford's Acid Phosphate was no longer being sold and the majority of soda brands had switching to citric acid. This made drinks like the chocolate, cherry and lemon phosphate extinct.

There are still a few soda fountains around, not many are traditional and very few, if any, use acid phosphate in the drinks. Most modern soda fountains use manufactured syrups, that already included the acid, usually citric.

The use of phosphoric acid in cola beverages shouldn't be thought of as a true "phosphate". The reason cola based drinks still use phosphoric acid is that the flavour compliments the cola better than citric acid. The taste of phosphoric acid is described as astringent, dry and sharp in flavour while lacking the bright fruitiness of citric and tartaric acids. This is what made the phosphate class of drinks so interesting. The dry, astringent flavour must have worked well, otherwise they wouldn't have been popular for over 75 years.

It should be noted that acid phosphates are different than pure phosphoric acid because the phosphoric acid is mixed with the mineral salts of potassium, calcium, and magnesium. These salts are alkaline (basic pH) and when mixed with phosphoric acid react to create phosphate salts. This also neutralizes some of the phosphoric acid, making it less acidic. The same principal can be seen when vinegar is mixed with baking soda.

The formula does leave a small excess of phosphoric acid, which provides the characteristic dry, tart flavour. The pH of the acid phosphate solution is between 1.7 and 2.0, or equivalent to that of fresh squeezed lime juice. In an 8 ounce glass of soda water, adding one teaspoon (5 ml) of acid phosphate gives the drink a pH of about 2.5, or the same as a can of cola.

The phosphate salts help give phosphate'd sodas their unique appeal and flavour. The minerals in acid phosphate included potassium phosphate monobasic, a compound used in hydrating sport drinks, like Gatorade; calcium phosphate is widely used in the food industry and is a key element in our skeletal system. It is often found in calcium supplements and antacids; magnesium phosphate is another mineral found in bones and teeth and is commonly used in the food industry.

The use of phosphoric acid and phosphate salts evolved from early medicine, but combined with soda it created a wildly successful class of beverages.

Acid Phosphates with Iron

Pharmacists offered "Phosphates of Iron" as a tonic that helped invigorate the blood and calm frazzled nerves. Iron was believed to be a common deficiency at the time, and taking supplemental iron was considered healthy. It is still estimated that 10% to 30% of North Americans are iron deficient.

Iron is no longer an ingredient in soda, and iron does not add any beneficial flavour to a drink. Flavoured soda waters were originally used to disguise the detestable flavour of the iron salts.

Syrup of Acid Phosphates

To save time, many operators combined the acid with the sugar or flavour syrup. This wasn't the preferred method as the acid discoloured the syrup and caused the phosphate salts to precipitate out. Some phosphate salts are only moderately soluble in water, but are readily dissolved in an acidic solutions, like dilute phosphoric acid. However, sugar interferes by reacting with the acid (i.e. inversion) which can increase the pH. The sugar syrup also has less water, making it harder for the phosphate salts to stay in solution.

Lactic Acid

The Avery Chemical Company introduced a new acid for aerated beverages in 1885, called "Lactart Acid of Milk". This was another proprietary composition, with the key ingredient being lactic acid. In the early 1900s, it was a very popular addition to soda fountain drinks.

It was advertised as a healthy, natural acid specifically for use in carbonated drinks. But like all good products of the time, certain health claims were made, including the ever popular dyspepsia cure. There is anecdotal evidence to suggest this might be true. One of the common methods for suppressing a disgruntled gastrointestinal track was a daily dose of buttermilk. Thin buttermilk is a weak solution of lactic acid and is still considered an effective way to deal with indigestion. Pharmacists also dispensed a compound called Acidum Lacticum, which was diluted lactic acid, for dyspepsia.

Analysis of Lactart concluded that it contained about 24% lactic acid. The formula contained 25% "other" solids, due to production methods. These solids were mannitol, a sugar alcohol, other carbohydrates and albumen.

Lactic acid is still widely used in the food and beverage industry. It has a mildly tart and agreeable flavour. It is naturally found in dairy products, but another example of its flavour would be lambic and wheat style beers. The bacteria that ferments in these beers creates lactic acid and gives the beers their unique flavour.

Even though lactic acid is associated with dairy products, there is very little, if any, lactic acid derived from milk products today. The majority of it is created using bacterial fermentation of sugar sources like molasses, grains and beets. The food industry uses lactic acid as an acidulent and flavour enhancing additive.

Citric and Tartaric Acid

The most common beverage acidifier today is citric acid. It is used in almost every soda pop—except the cola varieties—flavouring syrup and liqueur. It is a natural choice since it is commonly found in fruit. Citric acid is not a direct replacement for acid phosphate, because of their different flavour characteristics.

Citric acid was often employed in fruit flavoured beverages with lemon and lime juice being the preferred source.

Early methods for manufacturing crude citric acid used any available citrus fruit as the raw materials. The extraction process often contaminate the acid with lead because it was easy to make extraction vessels from this malleable metal. Because of lead's toxicity pharmacists avoided crude citric acid.

One of the more common adulterants found in wholesale citric acid was tartaric acid. Even though tartaric acid is a natural acid found in grapes, it reacted with aniline colourings making them transparent. Tartaric acid also reacts with certain calcium and magnesium salts, forming a precipitate which was not good for bottlers. These issues made citric acid the preferred choice for fruit flavoured beverages.

Citric acid is soluble in alcohol, making it a very versatile acid for beverages.

Citric and tartaric acid are both organic acids—in the chemical sense—which means that certain bacteria can ferment them into acetic acid. Solutions of citric and tartaric acid should be checked regularly to ensure they are not decomposing as this can cause a harsh vinegar like flavour in drinks.

www.artofdrink.com

Phospho-Citric Acid

The acidic tang of soda was an integral part of the soda fountain experience and pharmacists recognized this. If citrus fruit or pure citric acid were not available, this could cause them to loose business. To prevent this they developed a number of alternative, shelf stable acids for sodas.

One such composition was Phospho-Citric acid, a combination of phosphoric and citric acid, with additional salts. The principal benefit of this acid was increased shelf life, compared to pure citric acid. It was also said to taste good.

Citrochloric Acid

This is another compounded acid created to replace citric acid in beverages. The main benefit of citrochloric acid was that it had a very long shelf life. The extended life was due to the use of hydrochloric acid.

There is no reason or benefit to use this mixture. The use of hydrochloric acid, in a beverage, should be discouraged, since it is a very strong acid and has a disagreeable flavour. Citric acid is cheap, lead free, and readily available today.

Vinegar

Acids make an excellent medium for preserving foods, with vinegar (acetic acid) being well know across time and cultures as a method of pickling foods.

Vinegar was also a common drink for peasants in the middle ages, when beer was beyond their meagre means. American farmers were fond of a vinegar based beverage called Switchel (Haymaker's Punch). This drink was brought north by slaves in the West Indies, who called it "swizzle". The recipe is a simple combination of vinegar, a sweetener—usually molasses—and water.

Because vinegar was cheap and wasn't prone to spoiling like fruit acids, some proprietors used it in fountain drinks. However, beverage bottlers were condemned for its use in soda drinks, as the flavour was considered harsh.

Some soda beverages do call for vinegar, but not the distilled product. Instead they used infused wine and fruit based vinegar. The most successful flavours were raspberry and vanilla vinegar, but they never came close to matching the popularity of their phosphate and citric acid brethren.

Horsford's
Acid Phosphate,

Prepared according to the directions of Prof. E. N. HORSFORD,
of Cambridge, Mass.

FOR DYSPEPSIA,

Indigestion, Headache, Mental & Physical Exhaustion, Nervousness, Hysteria, Night Sweats of Consumption, etc.

There seems to be no difference of opinion in high medical authority, of the value of phosphoric acid, and no preparation has ever been offered to the public which seems to so happily meet the general want as this.

Every mental and physical exertion induces an augmented waste of the phosphates. This Acid Phosphate supplies that waste, and imparts new energy to the system, giving the feeling and sense of increased intellectual and physical power.

It is not nauseous, but agreeable to the taste.

No danger can attend its use.

Its action will harmonize with such stimulants as are necessary to take.

It makes a delicious drink with water and sugar only.

Pamphlet giving further particulars mailed free on application to manufacturers,

Rumford Chemical Works, Providence, R. I.

FOR SALE BY
JOSEPH T. BROWN & CO.
DRUGGISTS & CHEMISTS,
504 Washington Street, cor. Bedford,
BOSTON.
Drugs and Chemicals at Wholesale Prices.

Druggists' Sundries

Unlike the local confectioner or barkeep, pharmacists had privileged access to many compounds and the knowledge to mix them. This unique information allowed them to create drinks others could not. The specialized ingredients in sodas are what made them unique to the world of drinks. Many of them were mixtures designed to treat some form of ailment, but eventually were just used as flavouring component. Coca-Cola was formulated to treat dyspepsia and headaches, now it is consumed for its inimitable flavour.

Many of the compounds used by druggists are now widely available to the general public. This is especially true of the essential oils that were universally used in sodas.

The use of essential oils should not be considered heresy in mixed drinks. Good quality oils are the pure extract of the original material, usually procured through steam distillation. This isn't unlike other distilled products like rum, brandy or whisky. The key is to find pure, unadulterated, food grade oils.

Essential oils are very potent aroma and flavour compounds that must be diluted before use. In many instances, a few drops of the oil is all that is needed to make a litre of flavoured syrup.

Making Elixirs and Extracts

The use of essences and extracts was standard practice for pharmacy soda fountains. Aside from the medicinal applications, there were many reasons extracts were used including ease of use, stability and the ability to create unique flavours.

When soda fountains became popular refrigeration was still in its infancy. This made it impossible to store perishable ingredients for long periods of time. Extracts were the solution. These preparations could be made and then stored for months, even years, without a problem because the flavour compounds were separated from the perishable material. Extracts were made using high proof alcohol, which was a very effective preservative.

Combining extracts to make syrups was an evolutionary step in soda creation that opened up a whole new world of flavours. Where it was once a newsworthy event when some strange foreign fruit arrived by boat, soda fountains could create unique flavours at will, with extracts and chemicals. Coca-Cola was, and still is, one of the most successful extract and essential oil combination ever created.

Most extracts were standardized to ensure the dose was equivalent. A typical tincture was made of 31 grams (1 troy ounce) of pure drug in 237 ml (8 fluid ounces) of tincture. For example, an Allspice tincture would contain 31 g of Oil of Allspice and enough alcohol to make a total volume of 237 ml of tincture. A few millilitres of the tincture would then be used to make the flavour syrup.

The use of essential oils was the normal procedure, since the raw materials would contain a variable quantity of the oils. The oils were usually distilled by chemical houses, from the raw materials, and sold in bulk to pharmacists. This process ensured that there was a level of consistency in the drugs and syrups.

For some medicines the raw materials were used, like Cinchona and Angostura bark, because the active ingredients were water soluble and not easily purified. In these cases, the pharmacopoeia detailed the standardized preparation method.

When making extracts, the most important thing is to find a flavour that works and then being able to reproduce it each time it is made. Good documentation and quality starting material will help.

Soluble Extracts

One of the issues with using essential oils is that they are not completely soluble in water. The addition of alcohol or glycerine helps increase the solubility of the oil, but for flavour syrups this is not always practical.

The limited solubility of essential oils can result in a hazy or turbid syrup. This is caused by insoluble materials that come out of solution when added to water. One of the ways to prevent this is to mix or "rub" the oil with either magnesium carbonate, purified talcum powder or fine pumice stone in a mortar, to make a thin cream. The cream is then mixed with the water and vigorously shaken to break down any lumps. The solution is allowed to stand until the clarifying agent settles. The liquid is then filtered and should remain clear.

The mineral powders work by binding the insoluble components of the oil. Since these powders are insoluble, they are easily filtered and take the objectionable material with them. The flavour compounds are left dissolved in the liquid.

For alcoholic extracts, magnesium carbonate and talcum can be used. For water based extracts pumice stone is recommended because magnesium carbonate and talcum powder change the pH of aqueous extracts, noticeably changing the flavour.

Gum arabic can also be employed to help emulsify oils and extracts. Very fine gum arabic powder is best for this application. Mix just enough of the gum and oil to form a sloppy paste. Allow it to rest for a few minutes and then add a couple tablespoons of cooled simple syrup and mix thoroughly. The resting stage will help prevent clumping when mixed with the simple syrup.

To further stabilize the oil-water emulsion, take the flavour syrup and use an immersion blender (stick blender) that is set to the highest speed, and blend for a minute. This technique breaks down any large droplets of oil into microscopic particles. The sugar and gum arabic will prevent the oil drops from reforming.

Many of these flavour syrups may remain cloudy, especially if gum arabic is used to emulsify the oil. However, once mixed with soda water they produce a crystal clear drink. It should also be noted that heating the syrup with the essential oil is not recommended because the heat can evaporate a portion of the essential oil.

Aromatic Elixir

In the 19th century, taking medicine usually meant a vile tasting liquid was going to be served. To help people choke their medicine down, druggists developed Aromatic Elixirs. The mixture's sole purpose was to mask disagreeable flavours. However, some people found the masking flavour more disagreeable than the medicine. To combat this, there were numerous formulas created.

There was one official version of Aromatic Elixir, but the formula changed depending on which "Aromatic Spirit" was used, and there were eight of those. To confuse things even more, they were also called Simple Elixir.

The original Simple Elixir was a mixture of sweet orange oil, sugar, alcohol and water. Sometimes lemon oil was substituted for—or combined with—the orange oil. This worked for some people, while others balked at the flavour. Eventually one version of Simple Elixir combined a number of spices (cinnamon, nutmeg, cloves, anise, coriander, etc.) along with the citrus oils, to create a unique flavour that was generally viewed as favourable.

Many pharmacists created their own elixirs. Creating a compound that was more agreeable, to a specific clientele, would make them loyal customers. This behaviour wasn't unprecedented, considering the flavour battle the soda fountains waged.

These Aromatic Elixirs were often used in soda, as an aromatic enhancement to drinks, much like aromatic bitters used in cocktails, except the bitter agents were left out. The use of bitters in soda and cocktails happened because America was suffering from a raging case of dyspepsia. If it wasn't for the gastrointestinal distress, cocktail bitters may have taken a backseat to Aromatic Elixirs.

Simple Elixir No.3

Cinnamon, powder	4 g	1 tsp
Star Anise, powder	4 g	1 tsp
Coriander, powder	4 g	1 tsp
Nutmeg, powder	4 g	1 tsp
Caraway, powder	4 g	1 tsp
Oil Sweet Orange	2 g	½ tsp
Dilute Alcohol 20%	1 L	2 pints
Simple Syrup	1 L	2 pints

Percolate the spices with the alcohol previously mixed with the Oil of Orange continuing the percolation until two pints of Aromatic Tincture are obtained and mix with the simple syrup.

Aromatic Elixir

Aromatic Spirit	480 ml	16 oz
Simple Syrup	720 ml	24 oz
Water	720 ml	24 oz
Purified Talcum	30 ml	1 oz

Mix the Aromatic Spirit with twelve 12 oz of syrup and add the water to incorporate the purified talcum thoroughly with the mixture set the latter aside for a few days if possible, occasionally agitating then stir it well and filter it through a wetted filter returning the first portions of the filtrate until it runs through clear Finally mix the filtrate with the remainder of the simple syrup.

Aromatic Spirit of Ammonia

Another pharmaceutical addition to soda was Aromatic Spirit of Ammonia. It was most often called for in a Coca-Cola, or as it was ordered "an Ammonia Coke". The recipe was simple with the soda jerk adding a few dashes of the Aromatic Spirit of Ammonia to a glass of Coca-Cola, or any other soda flavour.

It may sound terrifying to add "ammonia" to a drink but it is important to note that this ammonia is not concentrated household ammonia used for cleaning. The principal ingredients are ammonium carbonate and a 10% solution of ammonia diluted with alcohol and water making a weak 1% solution of free ammonia. This spirit also contains the essential oils of lemon, nutmeg and sometimes lavender along with valerian root. When added to an 8 ounce soda, the ammonia is very dilute, but still perceptible.

The primary function of this tincture was to relieve an upset stomach and act as an antispasmodic for the digestive tract. It was said to be quite effective, most likely because the ammonia is basic and it functioned like an antacid.

Another common use of Aromatic Spirits of Ammonia was to relieve nervousness, faintness and hysteria. When people felt overwhelmed, a small amount in a glass of water was the solution. If someone had a fear of going to the dentist or another traumatic event, a preemptive dose was said to reduce a person's anxiety.

Lastly, it was used as a stimulant. Lethergy was commonly fixed with a dose of ammonia. For slightly intoxicated individuals, ammonia was said to mend that too. Being excessively intoxicated was beyond the capability of ammonia, but a hangover could be eased by a dash or two of this compound.

A typical dose ranged from a few drops for nervousness to ¾ of a teaspoon for the stimulating effects and hangover repair. It was always diluted, usually with sweetened water, prior to consumption. The soda fountain version used Coca-Cola as the sweetener and diluent.

More on Aromatic Spirit of Ammonia at http://www.artofdrink.com/2009/10/ammonia-coke.php

Aromatic Spirit of Ammonia is still sold at some pharmacies and can be bought online for about $2.00 for a 60 ml (2 oz) bottle, which is enough for at least 60 Ammonia Cokes or 15 hangovers.

Elixir of Calisaya

The bark from the Peruvian cinchona tree, often called calisaya, is the ingredient that gives this elixir its bitter tang. The main component is quinine.

Quinine has been used for centuries as a medicinal ingredient in the fight against malaria, but it has other properties as well. It is said to reduce fever, calm nerves, stimulate digestion and prevent leg cramps.

Over consumption of therapeutic doses of quinine or cinchona can lead to cinchonism. The symptoms are ringing of the ears (tinnitus), flushness, blurry vision, confusion, headache, abdominal pain, rashes, photosensitivity, dizziness, dysphoria, nausea, vomiting, and diarrhea. Fundamentally, the same symptoms as a hangover from a Green Day or Pink Floyd concert.

Cinchonism is rarely caused by consumption of tonic water. In the US, the government regulates the amount of quinine in tonic water at 83 mg/L but commercial bottlers use half that amount (40 mg/L). For a Gin & Tonic this means about 5 mg to 10 mg of quinine per drink. For comparison, a typical starting dose of quinine for malaria prevention starts at 300 mg per day, and for the actual treatment it's 600 mg three times daily. It would take 30 Gin & Tonics to match the basic prophylaxis dose.

Cinchona Wine or Elixir of Calisaya was a favourite drink of "soda flies" because of its "medicinal properties". This elixir was made with a lot of alcohol, but it contained so many aromatic spices that the aroma of alcohol was hard to detect on the breath of the imbiber. This was a great benefit to those gentlemen who preferred a cocktail at the saloon, but were under strict orders from their spouse to avoid such places. Calisaya can still be found, not at the pharmacy, but in the liquor store where it belongs.

⤜ Elixir of Calisaya ⤛

Calisaya bark	60g	2 oz
Fresh orange peel	30g	1 oz
Ceylon cinnamon	15g	½ oz
Coriander seed	8g	½ oz
Fennel seed	4g	1 tsp
Caraway seed	4g	1 tsp
Cardamom seed	4g	1 tsp
Cochineal	4g	1 tsp
Brandy	600ml	20 oz
Alcohol 90%	240ml	8 oz
Water	720ml	24 oz
Simple syrup	600ml	20 oz

Reduce the orange peel to a pulp in a mortar, and grind the spices to a coarse powder and then combine with the orange pulp. Mix the brandy, alcohol, and water, and moisten the powder with an amount sufficient to prepare it for percolation. Pack the moistened powder in a percolator, and begin the extraction with the remainder of the liquid. Lastly, mix this percolate with the simple syrup.

Ginger Extract

Anyone who has worked with ginger extract has noticed that the pungent ginger flavour starts to fade within a few hours of bottling. This is due to the reactive nature of the volatile oil (gingerol) found in the root. This oil will rapidly break down in very acidic environments or when bottled in a sucrose solution.

To stabilize the gingerol, using inverted sugar will avoid some of the degradation. It is also important to avoid adding any excess acid to the extract or syrup. It should be added when the drink is dispensed. Research shows that the oils from ginger are most stable between a pH of 4 and 5.

> ! Adding 1.5 g of sodium citrate and 1.0 g of citric acid to a litre of syrup will give you a pH of 4-5

The best method for making a ginger extract is to use high proof alcohol, preferably 90%, which is how Jamaican Ginger Extract was made. This preserves the gingerol and helps retain its pungency for a longer period of time. The downside is that the alcohol also extracts other resinous material, which can make a prepared syrup cloudy. The best method is to add a few drops or a teaspoon of tincture when preparing the drink.

When pockets of prohibition began appearing in the US, hardened drinkers would head for the local pharmacy and order a shot of Jamaican Ginger Extract since it was mostly alcohol, but still considered medicine.

Colouring

Science has demonstrated that the appearance of food and drink plays an important role in what people choose to eat. This evolutionary trait protects people from bad food choices. Bright, natural colours are perceived as good choices, like fresh fruit and vegetables. Brown, green and yellow can trigger a cautious response in people because they resemble contaminated water, rotting food or excrement.

The problem for many compounders of drinks was the flavour extracts were usually an unappetizing combination of browns, yellows and greens. The solution to this problem was to add bright colouring agents. Natural colours were employed, like cherry juice and saffron, but most early colourings were synthetic.

There was a significant amount of controversy about the use of synthetic colours, and rightfully so. Prior to the Pure Food Act of 1906, there were few rules regarding colouring agents. Many petrochemical companies, like Standard Oil, found uses for their coal tar waste as soda colouring in the form of aniline.

The colours produced from aniline were very vibrant and easily dominated the earthy colours in syrup. Some of the early formulated colours were mauve, fuchsia, brilliant blue, and malachite green. All very attractive colours, but toxic. Repeated exposure to these aniline dyes affected the nervous and circulatory system which caused fatigue, loss of appetite, headaches and dizziness. Ironically, the promoted health benefits of soda, as aiding the symptoms of aniline exposure, were being caused by the aniline coloured soda.

Many of the aniline colourings were eliminated with the *Pure Food and Drug Act*, but many pharmacists and doctors had already recognized the harmful nature of these substances and stopped using them. However, many soda syrup manufacturers continued to use them, since they were cheap and abundant.

There are many natural colourings that can be used to improve the appearance of sodas. The key issue is that these colourings are not as potent as synthetic colours.

Some common natural colouring agents are; chlorophyll from grass or spinach, curcuma from the spice turmeric, carmine which comes from the shell of an insect, caramel from burnt sugar, and saffron.

These colours work well on clear solutions, but if there is a competing colour they are more likely to tint the drink with a mixed colour.

Saffron makes a beautiful golden colour, but is expensive and can stain clothing. Turmeric is cheaper and produces a similar colour. Turmeric also fluoresces, similar to quinine, in ultraviolet light.

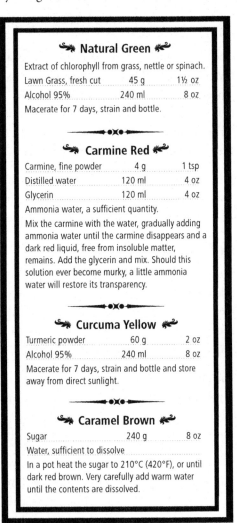

❧ Natural Green ❧
Extract of chlorophyll from grass, nettle or spinach.

Lawn Grass, fresh cut	45 g	1½ oz
Alcohol 95%	240 ml	8 oz

Macerate for 7 days, strain and bottle.

❧ Carmine Red ❧

Carmine, fine powder	4 g	1 tsp
Distilled water	120 ml	4 oz
Glycerin	120 ml	4 oz

Ammonia water, a sufficient quantity.

Mix the carmine with the water, gradually adding ammonia water until the carmine disappears and a dark red liquid, free from insoluble matter, remains. Add the glycerin and mix. Should this solution ever become murky, a little ammonia water will restore its transparency.

❧ Curcuma Yellow ❧

Turmeric powder	60 g	2 oz
Alcohol 95%	240 ml	8 oz

Macerate for 7 days, strain and bottle and store away from direct sunlight.

❧ Caramel Brown ❧

Sugar	240 g	8 oz

Water, sufficient to dissolve

In a pot heat the sugar to 210°C (420°F), or until dark red brown. Very carefully add warm water until the contents are dissolved.

Other natural colours can be made using the skin and juice of certain fruits. Blueberries skins can tint liquids a dark purple colour. Cherry and elderberry juice are often used as red colouring agents. To get the best colour, use dried fruits in a small quantity of solvent. Using dilute (20%) or proof spirit (57%) will create a more stable product and sometimes better colour. Water based extracts are liable to ferment, which can create off flavours.

Many natural colours can be effected by the pH of the liquid they are in. For example blueberries will remain purple-blue until a pH of 3 or lower is reached. At this point the colour turns to a red-pink shade.

Blue is the most difficult colour to produce naturally in an acidic environment. Because most drinks are acidic, it is rare to find a natural blue dye.

Natural colouring should be stored in a cool, dark place.

Notes on Ingredients

Eggs

Many recipes call for the inclusion of raw eggs, and to some people this may be a concern. The potential for salmonella infection is 1 in 20,000 from a raw egg. That is an extremely safe number because there is a better chance of fatally slipping in the shower (1 in 2232) or getting a hole-in-one (1 in 5000).

It is understandable for people to feel uncomfortable consuming raw eggs. We have been continuously blasted by the media about the dangers of salmonella. Outdated facts account for many of the issue. Most grocery stores do not stock free range eggs, and many of the large egg farms use specialized equipment to identify bad eggs.

When selecting eggs, pick the freshest ones possible. Sadly, most grocery stores have supply chains that make the eggs weeks old before they arrive in the store. Smaller stores and farmers markets deal more directly with farmers and the eggs tend to be fresher. The other option is to buy cartons of pasturized eggs and egg whites. They can be found in the dairy section of the grocery store.

If raw eggs are still a concern, then powdered eggs are an option. These eggs have been processed, usually freeze dried, or completely dehydrated. They are also tested to ensure that there is no contamination, such as salmonella. If ordered in bulk, a certificate of analysis can be requested.

Phosphoric Acid

Phosphoric acid has come under scrutiny lately for its potential role in osteoporosis. It is a fact that phosphoric acid does reduce bone density over the long term. But, short term exposure is not an issue. The reduction in bone density comes from years of continuous over consumption and poor diet. Calcium is a necessary element for bone building, but phosphorus is just as important. An excess of anything is bad. Consumption of a six pack of pop or a 44 ounce Slurpee daily, along with a diet poor in calcium, is of course going to cause health problems. But, a person drinking a couple of soda-pops a week, who eats well, and exercises moderately are unlikely to have problems. Moderation is key. The quantity of phosphoric acid in the drink recipes is equal to that used in a can of cola. On the flip-side of the negative health issues, there are people using phosphoric acid drops (57%) for healthy cells and to dissolve kidney stones. The medical community hasn't concluded either way, but moderation is a safe bet.

Another issue with the "acid phosphates of soda" is the solution can corrode non-stainless steel metals. This limits what types of containers it can be stored in behind the counter. Pump bottles seem ideal, but they contain a metal spring which will quickly react with the acid, eventually rendering it useless. Stainless steel syrup pumps are available, but are costly and usually hold a huge quantity. The best option is to purchase a brand new stainless steel soap dispenser. They range in price from $10 to $30, look fairly stylish, and should resist corrosion and dispense 1 ml to 2 ml per pump, which is perfect.

Sassafras

Old root beer recipes call for sassafras but the FDA no-longer considers sassafras a safe ingredient because of the chemical safrole, which is hepatotoxic and possibly carcinogenic. A few drops of pure safrole can seriously harm a child and a teaspoon of safrole is enough to bring about a personal meeting with ones maker.

A possible substitute is a product called File (pronounced: fee lay), which is used in Cajun and Creole cooking, and a necessity for gumbo. The leaves have an insignificant quantity of safrole, making them safe for use. Obviously, real sassafras can be purchased on the Internet, or found in a local wood lot.

Even though sassafras is considered potentially hazardous by the FDA, many spices contain safrole, like nutmeg (2.3%), cinnamon (1.3%) and black pepper (0.04%). These common spices also contain similar compounds, like myristicin found in nutmeg, which has toxic properties.

Tonka Bean

The tonka bean is another ingredient that is banned in some countries (US, Canada, Australia) but available in others, like France. Its fragrance is reminiscent of vanilla, almonds, cinnamon, and cloves and was used as a vanilla substitute.

The seed contains coumarin, which is a blood thinner (anti-coagulant) and is moderately toxic in high doses. Doctors prescribe coumarin under the brand name Warfarin to prevent blood clots and other cardiovascular issues.

An average Tonka Bean has 2% to 3% of its mass as coumarin, which is about 26 mg/g or 800 mg per ounce. The maximum dose of Warfarin is 10 mg which makes consumption of Tonka bean potentially dangerous, especially for people taking medication known to interact with coumarin.

Cassia Cinnamon is naturally high in coumarin (3330 mg/kg), but true cinnamon from Ceylon/Sri Lanka contains no coumarin. Any concentrated cinnamon infusion, made from cassia, will have high levels of coumarin.

Substitution of an equal mixture of vanilla extract and almond oil, with a pinch of allspice, was said to be a rough approximation of the tonka bean flavour.

Wine of Coca

One of the more common ingredients in old soda fountain guides is Wine of Coca. This is the ingredient that gives Coca-Cola half its name and is the ingredient that imparts its "addictive" flavour. It comes from the coca leaf and contributes cocaine, the extremely addictive narcotic, to beverages that used it.

In the late 19th century, Wine of Coca was regularly incorporated into drinks. One of the earliest was Vin Mariani, which containing about 7 mg of cocaine per serving. Royalty, politicians and religious figures like Pope Leo VIII and Pope Saint Pius X were fond of Vin Mariani. Even Thomas Edison was an admirer of the product. Pope Leo VIII carried a flask of Vin Mariani around with him and loved it so much he awarded it a Vatican gold medal. He even endorsed the product by allowing his image to appear in posters.

Coca-Cola was influenced by Vin Mariani and was originally called Pemberton's French Wine Coca. Coca-Cola up'd the cocaine ante to 9 mg though.

Coca leaf is still a legal food additive, otherwise Coca-Cola wouldn't taste the way it dose. The key is that the coca leaf must be "decocainized". The Stephan Company of New Jersey imports 175,000 kilograms (385,000 lbs) of coca leaf into the United States each year. They are licensed by the DEA to remove the cocaine from the leaves and sell the flavour extract, almost exclusively to Coca-Cola.

It is still possible to get decocainized coca leaf in North America. A company called Mysterious Bolivia, located in the US, currently sells coca leaf tea via the Internet. It contains no cocaine and can be purchased legally. Do not order coca leaf from companies outside of the US or Canada, as the cocaine content is unknown. Doing so may bring a visit from the DEA or the RCMP.

Possible substitutes for coca leaf wine are Green Tea and Hojicha, a Japanese roasted tea. Hojicha has less astringent and vegetative qualities, and more toasted caramel flavours, than green tea.

Ingredient Choice

The thrill of trying a "forbidden fruit" is mostly a psychological curiosity, which influences our expectations of taste. That's why many people will often state root beer made with sassafras is the best, and no other products come close. For comparison, it's like saying a Riesling from Germany is different than one from France. The reality is that they do taste different, but anyone who's tasted wine will still describe them as Riesling. The key difference is personal preference, which has nothing to do with the wine and more to do with psychology.

Absinthe was once "forbidden" and through the efforts of a small group, it was reintroduced to the market. With the increased availability, many curious people sampled it, only to be disappointed that its primary flavour is anise (liquorice). But the fact that it was forbidden at one time still compels people to buy it.

The choice of ingredients for individual consumption is always a personal decision. Many things in life are bad for us, including drinking alcohol, but in small doses, the rewards can sometimes outweighed the risks.

People who serve drinks to the public are obliged to heed the law. The ingredients mentioned above are regulated by the US government, for good or bad.

The Last Gulp

The revelation that cocktails and soda existed in parallel time-lines may surprise some people, but it shouldn't. The macrocosm of mixed drinks was created in America during the 1800s, and it's not unreasonable to believe that they influenced one another during their heyday.

These mixed drinks evolved under different circumstances, but the similarities are striking. The fates of both can be explained as: a hard-core rebellious period, at times schizophrenic, bouncing between well mannered gentlemanly compositions and gutter dwelling benders of narcotics and alcohol. Cocktails had a stay in the "big house" from 1919 to 1933 and a lifetime of probation, but kept its drug like properties, while soda got house arrest in exchange for ditching the drug habit. Sodas and cocktails have both witnessed ever increasing quantities of sugar, which has become their modern crutch.

Unlike most processes that cycle through peaks and valley's before attaining equilibrium at some mid-point, mixed drinks peaked and plummeted. It would be difficult to say that a can of soda is the finest representation of the art. What can be said is that in modern times speed and price are more important than quality.

The convenience factor of bottles, cans and modern dispensing equipment was the most likely reasons for the decline of the soda fountain. It can also be noted that convenience nearly killing the cocktail. In either case, prepackaged products, requiring no skill to operate, replaced quality and craftsmanship.

Quality mixed drinks have not resonated with people in the last half century for a number of reasons. Marketing became a major industry and if a person viewed an advertisement enough, they would start believing it. Companies with large marketing budgets could artificially create the image of a quality product. The Coca-Cola company has executed this masterfully. Secondly, the pace of modern life has made waiting three minutes to get a drink seem like an eternity. Time guarantees have become part of drink service for many restaurants for this reason. Lastly, price is a key factor. A case of 12 cans of pop costs about $4 in North America. That's about 33¢ per 12 oz serving. This makes it impossible for a traditional soda fountain to compete on price alone.

When you combine advertising, price, modern life's pace and the convenience factor traditional soda fountain drinks did not stand a chance. Doing more faster and cheaper is the bane of mixed drinks.

Soda's Influence on the Cocktail

After prohibition, the soda fountain's influence on alcoholic drinks is hard to ignore. There was a definitive shift away from strong cocktails and a rapid acceptance of sweet drinks. Thirteen years of prohibition did not help because it made malted milkshakes and syrupy sweet soda the defacto drink choices for many people. The taste for strong drinks was greatly diminished.

Most people point to prohibition's "bathtub gin" for America's change in taste because it was so bad that it required gads of sugar to cover up the flavour. There is no doubt that cocktails changed during the 1920s, but sugar was already playing an increasing role in soda concoctions.

In the 1920s, the most popular items at soda fountains were ice cream based treats like the milkshake, sundae and the banana split. A 1929 survey from the *New York Chain Store Research Bureau* stated that chocolate factored into 70% of confections sold at soda fountains. These fatty, sugar laden kickshaws were the closest legal stand-in for the dopamine inducing effects of alcohol.

The appetite for sweet beverages would have been hard to reverse after prohibition. Instead of reverting back to potent cocktails, the worlds of cocktails and soda began to intermingle, creating new preferences in alcoholic beverages.

The soda fountain's influence is especially hard to dismiss when the first new alcoholic drinks created after prohibition were so very different than those 13 years prior. One class of drinks introduced in 1934 were known as exotics, or tiki drinks as we call them today. Even though many of these exotic drink recipes are devoid of soda water, they do include a significant number of compound syrups (mixtures of multiple flavours) and a lot of fruit juices, two pillars of the soda fountain. It's also important to note that pre-prohibition bartenders frowned upon the electric mixer, but it became a necessity at tiki styled bars.

Whether these exotic tiki style drinks developed from international observation or internally, via the soda fountain, is hard to say. Most likely it was a gradual fusion of both. There is no doubt that Americans became fascinated with these drinks and it's quite possible that exotic drinks were just the serendipitous union of alcohol and soda flavours at a time when America's tastes were changing.

Bartenders have always incorporated fruit juices into drinks. Citrus fruit were primarily used as an acid or sour flavour. Pineapple, raspberry and grenadine were used for their sweetening and colouring properties. The key difference was that prior to prohibition most fruit flavours were introduced into cocktails via cordials like curaçao and maraschino. Early bars rarely used compound syrups the way soda fountains did, but that would change when cordials became the fruit flavoured alcohol syrups sold today.

The fusion of soda and cocktails continues with the increased production of fruit liqueurs after World War II. Instead of being used as the traditional digestif application, liqueurs were being marketed for use in cocktails.

In 1952, the *Wall Street Journal* noted that whiskey sales were decreasing while liqueur sales were steadily increasing. The stated reason was "*...the increased use in cocktails. It's a trend much encouraged by the cordial makers who credit such concoctions as the Pink Squirrel for making more sales. In the pre-war years, liqueurs were pretty much restricted to use after dinner...*"

Drinks like the Pink Squirrel, Hop-Toad and the Two Striper were made with straight liqueurs and devoid of any base spirit like whisky, rum or brandy. These new drinks were focussed on elevating sweetness, which was the key selling point. This change in cocktail taste was a mirror image of the soda fountain's earlier transition from soda water to milkshakes and floats.

Increasing liqueur sales was profitable for the manufacturers because they paid less tax on the lower alcohol content, but could charge relatively the same price as a bottle of whisky. It was a bonus that warehousing and aging was not required, reducing operating costs even further.

The domains of soda and cocktails were amalgamated when the 7&7, Mojito, Moscow Mule, and the Cuba Libre became the defacto drinks of most bars. Soda-pop and cocktails were an American passion, so it only made sense to merge them. It was also cheaper, easier and faster to mix a Rum & Coke than a proper Manhattan. The convenience factor was too easy to resist. Well crafted cocktails were relegated to a fourth line role behind liqueurs, powdered sour mix and blender drinks and even then cocktails were still made with flippant disregard.

Beverages continued to change and the world of mixed drinks bottomed out in the 1980s and 90s. Coca-Cola was now the uncontested leader in the carbonated beverage market. Even with a stranglehold on the market, their hubris led them to reformulate the product that made them the alpha male of soda manufacturers. That idea didn't go over well with Coca-Cola loyalists.

The rest of the soda-pop market was apportioned to a small group of name brands like Pepsi, Canada Dry, Dr. Pepper, 7-Up, Schweppes, and A&W all controlled by a handful of companies. Regional varieties like Faygo, Moxie and Vernors were available in select markets, but overall soda choice was limited.

In restaurants the selection was even more dismal because of fierce competition between Coca-Cola and Pepsi. Most major restaurants and fast food chains have contractually obliged themselves to one manufacturer for monetary reasons. This may have been good for profits, but was bad for choice. Most allied businesses had five soda choices, usually cola, diet cola, lemon lime, ginger ale and maybe root beer or orange crush. Convenience usurped choice once more.

The dark ages of drinking didn't stop with soda in the 1990s. Whisky producers were releasing "light whisky" with fewer calories and 27% alcohol. Brewers released light beer alternatives like Zima, and artificially flavoured liqueurs were all the rage. The concept of quality was non-existent in corporate board rooms.

The bottoming out of the mixed drink category opened a door for keen marketers. Products like vodka—now toting the premium and ultra premium banners—were being sold at higher prices and catered to those who wanted better things in life. It was rare to find quality ingredients in most bars and well balanced drinks had morphed into sweet syrupy slush dispensed from a blender. This allowed vodka to take up the "premium" moniker with no resistance at all, quickly felling the former premium spirits like whisky, rum and cognac to become the dominant spirit for a new generation of aspiring drinkers.

This decline in drink quality resulted in a new generation of company that created products to fill the premium void. Micro-breweries began brewing flavourful beer, pulling beer from the brink of self-immolation. Classic cocktails started to see the beginnings of a renaissance. The idea of quality was starting to resonate.

Soda-pop hasn't seen the resurgence other drink categories have had. Many of the major soda brands are solidly entrenched in the minds of consumers—who have also developed fierce brand loyalty. But there are some small soda-pop producers like Jones Soda making inroads.

The revival of the classic soda fountain would require a monumental effort. The ubiquity of major soda brands in every store, big and small, along with the convenience of bottles, creates an almost unchallengeable force. However, the ability to reproduce classic soda fountain drinks is not outside the skills of the professional bartender.

The fact that the non-alcoholic beverage category is astonishingly bleak makes soda recipes a natural match for bartenders. Classic soda recipes offer such a wide variety of tastes that it could be a boon for bars and restaurants. Offering unique drinks that span the flavour range from sweet to bitter, in a non-alcoholic form, could be the key to getting more people to drink in a social atmosphere, without the negative effects of excess alcohol consumption.

Wanted: Soda Jerks

The days of the gold gilded onyx soda fountain are long gone and most likely never to return. A few physical reincarnations from the 1950s may appear from time to time, but not the authentic soda fountain from the 1800s. This doesn't mean the drinks are lost forever, they just need champions to revive them.

There are thousands of soda recipes locked up in old publications awaiting rediscovery. These recipes are the last tangible remains of the classic soda fountain and are under siege from companies trying to claim ownership of the American soda.

Beyond the mere curiosity of tasting a long lost drink, these recipes represent an opportunity to reintroduce a respected non-alcoholic beverage. The mocktail and virgin cocktail have bombed as a friendly alternative for the abstainer. Social order has made ordering a virgin cocktail a negative experience—real or imaginary—bringing shame or a sense of embarrassment upon the imbiber.

The tip based system of compensation for bartenders has made non-alcoholic drinks a low priority because they do not command the high price that alcohol based drinks do. For most bartenders this means less income, and for others these drinks lack the complexity that challenges their skills. In either scenario, bartenders often glower and huff at patrons requesting such drinks.

Vintage soda recipes offer an opportunity for serious bartenders to resolve some of the salient issues with alcohol free drinks. Well crafted temperance drinks can improve profits and remedy social concerns about excess consumption.

The skill required for soda preparation is something that can be reasonably charged for—unlike cracking open and pouring a can of pop. Even though some establishments try to justify charging unreasonable prices hikes of 10 to 20 times for cola on the rocks, it is rarely ever perceived as fair by the customer. These negative reactions usually result in lower tips and lost customers.

On the other hand, a uniquely crafted drink can sustain a higher price, which benefits the establishment, bartender and customer. A person can buy a bottle of name brand pop anywhere for a fraction of the price, but they can only get those unique sodas from one place, which automatically increases their value.

Excess consumption is a recognized problem that has vexed proprietors of alcoholic beverages for centuries. There are no simple solutions, and this book does not claim to have an answer, but there are ways to mitigate the damage. Drink diversity is a simple method to get people to order something they normally wouldn't.

Very few restaurants offer anything tantalizing in the non-alcoholic category. Most provide the basic four or five soda types and maybe a few predictable juice combinations. There is nothing compelling about these choices when compared to the vibrant world of beer, wine and cocktails. Classic soda recipes offer a novel choice that will peak people's curiosity. A soda phosphate made with gentian, aromatic elixir and cognac essence is unique, and not something for the standard sugar addict, but may appeal to lovers of amaro or bittered cocktails.

Beyond the need for non-alcoholic options, the techniques and methods employed by pharmacists and soda jerks offer a new arena for bartenders and mixologists to explore. Aromatic elixirs and house mineral waters add another level of detail to the realm of mixed drinks and the drinking experience.

Cocktails and sodas may have started as singletons, but their similarities inevitably attracted one-another, intermingling and blurring their defining characteristics. Like a perfect marriage, it's unlikely there will ever be a separation between the two and attempting to break it up would be futile. Embracing the union and harnessing the synergy could create the offspring that unites the mixed drink category once and for all. Unifying the best characteristics of each can only lead to better drinks, for both alcoholic and non-alcoholic drinks alike.

Fountain Recipes

Recipe Conventions

The recipes on the following pages were gathered from a long list of pharmaceutical journals, soda fountain books and beverage manuals. The units of measure used for the recipes varied widely, depending on the source. For convenience the units have all be converted to metric and the American system.

For the most accurate recipe use the metric measurements. Because many of the original recipes used grains, drachms and minims they could be accurately converted to metric. With the American units many of the recipes had to be rounded to fractions of an ounce or teaspoon. When converting to the metric system, numbers were also rounded. For example 1 quart is 960 ml, but for this book 1 quart was rounded to 1 litre.

Many of the recipe sources used either troy, apothecary or avoirdupois ounces which are all slightly different. There is no differentiation made in the following recipes and 1 ounce = 30 g or 30 ml in the recipes. Also, the "drop" unit of measure changed over time. It once defined a minim or 0.0616 ml, but the official measurement for a drop is now 0.05 ml. This book uses the later measurement.

Extracts & Essences

Absinthe Extract

Wormwood	7.5 g	¼ oz
Centaury	7.5 g	¼ oz
Blessed Thistle	7.5 g	¼ oz
Gentian	4 g	1 tsp
Cinchona	4 g	1 tsp
Bitter Orange Peel	4 g	1 tsp
Orris Root	3 g	¾ tsp
Grains of Paradise	10 g	⅓ oz
Alcohol	360 ml	12 oz

Combine the herbs and spices in a mortar and reduce to a fine powder. Transfer to a bottle and add the alcohol. Allow to stand for a few hours, with regular shaking. Filter and bottle.

Adjuvant Elixir

Sweet Orange Peel, dried	15 g	½ oz
Wild Cherry Bark	30 g	1 oz
Glycyrrhiza, peeled	60 g	2 oz
Coriander	2 tsp	
Caraway	2 tsp	
Simple Syrup	240 ml	8 oz
Alcohol 40%	720 ml	24 oz

Grind the Wild Cherry to a coarse powder, moisten it with 4 oz of water and set it aside for 12 hours. Reduce the other solids to a coarse powder, mix with the Wild Cherry and moisten the powder with four 4 oz alcohol. Pack tightly in a percolator, then gradually pour the alcohol on top until 96 oz of percolate are obtained. Mix this with 32 oz of simple syrup and filter.

Aloes, Elixir of

Aloes	90 g	3 oz
Saffron	90 g	3 oz
Tincture Myrrh	1 L	1 qt

Reduce the drugs to a coarse powder and macerate in the alcohol for fourteen days, stirring the mixture thoroughly each day; then filter.

Allspice Extract

Oil of allspice	45 ml	1½ tsp
Powdered Allspice	60 g	2 oz
Alcohol, sufficient	480 ml	16 oz

Rub the oil with the powdered allspice and pack the mixture in a percolator. Cover with alcohol, and macerate for a period of 24 hours; then percolate slowly until one pint of percolate is obtained. The strength may be increased or diminished to suit the taste of the operator.

Amazon Flavour

Amazon Wine Bitters	240 ml	8 oz
Extract of Roses	60 ml	2 oz
Vanilla Extract	30 ml	1 oz
Lemon Extract	30 ml	1 oz

Combine and bottle.

Aromatic Elixir

Sweet Orange Peel	60 g	2 oz
Lemon Peel	30 g	1 oz
Vanilla Bean	15 g	½ oz
Cinnamon Powder	15 g	½ oz
Coriander Powder	15 g	½ oz
Anise Powder	15 g	½ oz
Sugar	570 g	1¼ lbs
Alcohol 90%	600 ml	20 oz
Water, sufficient	2 L	2 qt

Macerate the solids in alcohol for 48 hours, then add 480 ml (16 oz) of water and macerate for another 48 hours. Pour off the liquid and transfer the solids to a percolator and pass the tincture through the percolator. Then add water through the percolator to make a total of 1.7 L (38 oz) of extract. Filter clear through a little magnesium carbonate, dissolve the sugar, adding water if necessary, to make 2 L.

Aromatic Spirit

Sweet Orange Zest	60 g	2 oz
Lemon Zest	15 g	½ oz
Coriander Seed	15 g	½ oz
Oil of Star Anise	4 drops	
Alcohol 90%	1 L	1 qt

Macerate the solids for 4 days in the alcohol. Filter and add the Oil of Star Anise. Bottle.

Aromatic Tincture

Cinnamon Powder	150 g	5 oz
Ginger Powder	60 g	2 oz
Galangal Root Powder	30 g	1 oz
Long Pepper	30 g	1 oz
Cardamom	30 g	1 oz
Dilute Alcohol (40%)	1500 ml	50 oz

Moisten the powders with 60 ml (2 oz) of alcohol and pack tightly in the percolator. Add more alcohol and allow to percolate until 1.5 L (50 oz) of extract had passed through.

Belfast Ginger-Ale Extract

Ginger, powder	180 ml	6 oz
Orange peel	75 g	2½ oz
Nutmeg, grated	1 tbsp	
Ceylon Cinnamon	1 tbsp	
Vanilla Bean	2 tsp	
Capsicum	1 tsp	
Alcohol, to make	480 ml	16 oz

Black Pepper Extract

Ground Black Pepper	60 g	2 oz
Alcohol	600 ml	20 oz
Water		

Pack the powder into a percolator. Cover with alcohol, and when the percolate appears close the exit of the percolator and macerate for a period of twenty-four hours. Then percolate slowly until one pint of percolate is obtained. The strength may be increased or diminished to suit the taste of the operator, the quality desired governing in this direction.

Capsicum Extract

| Cayenne Pepper | 120 g | 4 oz |
| Alcohol | 1 L | 1 qt |

Mix them together and colour with Curcuma, modified with cochineal, to suit the taste.

Celery Extract

| Celery Seed, bruised | 60 g | 2 oz |
| Diluted Alcohol (50%) | 480 ml | 16 oz |

Mix and macerate for 7 days, agitating regularly. Filter and bottle.

Cinchona Wine

Cinchona Tincture	480 ml	16 oz
Glycerine	480 ml	16 oz
Sherry Wine	1.4 L	1½ qt

To make Cinchona Syrup simply mix 2 parts of the wine with 3 parts of simple syrup.

Cinnamon Extract (Soluble)

Cinnamon Oil	40 ml	1¼ oz
Magnesium Carbonate	60 g	2 oz
Alcohol 90%	360 ml	12 oz
Water, sufficient	1 L	1 qt

Dissolve the oil in the alcohol and then add the magnesium carbonate. Agitate until any clumps are gone. Allow to macerate for at least a week, shaking daily. Filter through paper and then pour water, through the filter, to get 1 quart.

Cinnamon Tincture

Cinnamon	16 g	4 tsp
Cardamom	4 g	1 tsp
Cloves	4 g	1 tsp
Galagal	4 g	1 tsp
Ginger	4 g	1 tsp
Alcohol 90%	210 ml	7 oz

Digest for 8 days, express and filter.

Cinnamon Water

Oil of Ceylon Cinnamon	2 ml	⅓ tsp
Magnesium Carbonate	4 g	1 tsp
Distilled Water	1 L	1 qt

Rub the oil with the magnesium and then add water. Mix until free of lumps. Filter.

Cinnamon Wine

Cinnamon, powder	2 g	½ tsp
Cloves	2 g	½ tsp
Mace	2 g	½ tsp
Cardamom	2 g	½ tsp
White Wine	750 ml	26 oz
Sugar	300 g	10 oz

Digest for 24 hours, filter and then add sugar. Use as a cordial stomachic.

Clove Extract (Soluble)

Clove Oil	40 ml	1¼ oz
Magnesium Carbonate	60 g	2 oz
Alcohol 90%	360 ml	12 oz
Water	1 L	1 qt

Dissolve the oil in the alcohol and then add the magnesium carbonate. Agitate until any clumps are gone. Allow to macerate for at least a week, shaking daily. Filter through paper and then pour water, through the filter, to get 1 quart.

Coffee Extract

Mocha Coffee	300 g	10 oz
Java Coffee	300 g	10 oz
Glycerin	120 ml	4 oz
Water	360 ml	12 oz

Grind the two coffees into a fine powder. Mix the glycerine and water and moisten the ground coffee with 4 oz. Pack tightly into a percolator. Heat up the remaining glycerine mixture and add to the percolator. Extract 16 oz of fluid.

Cognac Essence

Acetic Ether	60 ml	2 oz
Spirit of Nitrous Ether	45 ml	1½ oz
Pyroligneous Acid	45 ml	1½ oz

Mix with cognac oil and dilute alcohol.

Gentian Elixir

Gentian Root	75 g	2½ oz
Bitter Orange Peel	45 g	1½ oz
Coriander Seeds	30 g	1 oz
Cardamom Seeds	30 g	1 oz
Percolating Menstrum	3.8 L	7½ pt
Soluble Flavouring	240 ml	8 oz
Sugar	1150 g	2½ lbs

Macerate the ground spices for 48 hours in the menstrum. Filter and add the soluble flavouring and the sugar.

Ginger Extract

Ginger Root, ground	240 g	8 oz
Alcohol 90%	120 ml	12 oz
Water	360 ml	12 oz
Magnesium Carbonate	30 g	1 oz

Mix the ginger and alcohol, and let stand for several hours. Next, pack the material in a percolator and obtain 12 oz, adding additional alcohol to the percolator, if necessary. To this tincture, add the magnesium carbonate, shake well and add 12 oz of water. Shake again and filter. If the solution remains cloudy, add more magnesium carbonate, shake and filter again. This extract may form a deposit after a few days. Filter again, and it will stay clear.

Ginger Ale Extract

Ginger Powder	240 g	8 oz
Lemon Peel	45 g	1½ oz
Red Pepper, powder	15 g	¼ oz
Potassium Bicarbonate	1 tbsp	
Alcohol 20%	2 L	2 qt

Mix the potassium bicarbonate with the alcohol and macerate the spices for 24 hours and filter.

Grenadine Extract

Oil of Cloves	6 drops	
Oil of Orange Peel	18 drops	
Tincture of Ginger	¾ tsp	
Vanilla Extract	1 tsp	
Phosphoric Acid (10%)	15 ml	½ oz
Maraschino Liqueur	60 ml	2 oz
Tincture of Cochineal	60 ml	2 oz
Distilled Water	60 ml	2 oz
Alcohol, to make	480 ml	16 oz

Mix the oils and extracts with the alcohol then mix the phosphoric acid, Maraschino and cochineal with the water. Combine the two liquids.

Grog Extract

Arrack or Jamaica Rum	240 ml	8 oz
Alcohol (90%)	180 ml	6 oz
Sugar	240 g	8 oz
Water, to make	1 L	1 qt

Dissolve the sugar in the water, add the other ingredients, and strain or filter if necessary.

Hop Tonic Extract

Hops, fresh	120 g	4 oz
Quassia powder	60 g	2 oz
Alcohol	180 ml	6 oz
Water	360 ml	11 oz

Mix the hops and quassia with 12 ounces of boiling water and steep for 2 hours, agitating occasionally. Add the alcohol and macerate for several days. Filter and bottle.

Hot Drops
(Tincture of Capsicum and Myrrh)

Capsicum, powder	30 g	1 oz
Myrrh, coarse powder	60 g	2 oz
Alcohol 90%	480 ml	16 oz

Mix the powders with an equal bulk of clean fine sand and percolate them with the alcohol until sixteen 16 oz of percolate are obtained.

Hot Tom Extract

Gentian (ground)	60 g	2 oz
Ginger (powder)	15 g	½ oz
Orange Peel	15 g	½ oz
Capsicum	4 g	1 tsp
Alcohol (90%)	180 ml	6 oz
Water	420 ml	14 oz

Combine the ingredients and macerate for up to 7 days, aggitating occassionaly.

Kola Extract

Kola Nut Oil	30 ml	1 oz
Alcohol 90%	210 ml	7 oz

Combine the two ingredients and shake. If it forms a hazy solution, add magnesium carbonate, shake and let stand 24 hours. Filter.

Kola Nut Essence

Fluid Extract of Kola	120 ml	4 oz
Tincture of Canella	15 ml	½ oz
Tincture of Orange	60 ml	2 oz
Cherry Essence	12 ml	2½ tsp
Clove Essence	4 ml	¾ tsp
Alcohol (57%)	600 ml	20 oz

Combine the ingredients with the alcohol, shake and bottle. Allow to stand for 48 hours and filter if necessary.

Lemon Extract (Soluble)

Lemon Oil	40 ml	1¼ oz
Magnesium Carbonate	60 g	2 oz
Alcohol 90%	360 ml	12 oz
Water, sufficient	1 L	1 qt

Dissolve the oil in the alcohol and then add the magnesium carbonate. Agitate until any clumps are gone. Allow to macerate for at least a week, shaking daily. Filter through paper and then pour water, through the filter, to get 1 qt.

Lemon Oil Solution

Oil of lemon	30 ml	1 oz
Alcohol	450 ml	15 oz

Mix and let rest for a few days. Filter if a precipitate forms. Then colour with tincture of Curcuma.

Lime Extract (Soluble)

Lime Oil	40 ml	1¼ oz
Magnesium Carbonate	60 g	2 oz
Alcohol 90%	360 ml	12 oz
Water, sufficient	1 L	1 qt

Dissolve the oil in the alcohol and then add the magnesium carbonate. Agitate and macerate for one week, shaking daily. Filter through paper and add water, through the filter, to get 1 qt.

Macaroon Essence

Apricot Oil	60 ml	2 oz
Peach Oil	90 ml	3 oz
Raspberry Distillate	150 ml	5 oz
Brandy	300 ml	10 oz
Coffee Essence	45 ml	1½ oz
Maraschino Essence	60 ml	2 oz
Cacao Essence	75 ml	2½ oz
Walnut Essence	90 ml	3 oz

Combine the essences with brandy and mix to combine. Use 60 ml (2 oz) for 4 L (1 gal) of spirit.

Mace Extract

Mace, powder	30 g	1 oz
Alcohol 90%	180 ml	6 oz

Macerate for 14 days. Filter and bottle.

Malt Wine

Cinchona Bark Extract	60 ml	2 oz
Soluble Flavouring	120 ml	4 oz
Sherry Wine	2 L	4½ pt
Alcohol 90%	480 ml	16 oz
Malt Extract	1.5 L	3 pt

Mead Extract

Sarsaparilla	300 g	10 oz
Sassafras	90 g	3 oz
Ginger Root	30 g	1 oz
Cloves	30 g	1 oz
Allspice	30 g	1 oz
Vanilla Extract	60 ml	2 oz
Lemon Oil		½ tsp
Wintergreen Oil		½ tsp
Sassafras Oil		½ tsp
Alcohol 90%	1 L	1 qt
Water, sufficient for	2 L	2 qt

Grind the spices to a course powder. Combine with alcohol and 250 ml of water, macerate for 3 days. Filter, then add the oils to 1 oz of alcohol and mix with other components. Colour with caramel, set aside for 48 hours, then filter.

Milkshake Extract

Vanilla Extract	60 ml	2 oz
Pineapple Juice	420 ml	14 oz

Mix

Myrrh, Tincture Of

Myrrh, powdered	120 g	4 oz
Alcohol 90%	1 L	1 qt

Infuse for twelve days, strain and bottle.

Orange Extract (Soluble)

Orange Oil	40 ml	1¼ oz
Magnesium Carbonate	60 g	2 oz
Alcohol 90%	360 ml	12 oz
Water, sufficient	1 L	1 qt

Dissolve the oil in the alcohol and then add the magnesium carbonate. Agitate until any clumps are gone. Macerate for 7 days, shaking daily. Filter through paper to get 1 qt.

Orange Wine

Sweet Orange Essence	480 ml	16 oz
Sweet Catawba Wine	2 L	2 qt

Mix.

Peppermint Extract

Peppermint Oil	30 ml	1 oz
Magnesium Carbonate	60 g	2 oz
Alcohol 90%	360 ml	12 oz
Water, sufficient	1 L	1 qt

Dissolve the oil in the alcohol and then add the magnesium carbonate. Agitate until all clumps are gone. Macerate for a week, shaking daily.

Persico Essence

Lemon Oil	22 ml	¾ oz
Clove Oil	50 ml	1¾ oz
Cinnamon Oil	105 ml	3½ oz
Bitter Orange Oil	120 ml	4 oz
Brandy	480 ml	16 oz
Grape Tincture (1:5)	45 ml	1½ oz
Peach Essence	45 ml	1½ oz
Distilled Water	450 ml	15 oz
Alcohol 90%	2 L	2 qt

Dissolve the oils in the water alcohol mixture. Use 30 ml of extract in 4 L of syrup.

Royale Essence

Ambergris	2.6 g	⅔ tsp
Musk	1.3 g	⅓ tsp
Civet	0.7 g	¼ tsp
Carbonate of Potash	0.7 g	¼ tsp
Oil of Cinnamon		6 drops
Oil of Rhodium		4 drops
Otto of Roses		4 drops
Brandy	480 ml	16 oz

Macerate for 10 days or longer.

Rose Extract

Red Rose Petals	15 g	½ oz
Oil of Rose	5 drops	
Alcohol	180 ml	6 oz
Water	300 ml	10 oz

Dissolve the oil in the alcohol, add the water and rose petals, macerate for 7 days, agitating occasionally. Filter and bottle.

Rose Extract (Soluble)

Red Rose Petals	450 ml	15 oz
Glycerine	30 ml	1 oz
Alcohol 90%, sufficient		

Mix the glycerine with 15 oz of alcohol, and use 7 oz to moisten the rose petals. Pack the roses in a percolator, add more glycerine mixture to cover and macerate for 48 hours. Percolate until 12 oz are obtained. Continue percolating with the remainder of the alcohol. Dissolve the first portion and make up to 16 oz with proof spirit.

Sarsaparilla Extract

Oil of wintergreen	15 ml	½ oz
Oil of sassafras	15 ml	½ oz
Alcohol 60%	450 ml	5 oz
Caramel	sufficient	

Mix the oils with magnesium carbonate to form a thick cream, then mix with alcohol and water, and filter. Colour a dark brown with caramel.

Saxe's Orange Extract

Zested Peel of Oranges	60	
Orange Oil	30 ml	1 oz
Glycerine	180 ml	6 oz
Water	3 L	3 qt
Alcohol	3 L	3 qt

Combine and macerate the zest for 2 to 3 weeks. Strain and then add the orange extract.

Spice Extract

Black Pepper	30 g	1 oz
Pimento Berry	15 g	½ oz
Nutmeg	2 tsp	
Brandy or Alcohol	240 ml	8 oz

Extract by slow percolation.

Soluble Flavouring

Sweet Orange Oil	120 ml	4 oz
Cassia Oil	1½ tsp	
Coriander Oil	1½ tsp	
Clove Oil	1½ tsp	
Nutmeg Oil	¾ tsp	
Magnesium Carbonate	120 g	4 oz
Alcohol 90%	2.2 L	2¼ qt
Water	1.7 L	1¾ qt

Mix the oils with the alcohol and the magnesium carbonate with the water; gradually combine the two mixtures. Allow the mixture to stand for 48 hours, with occasional agitation. Decant the clear liquid and bottle.

Soup Herbs Extract

Thyme	30 g	1 oz
Sweet Basil	30 g	1 oz
Marjoram	30 g	1 oz
Summer Savory	30 g	1 oz
Celery Seed	1 tsp	
Alcohol 40%	480 ml	16 oz

Extract by slow percolation. Use is savory drinks.

Taraxacum, Elixir of
(Elixir Of Dandelion)

Dandelion Extract	60 ml	2 oz
Simple Elixir	420 ml	14 oz
Magnesium Carbonate, a sufficient quantity		

Mix the extract of dandelion in a mortar with magnesium carbonate to form a paste. Slowly add the simple elixir, stirring well, and filter.

Tonka Essence

Tonka Bean, bruised	120 g	4 oz
Orris Root, powder	15 g	½ oz
Alcohol 20%	1 L	16 oz

Create fine powder with the Orris and Tonka, add the alcohol and macerate for 14 days. Filter.

Tonic Extract

Red Cinchona	15 g	½ oz
Coriander	2 tsp	
Canella	2 tsp	
Angelica	2 tsp	
Cinnamon	2 tsp	
Cardamom (no shells)	1 tsp	
Cochineal	¼ tsp	
Cloves	¼ tsp	
Alcohol 40%, sufficient	480 ml	16 oz

Reduce the spices to a fine powder and extract by slow percolation to obtain 16 oz of extract.

Wine of Beef

Extract of Beef	1 tbsp	
Hot Water	30 ml	1 oz
Sherry Wine, to make	480 ml	16 oz

Pour the hot water upon the extract of beef contained in a mortar and triturate until a smooth. Then add while stirring 14 ounces of sherry wine. Transfer the mixture to a bottle and refrigerate for 2 days then filter. Each teaspoon represents 2 grains of Extract of Beef.

Wine of Coca

Extract of Coca	30 ml	1 oz
Alcohol	40 ml	1¼ oz
Sugar	30 ml	1 oz
Port Wine	390 ml	13 oz

Dissolve the sugar in 8 oz of the wine, add the Coca extract and alcohol. Mix and then add the remainder of the Port Wine and set to rest for 2 days. Filter and bottle.

Wintergreen Extract (Soluble)

Wintergreen Oil	30 ml	1 oz
Magnesium Carbonate	60 ml	2 oz
Alcohol 90%	360 ml	12 oz
Water, sufficient	1 L	1 qt

Dissolve the oil in the alcohol and then add the magnesium carbonate. Agitate until any clumps are gone. Allow to macerate for at least a week, shaking daily. Filter through paper and then pour water, through the filter, to get 1 qt.

Wintergreen II

Oil of wintergreen	30 ml	1 oz
Alcohol	450 ml	15 oz

Mix them together.

This extract may be made of the fresh berries, but not of the flavour strength produced by the foregoing formula. There is perhaps a freshness in the extract that is made of the berries that is wanting in the solution of the oil, but few persons, however, can procure fresh wintergreen berries. In selecting oil of wintergreen, it is to be borne in mind that the commercial oil is likely to be either oil of white birch or synthetical oil.

World's Fair Root Beer Extract

Sarsaparilla Extract	30 ml	1 oz
Wild Cherry Extract	30 ml	1 oz
Yellow Dock Extract	30 ml	1 oz
Wintergreen Extract	30 ml	1 oz
Oil of Coriander	15 ml	½ oz
Oil of Lemon	7.5 ml	¼ oz
Oil of Sassafras	7.5 ml	¼ oz
Magnesium Carbonate	45 g	1½ oz
Caramel Colouring	15 ml	½ oz
Alcohol (90%)	480 ml	16 oz
Water	480 ml	16 oz

Dissolve the oils in the alcohol and separately dissolve the magnesium carbonate in the water. Add the fluid extracts and caramel colouring. Combine the three solutions and allow the mixture to rest for two to three days, agitating occasionally. After resting, filter the extract if necessary.

DRINK
CHAMPAGNE GINGER.

A choice table drink, invigorating, but not intoxicating. Sold everywhere.

Manufactured by

G. D. DOWS & CO., Boston.

Syrups & Drinks

The base of most soda fountain drinks is the flavouring syrup. These syrups could be viewed as the equivalent of the bartenders back bar.

Compound Syrups are a mixture of two or more base syrups. If a particular drink was popular, the pharmacist would just pre-mix the two flavouring syrups for convenience. An example would be the very popular Ambrosia and Nectar syrups.

Phosphate Concentrates are similar to plain or compound syrups, but they pre-mixed the acid phosphate solution into the syrup. This ensure consistency and helped avoid handling bulk acids behind the counter.

Fancy Syrups are complex mixtures that were created using fruits, tinctures and extracts. These were usually signature recipes that the pharmacy kept secret, as a competitive advantage. This is how Coca-Cola started.

The best soda syrups are made from fresh pressed fruit juice, treated in a manner that preserves its quality. To do this, a high quality fruit juicer is recommended. The cheaper varieties can "grind" the fruit, creating an excess of pulp and bitter compounds from peels. For soda syrups, it is important that they are clear and free of flotsam, as this pulpy material will cause excess foaming when soda water is added.

Base Syrups

Arrack Punch Syrup

Batavia Arrack	480 ml	16 oz
Lemon Juice	2 L	2 qt
Sugar	1140 g	2½ lbs
Water	480 ml	16 oz

Combine sugar, water and lemon juice, and stir till the liquid is clear; add ½ gallon Batavia arrack, then filter.

Barnaby's Prize Chocolate Syrup

Cocoa Powder	454 g	1 lb
Granulated Sugar	900 g	2 lb

Mix thoroughly, in a pot, then add just enough hot water to make a thick paste-taking care to rub out all the lumps. Add boiling water to make a molasses consistency; in a water bath, cook for 15 minutes with the water boiling.

To serve, place small ladle full of mixture in a coffee cup, add 30 ml (1 oz) of standard cream, and fill with soda or hot water.

Bisque Syrup

Roasted almonds	120 g	4 oz
Extract of vanilla	15 ml	½ oz
Soda syrup	1 L	32 oz

Break up the almonds to coarse powder, boil for a few minutes with about 8 ounces of the syrup, allow to cool, strain, and add the extract and the remainder of the syrup. This is to be served in a 12 oz glass with or without ice cream.

Birch Syrup

Birch Essence	60 ml	2 oz
Simple Syrup	2 L	64 oz
Soda Foam		sufficient

Serve 1 oz of syrup "solid" in an 8 oz glass.

Capillaire
(Maidenhair Syrup)

Maidenhair Herb	30 g	3 oz
Boiling Water	1 L	32 oz
Sugar	7.2 kg	16 lbs
Orange-flower water	60 ml	2 oz
Egg White	1	

Combine the maidenhair with boiling water and macerate until cold. Strain without pressing, to get 1 gallon; beat the egg white to a froth, and mix with the infusion; dissolve the sugar and bring to a boil; skim off any scum that rises and when clear, cool and add the orange-flower water.

Champagne Syrup

Rhine Wine	1 L	32 oz
French Cognac	60 ml	2 oz
Sherry Wine	30 ml	1 oz
Sugar	1350 g	3 lbs

Dissolve the sugar in the wine without heat

Champagne Syrup III

Crabapple Extract	10 ml	⅓ oz
Pineapple Juice	60 ml	2 oz
Citric Acid	45 ml	1½ oz
Simple Syrup	1.2 L	40 oz

Combine ingredients and bottle.

Checkerberry Syrup

Checkerberry Extract	15 ml	½ oz
Simple Syrup, to make	1 L	32 oz

Checkerberry is the same as Wintergreen.

Claret Syrup

Red Bordeaux Wine	300 ml	10 oz
Syrup	180 ml	6 oz
Soda Foam		sufficient

Mix and bottle. Use 1 to 2 ounces of syrup.

Cherry Kicker (Hot)

Cherry Juice	240 ml	8 oz
Sugar	360 g	12 oz
Water	120 ml	4 oz

Make a syrup. Dispense 45 ml (1½oz) in a coffee mug, add 1 teaspoon of acid phosphate and wedge of lemon and fill with hot water.

Cherry Syrup

Sour Cherry Juice	240 ml	8 oz
Sugar	360 g	12 oz
Alcohol, 90%	30 ml	1 oz

Take the juice of fresh sour cherries and set aside in a container for 24 hours. Carefully decant the liquid from any solids. Add the sugar and bring the mixture to a boil, turning the heat off once it has reached that point. Add the alcohol to a clean bottle, ensuring the inside of the bottle is fully coated. Add the cherry syrup.

Chocolate Syrup

Cocoa Powder	112 g	4 oz
Sugar	1600 g	3½ lbs
Water	1.2 L	40 oz
Vanilla	15 ml	½ oz

Make cocoa into a thick paste with hot water, gradually add rest of water then the sugar; boil for one minute, stirring constantly. Strain while hot, and when cool add extract of vanilla.

Cinnamon Syrup

Cinnamon Oil	2 ml	⅓ tsp
Sugar	1.68 kg	56 oz
Water	1 L	32 oz
Magnesium Carbonate	4 g	1 tsp
Gum Arabic	30 g	1 oz

Rub the oil with the magnesium carbonate and gum, then gradually add the water. Filter this mixture through filter paper and then dissolve the sugar without heat.

Coffee Syrup

Coffee (fresh ground)	150 g	5 oz
Sugar	700 g	24 oz
Water, to make	1 L	32 oz
Soda Foam	sufficient	

Combine the ground coffee with half the water, cool, and steep over night. Place in a pot and bring to a simmer for two minutes, don't boil. Strain and let stand for two to three hours. Filter off the clarified liquid, and avoid the dark precipitate. In the other half of the water, dissolve the sugar and soda foam then combine and bottle. Serve 2 oz in a 12 oz glass.

Cranberry Syrup

Cranberry Conc.	210 ml	7 oz
Simple Syrup	810 ml	27 oz
Lemon Extract	½ tsp	

Mix and bottle. Use 1 to 2 ounces of syrup.

Damascus Plum Syrup

Port Wine	240 ml	8 oz
Citric Acid Solution	1 tbsp	
Vanilla Extract	1½ tsp	
Simple Syrup	2 L	2 qt
Soda Foam	sufficient	
Colour Red	Sufficient	

Gentian Syrup

Gentian Extract	1½ tsp	
Sarsaparilla Extract	3 tsp	
Simple Syrup	1 L	32 oz

Use to add bitterness to a drink.

Ginger Syrup

Jamaica Ginger Extract	30 ml	1 oz
Simple Syrup	1 L	32 oz
Caramel	10 ml	⅓ oz

Combine the ingredients and filter if required.

Imperial Chocolate Syrup

Cocoa powder	180 g	9 oz
Sugar	900 g	2 lbs
Gelatin	7.5 g	¼ oz
Water	1.2 L	40 oz
Vanilla Extract	30 ml	1 oz
Eggs	4	

Dissolve the gelatin in 4 oz of water, add the cocoa, sugar and remainder of the water. Bring to a boil, stirring constantly. Strain when cool. Add the eggs, beaten, and the vanilla. Mix thoroughly. Serve like Chocolate Syrup.

Lemon Syrup

Lemon Juice (fresh)	480 ml	16 oz
Lemon Zest	60 g	2 oz
Sugar	700 g	24 oz
Soda Foam	sufficient	

Bring the lemon juice to boiling, remove from heat, add the peel and let the whole stand closely covered until cold. Filter and add water if needed to make 480 ml (1 pint). Dissolve the sugar without heat and add the soda foam.

Lime Fruit Syrup
Possible Green River

Lime Juice	180 ml	6 oz
Lime Oil	1 tsp	
Simple Syrup, to make	1 L	32 oz
Green Colouring	sufficient	

Mix and bottle. Use 1 to 2 ounces per glass.

Orange Syrup

Simple Syrup, to make	1 L	32 oz
Sugar	30 g	1 oz
Citric Acid	¼ tsp	
Oranges	5	

Grate the peel from the orange and rub it well with the sugar. Express the juice from the oranges, add the acid and mix with the simple syrup.

Orange Syrup II

Sweet Orange Oil	10 drops	
Simple Syrup	1.2 L	40 oz
Tartaric Acid	15 g	½ oz

Rub the oil with the acid then add to the syrup.

Orgeat Syrup

Sweet Almonds	240 g	8 oz
Bitter Almonds	90 g	3 oz
Sugar	1.5 kg	48 oz
Water	780 ml	26 oz
Orange Flower Water	120 ml	4 oz

Blanche the almonds and grind to a fine paste with 12 oz of sugar and 2 oz of water. Mix the paste with the remaining water, steep for 10 minutes, strain and strongly express the paste to get all of the liquids out. Dissolve the remaining sugar, using gentle heat if necessary. Cool and add the orange flower water.

Pear Syrup

Pear Juice	480 ml	16 oz
Simple Syrup	360 ml	12 oz
Soda Foam	sufficient	

Serve 1 to 1½ oz "solid" in an 8 oz glass.

Pineapple Syrup

Pineapple Juice	240 ml	8 oz
Water	150 ml	5 oz
Sugar	600 g	20 oz
Alcohol, 90%	30 ml	1 oz

Take the juice of fresh pineapple and set aside for 24 hours. Dissolve the sugar in the water, using a gentle heat. Add the pineapple juice and bring the mixture to a boil, turning the heat off once it has reached that point. Add the alcohol to a clean bottle, ensuring the inside of the bottle is fully coated. Add the pineapple syrup.

Pineapple Ginger Syrup

Pineapple Juice	240 ml	8 oz
Extract Ginger Sol.	120 ml	4 oz
Citric Acid	15 g	½ oz
Simple Syrup	1.2 L	40 oz

Makes a good phosphate syrup also.

Pomegranate Syrup

Pomegranate juice	480 ml	16 oz
Lemon Juice	15 ml	½ oz
Vanilla Extract	15 ml	½ oz
Simple Syrup	480 ml	16 oz
Soda Foam	sufficient	

Mix and serve "solid". Alternately the syrup can be made from ½ oz of Grenadine Extract, with 2 tsp citric acid and 16 oz of thin syrup.

Pistachio Syrup

Simple Syrup	480 ml	16 oz
Pistachio Essence	1 tsp	
Almond Essence	½ tsp	
Soda Foam	¼ tsp	

Mix to combine.

Raspberry Syrup

Raspberry Concentrate	150 ml	5 oz
Simple Syrup	450 ml	15 oz
Citric Acid	1 tsp	

Mix. For milk or cream drinks, omit the acid.

Raspberry Vinegar

Raspberry Juice	240 ml	8 oz
Cider Vinegar	60 ml	2 oz

Mix and bottle.

Red Bordeaux Syrup

Red Bordeaux	240 ml	8 oz
Simple Syrup	480 ml	16 oz

Mix. Use 1-2 ounces per 8 ounce glass.

Red Currant Syrup

Red Current Juice	480 ml	16 oz
Extract of red currant	30 ml	1 oz
Simple Syrup,	4 L	4 qt
Citric Acid Solution	60 ml	2 oz

Mix thoroughly. Serve solid; no milk.

Rhine Wine Syrup

Simple Syrup	480 ml	16 oz
Rhine Wine (Riesling)	480 ml	16 oz

Mix and serve solid in an 8 ounce glass.

Rose Syrup

Rose Extract	1 tsp	
Orris Extract	15 ml	½ oz
Vanilla Extract	2 tsp	
Red Colouring	1 tsp	
Simple Syrup	1 L	32 oz

Mix and strain.

Sarsaparilla Syrup

Sarsaparilla powder	240 g	8 oz
Licorice Root, powder	240 g	8 oz
Oil of Anise	10 drops	
Oil of Wintergreen	10 drops	
Oil of Cinnamon	2 drops	
Sugar	3 kg	6 lbs
Soda Foam	sufficient	

Digest the roots for 12 hours in 4 pints of warm water. Place the steeped liquid in a percolator and obtain 4 pints by adding sufficient water. Dissolve the sugar with a gentle heat. When the syrup is cold, add the oils by rubbing them with a little sugar then dissolving in the syrup. Finish by mixing in the soda foam.

Solferino Syrup

Cognac	150 ml	5 oz
Simple Syrup	300 ml	10 oz

Strawberry, Fresh Syrup

Strawberry Juice	360 ml	8 oz
Citric Acid	1 tsp	
Soda Foam	10 ml	⅓ oz
Simple Syrup	2 L	2 qt

The flavour will depend on the quality of the strawberries. If the flavour is weak, as more strawberry juice.

Strawberry, Wild (Syrup)

Strawberry Syrup	480 ml	16 oz
Almond Extract,	1½ tsp	
Cherry Juice	240 ml	8 oz
Extinct Acid Phosphate	30 ml	1 oz
Simple Syrup	210 ml	7 oz

Mix.

Tea Syrup

Green Tea	150 g	5 oz
Black Tea	120 g	4 oz
Soda Foam	30 ml	1 oz
Granulated Sugar	1 kg	36 oz
Boiling Water	750 ml	26 oz

Place 90 g (3 oz) of tea in a suitable vessel, pour upon it 250 ml (8 oz) of boiling water, cover and steep for a few minutes, express and set aside. Repeat twice more, using fresh tea each time. Mix the liquids and dissolve the sugar by agitation. Add the soda foam.

Vanilla Syrup

Vanilla Extract	10 ml	⅓ oz
Simple syrup	930 ml	31 oz
Citric Acid	1 tsp	
Foam Extract	1-2 tsp	
Tincture of Musk	¼ tsp	

The quality of the vanilla syrup is dependant on the vanilla extract used. If the syrup lacks enough vanilla flavour just add more extract.

Violet Syrup

Violet Essence	60 ml	2 oz
Magnesium Carbonate	15 g	½ oz
Sugar	700 g	24 oz
Water	480 ml	16 oz
Soda Foam	sufficient	

Thoroughly mix the violet essence with magnesium carbonate in a mortar and pestle. Add the water, mix thoroughly with shaking and filter. Dissolve the sugar and add the soda foam. The syrup can be coloured green with Chlorophyll.

White Wine Syrup

White Wine (dry)	150 ml	5 oz
Simple Syrup	300 ml	10 oz

Mix.

Wild Cherry Syrup

Wild Cherry Bark	60 g	2 oz
Glycerin	60 ml	2 oz
Sugar	600 g	20 oz
Citric Acid Solution	30 ml	1 oz
Water, to make	600 ml	20 oz

Mix the glycerin with 8 ounces of water and moisten the cherry bark powder. Macerate for 24 hours in a closed vessel. Extract my percolation, using additional water, until 20 oz is obtained. Dissolve the sugar, by agitation. And filter if required.

Wintergreen Syrup

Oil of Wintergreen	5 drops	
Simple Syrup	450 ml	15 oz
Alcohol 90%	30 ml	1 oz
Caramel	to colour	

Mix the oil with the alcohol to dissolve and then add to the simple syrup. Shake to combine. Add caramel to colour.

Compound Syrups

Adironda Mulberry

Mulberry Syrup	480 ml	16 oz
Bordeaux Syrup	120 ml	4 oz
Champagne Syrup	120 ml	4 oz
Mulberry Juice	360 ml	12 oz

Use 3 oz of syrup per 8 oz glass. Place shave ice into tumbler and draw "solid" with soda water.

Alhambra Cream

Peach syrup	60 ml	2 oz
Orange syrup	180 ml	6 oz
Vanilla syrup	270 ml	9 oz
Cream	210 ml	7 oz

Draw about 1 to 1½ ounces of this syrup into a 12-ounce glass, fill with soda water.

Ambrosia Syrup No.1

Strawberry Syrup	480 ml	1 pint
Vanilla Syrup	480 ml	1 pint
Riesling Wine	240 ml	8 oz

Mix and use 45 ml (1½ oz) per 240 ml (8 oz) glass.

Baltimore Cream

Peach Syrup	90 ml	3 oz
Orange Syrup	240 ml	8 oz
Vanilla Syrup	240 ml	8 oz
Strawberry Syrup	120 ml	4 oz

Mix thoroughly. Serve 2 oz "solid" in a 10 oz glass.

Caramel Syrup

Extract of Coffee	45 ml	1½ oz
Extract of Vanilla	15 ml	½ oz
Caramel	30 ml	1 oz
Chocolate syrup	240 ml	8 oz
Simple syrup, to make	1 L	32 oz

Serve in 12 oz glasses with or without ice cream.

Celery Syrup

Lemon Syrup	480 ml	16 oz
Celery Extract	30 ml	1 oz
Bitters	1 tsp	

Mix and use in a Celery soda or phosphate.

Champagne Smash

Champagne Syrup	90 ml	3 oz
Sweet Mint Syrup	90 ml	3 oz
Simple Syrup	480 ml	1 pint
Essence of Peppermint	2 drops	
Acid Phosphates	2 tsp	

Mix thoroughly. Serve 2 oz "solid" in a 10 oz glass.

Cherry Flip

Extract of Wild Cherry	30 ml	1 oz
Jamaican Rum	30 ml	1 oz
Citric Acid Solution	30 ml	1 oz
Simple Syrup	2 L	2 qt
Red Colouring	Sufficient	

Serve 1 oz in an 8 oz glass with soda water.

Chocolate Nectar

Vanilla extract	15 ml	½ oz
Orange flower water	120 ml	4 oz
Chocolate syrup	1 L	1 qt

Carmine solution to colour reddish-brown.

Draw 2 oz of this into an 8 oz glass, add 1 oz of cream, and fill with the coarse stream.

Claro

Strawberry juice	120 ml	4 oz
Raspberry juice	120 ml	4 oz
Solution of citric acid	180 ml	6 oz
Soda foam	120 ml	4 oz
Soda syrup	1.5 L	1½ qt
Juice of lemons	3	

Serve like other soda syrups in a 12 ounce glass.

Crescent Sherbet

Pineapple syrup	480 ml	16 oz
Orange syrup	480 ml	16 oz
Vanilla syrup	360 ml	12 oz
Sherry wine	120 ml	4 oz

Serve "solid" in an 8-ounce glass, using 1 to 1½ oz of syrup, filling the glass with the coarse stream.

Don't Care Syrup (Hiss)

Pineapple Syrup	120 ml	4 oz
Strawberry Syrup	120 ml	4 oz
Vanilla Extract	1 tsp	
Port Wine	60 ml	2 oz
Simple Syrup	1 L	1 qt

"Don't Care Syrup" was a response for customers who wanted a drink, but didn't care what they got. Smart operators created a syrup with this name and served it whenever somebody didn't care.

Don't Care Syrup (Saxe's)

Cognac	240 ml	8 oz
Simple Syrup	4 L	1 gal
Gum Foam	30 ml	1 oz
Fruit Acid	1½ tsp	

Serve 1 to 1½ oz solid in an 8 ounce glass.

English Peach, Honey And Cream

Peach Juice	360 ml	12 oz
Strained Honey	480 ml	16 oz
Simple Syrup	480 ml	16 oz
Rose Water	60 ml	2 oz
Foam Extract	15 ml	½ oz

Mix well. Serve in a 12 oz glass with 2 oz of syrup and 2 oz of sweet cream; fill up soda water.

Eumelan Currant

Black Currant Syrup	480 ml	16 oz
Black Currant Juice	300 ml	10 oz
Raspberry Syrup	60 ml	2 oz
Orange Syrup	30 ml	1 oz
Champagne Syrup	30 ml	1 oz

Mix and serve 1 to 1½ oz in an 8 ounce glass.

Excelsior Syrup

Wild Cherry Syrup	120 ml	4 oz
Port Wine	120 ml	4 oz
Simple Syrup	240 ml	8 oz

Mix and serve 1 to 1½ oz in an 8 ounce glass.

Fancy Syrup

Vanilla Syrup	1 L	32 oz
Pineapple Syrup	240 ml	8 oz
Raspberry Syrup	240 ml	8 oz

Mix and serve 1 to 1½ oz in an 8 ounce glass.

Florentine Syrup

Pineapple Juice	30 ml	1 oz
Strawberry Juice	30 ml	1 oz
Vanilla Syrup	420 ml	14 oz
Soda Foam	Sufficient	

Mix and serve 1 to 1½ oz in an 8 ounce glass.

Fruit Shrub

Pineapple juice	30 ml	1 oz
Grape juice	30 ml	1 oz
Raspberry juice	30 ml	1 oz
Extract of vanilla	15 ml	½ oz
Solution of citric acid	60 ml	2 oz
Simple syrup, to make	1 L	1 qt

Serve like other soda syrups in 12-ounce glass.

Grape Cup

Grape juice	420 ml	14 oz
Brewed Tea	420 ml	14 oz
Lime juice	120 ml	4 oz
Extinct Acid Phosphate	15 ml	½ oz

Serve like other soda syrups in 12-ounce glass.

Idlewild

Strawberry syrup	300 ml	10 oz
Orange syrup	300 ml	10 oz
Pineapple syrup	300 ml	10 oz
Lemon juice	60 ml	2 oz

Draw 1½ ounces of this into a 12 oz glass ⅓ filled with shaved ice, then fill the glass with the coarse stream, add a strawberry, slice of pineapple and a slice of orange, and serve with straws.

Malted Milk Syrup
(J. Milhau's & Son, New York)

Malted Milk	120 g	4 oz
Whisky	90 ml	3 oz
Maple Syrup	60 ml	2 oz
Simple Syrup	180 ml	6 oz
Water (hot)	480 ml	16 oz

Mix all the ingredients and stir until dissolved. Serve 60 ml (2 oz) in an 8 oz glass.

Marshmallow Syrup

Sugar	500 g	16 oz
Water, cold	1 L	1 qt
Gum Arabic	180 g	6 oz
Egg Whites	3	

Dissolve gum in ½ the water Dissolve the sugar in the other ½ of the water. Beat the egg whites until frothy, and combine with the sugar syrup. Combine the two solutions. Keep refrigerate.

May Queen Fizzette

Blood Orange Syrup	480 ml	16 oz
Raspberry Fruit Syrup	300 ml	10 oz
Sweet Catawba	300 ml	10 oz
Rose Syrup	90 ml	3 oz
Pineapple Syrup	75 ml	2½ oz
Fruit Acid	15 ml	½ oz

Mix well together. Place 2 oz of syrup in a tumbler, add shaved ice, fill with carbonated water. Garnish with raspberries and a piece of lemon.

Mountain Mist Syrup

Holland Gin	30 ml	1 oz
Lemon Syrup	450 ml	15 oz

Draw 1½ ounces of this into a 8 oz glass ⅓ filled with shaved ice, then fill the glass with the coarse streamand serve with straws.

Mountain Pink

Vanilla Extract	15 ml	½ oz
Lemon Essence	15 ml	½ oz
Pineapple Juice	60 ml	2 oz
Sugar	1125 g	2½ lbs
Sodium Bicarbonate	1 tsp	
Sweet Cream	1 L	1 qt
Sufficient Red Colouring		

The sodium bicarbonate is to neutralize fruit acid. Serve as an ice cream soda.

Nectar Syrup

Vanilla Syrup	480 ml	16 oz
Raspberry Syrup	210 ml	7 oz
Pineapple Syrup	90 ml	3 oz

Use 45 ml (1½ oz) per 8 oz (240 ml) glass.

Orange Chocolate

Extract of vanilla	1½ tsp
Orange-flower water	3 tsp
Chocolate syrup, to make 1 L	32 oz

This may be served with cream in a 12 oz glass.

Orange Ferrone

Orange syrup	480 ml	16 oz
Raspberry syrup	240 ml	8oz
Vanilla syrup	120 ml	4 oz
Elixir gentian with iron	120 ml	4 oz

Use 45 ml (1½ oz) per 8 oz (240 ml) glass.

Phantom Syrup

Vanilla Syrup	240 ml	8 oz
Pineapple Syrup	980 ml	32 oz
Orange Syrup	720 ml	24 oz
Orange Flower Water	60 ml	2 oz

Mix well. To serve add sweet cream to a 12 oz glass. This syrup makes a good egg drink.

Pink Tea (Hot)

Green tea	30 g	1 oz
Black tea	30 g	1 oz
Water	480 ml	16 oz
Sugar	300 g	10 oz

Make two teas with the water, strain the liquid, dissolve the sugar. Serve 30 ml (1 oz) in an 8 oz mug, fill with hot water, add a slice of lemon.

Polar Syrup

Root Beer Extract		4 tsp
Ginger Ale Extract		2 tsp
Soda Foam		sufficient
Simple Syrup, to make	480 ml	16 oz

Serve 30 ml (1 oz) in an 8 oz glass with cracked ice.

Sherbert Syrup

White Wine	240 ml	8 oz
Lemon Syrup	240 ml	8 oz
Pineapple Syrup	480 ml	16 oz
Soda Foam	sufficient	

Serve 45 ml (1½ oz) of syrup "solid" in a 12 oz glass.

Spice Of Life

Red Currant Syrup	600 ml	20 oz
Lemon Syrup	150 ml	5 oz
Raspberry Syrup	150 ml	5 oz

Serve 30 ml (1 oz) in an 8 oz glass with cracked ice.

St. Lawrence Blueberry

Blueberry Syrup	480 ml	16 oz
Blackberry Juice	240 ml	8 oz
Cherry Juice	120 ml	4 oz
Port Wine Syrup	120 ml	4 oz
Cinnamon Syrup	60 ml	2 oz
Orange Syrup	30 ml	1 oz
Lemon Syrup	30 ml	1 oz

Combine and serve 1 to 1½ oz in an 8 oz glass.

Tahiti Pineapple

Pineapple Syrup	480 ml	16 oz
Pineapple Champagne	180 ml	6 oz
Pineapple Juice	180 ml	6 oz
Orange Syrup	90 ml	3 oz
Vanilla Syrup	90 ml	3 oz

Use 3 oz of syrup per 8 oz glass. Place shave ice into tumbler and draw "solid" with soda water. Transfer to the shaker and shake and strain.

Turqua Syrup

Orange Juice	60 ml	2 oz
Lemon Juice	30 ml	1 oz
Raspberry Juice	15 ml	½ oz
Angostura Bitters	1 tsp	
Solution of Citric Acid	15 ml	½ oz
Simple Syrup	1 L	32 oz
Soda Foam	sufficient	

Combine and serve 1 to 1½ oz in an 8 oz glass.

Tutti Fruitti

Maple syrup	30 ml	1 oz
Spirit of lemon	¾ tsp	
Spirit of orange	¾ tsp	
Tincture of vanilla	¾ tsp	
Solution of citric acid	3 tsp	
Soda syrup, to make	1 L	1 qt

Serve like other soda syrups in 12-ounce glasses with or without ice cream.

Yum Yum Syrup

Vanilla Syrup	90 ml	3 oz
Orgeat Syrup	60 ml	2 oz
Pineapple Syrup	60 ml	2 oz
Orange Wine	30 ml	1 oz
Simple Syrup	to make 16 oz	

Combine and serve 1 to 1½ oz in an 8 oz glass.

White Violet Syrup

Strong Tincture of Orris	60 ml	2 oz
Magnesium Carbonate	15 g	½ oz
Sugar	720 g	24 oz
Water	480 ml	16 oz
Soda Foam	sufficient	

Mix the tincture with the magnesium carbonate to form a paste, add the water and mix thoroughly. Filter and add the sugar, aggitate to dissolve and then add the soda foam.

Zozia Syrup

Lemon Essence	¾ tsp	
Vanilla Extract	1½ tsp	
Angostura Bitters	15 drops	
Absinthe Essence	15 drops	
Citric Acid Solution	¾ tsp	
Simple Syrup, to make	1 L	1 qt
Soda Foam	sufficient	
Caramel	Sufficient	

Serve in the Zozia Fizz on Page 159.

Phosphate Syrups

Burbank Special

Pineapple Juice	300 ml	10 oz
Simple Syrup	4 L	4 qt
Plum Extract		1½ tsp
Quince Extract		1½ tsp
Fruit Acid		3 tsp

Mix well. Serve as a phosphate.

Black Cherry Phosphate

Black Cherry Syrup	3 L	3 qt
Lemon Syrup	480 ml	16 oz
Cinnamon Syrup	240 ml	8 oz
Acid Phosphate	240 ml	8 oz

Mix well. Serve like other phosphates.

Burgundy Phosphate

Burgundy Wine	480 ml	16 oz
Simple Syrup	480 ml	16 oz
Amazon Flavour	30 ml	1 oz
Acid Phosphates	60 ml	2 oz

Draw 6 oz of soda into an 8 oz glass and then add 2 oz of syrup. Stir gently with a spoon.

Calisaya Phosphate

Syrup of Roses	540 ml	18 oz
Cinnamon Syrup	240 ml	8 oz
Elixir of Calisaya	120 ml	4 oz
Acid Phosphate	60 ml	2 oz

Serve "solid" in 8-ounce glasses.

Catawba Phosphate

Sweet Catawba Wine	480 ml	16 oz
Simple Syrup	360 ml	12 oz
Syrup of Roses	90 ml	3 oz
Cinnamon Syrup	30 ml	1 oz
Acid Phosphates	60 ml	2 oz

Draw 6 oz of soda into an 8 oz glass and then add 2 oz of syrup. Stir gently with a spoon.

Champagne Smash

Champagne Syrup	480 ml	16 oz
Sweet Mint Syrup	480 ml	16 oz
Essence of Peppermint	5 drops	
Acid Phosphates	30 ml	1 oz
Simple Syrup	2.4 L	2½ qt

Mix thoroughly. To serve place about 2 ounces in a 10-ounce glass and fill with carbonated water.

Cherry Cola

Coca Cola Syrup	480 ml	16 oz
Cherry Syrup	1 L	1 qt

Serve solid in an 8 oz glass.

Chocolate Malt Phosphate

Extract of MAlt		2 lb
Chocolate Syrup		2½ qt
Vanilla Syrup		16 oz
Extinct Acid Phosphate		8 oz

Mix thoroughly. Serve "solid" in 8-ounce glasses.

Delhi Punch

Grape Juice	180 ml	6 oz
Orange Juice	120 ml	4 oz
Acid Phosphates	60 ml	2 oz
Cochineal colour	½ tsp	
Simple Syrup	2 L	2 qt

Mix thoroughly. Serve "solid" in 8-ounce glasses.

Egyptian

Grape Juice	180 ml	6 oz
Orange Juice	60 ml	2 oz
Raspberry Juice	60 ml	2 oz
Phosphate Solution	90 ml	3 oz
Foam Extract	30 ml	1 oz
Cochineal colouring	½ tsp	
Simple Syrup	2 L	2 qt

Mix thoroughly. Serve "solid" in 8-ounce glasses.

Harvest Rome

Tea Syrup	480 ml	16 oz
Maple Syrup	120 ml	8 oz
Acid Phosphate	15 ml	½ oz
Foam Extract	15 ml	½ oz
Simple Syrup	1.4 L	1½ qt

Mix and colour green with a solution made from spinach leaves or any vegetable green colour.

Madeira Phosphate

Maderia Wine	480 ml	16 oz
Simple Syrup	360 ml	12 oz
Vanilla Syrup	60 ml	2 oz
Peach Syrup	60 ml	2 oz
Acid Phosphates	60 ml	2 oz

Draw 6 oz of soda into an 8 oz glass and then add 2 oz of syrup. Stir gently with a spoon.

Malt Bitters Phosphate

Malt Bitters	2½ pt
Syrup of Roses	2½ pt
Vanilla Syrup	1½ pt
Cinchona Wine Syrup	1 pt
Extinct Acid Phosphate	8 oz

Malt Wine Phosphate

Malt Wine	1 qt
Simple Syrup	4½ pt
Aromatic Elixir	1 pt
Extinct Acid Phosphate	8 oz

Serve "solid" in 8-ounce glasses.

N.A.R.D. Favourite

Red Orange Syrup	600 ml	20 oz
Orange Wine	120 ml	4 oz
Pineapple Syrup	120 ml	4 oz
Acid Phosphate	15 ml	½ oz

Put two ounces in thin 8-ounce glass and fill with carbonated water coarse stream.

Oporto Port Phosphate

Port Wine	480 ml	16 oz
Simple Syrup	360 ml	12 oz
Black Cherry Syrup	90 ml	3 oz
Lemon Syrup	15 ml	½ oz
Cinnamon Syrup	15 ml	½ oz
Acid Phosphates	60 ml	2 oz

Draw 6 oz of soda into an 8 oz glass and then add 2 oz of syrup. Stir gently with a spoon.

Orange Phosphate Syrup

Orange Syrup	2 L	2 qt
Extinct Acid Phosphate	30 ml	1 oz

Mix. Blood orange phosphate syrup may be prepared in the same manner as blood orange syrup.

Pedro Ximénez Phosphate

Pedro Ximénez	480 ml	16 oz
Simple Syrup	480 ml	16 oz
Amazon Flavouring	30 ml	1 oz
Acid Phosphates	60 ml	2 oz

Draw 6 oz of soda into an 8 oz glass and then add 2 oz of syrup. Stir gently with a spoon.

Pepsin Phosphate

Glycerite of Pepsin	120 ml	4 oz
Raspberry Syrup	240 ml	8 oz
Acid Phosphate	60 ml	2 oz
Soda syrup, to make	1 L	32 oz

Serve "solid" in 8-ounce glasses.

Phosphorade

Orange Flower Water	30 ml	1 oz
Acid Phosphates	30 ml	1 oz
Phosphoric Acid 85%	45 ml	1½ oz
Simple Syrup	600 ml	20 oz
Water	240 ml	8 oz

Serve 1 oz "solid" in an an 8 oz glass. —Andrew Blair & Co., Philadelphia, Pa.

Pineapple Ale

Extract of ginger	60 ml	2 oz
Pineapple juice	60 ml	2 oz
Acid Phosphate	2 tsp	
Soda syrup	720 ml	24 oz

Serve "solid" in 8-ounce glass.

President's Phosphate Syrup

Blood Orange juice	60 ml	2 oz
Red Raspberry juice	30 ml	1 oz
Vanilla extract	½ tsp	
Juice from Oranges	2	
Acid Phosphate	30 ml	1 oz
Simple Syrup	1 L	1 qt

To serve, place 2 ounces in an 8-ounce glass, and fill with carbonated water, coarse stream.

Pineapple Phosphate Syrup

Orange Syrup	60 ml	2 oz
Vanilla Syrup	30 ml	1 oz
Acid Phosphate	15 ml	½ oz
Pineapple Syrup, to make	1 L	1 qt

Mix. Pour 2 oz into a mineral water glass, fill with soda water and serve.

Rapid Transit Syrup

Tea Syrup	480 ml	16 oz
Vanilla Syrup	240 ml	8 oz
Acid Phosphate	15 ml	½ oz
Foam Extract	15 ml	½ oz
Simple Syrup	1440 ml	1½ qt
Caramel, sufficient		

Mix. Serve 1 to 1½ oz "solid" in an 8 oz glass.

Raspberry Phosphate Syrup

Raspberry Syrup	480 ml	16 oz
Acid Phosphate	1-2 tsp	

Mix. Pour 2 oz into a mineral water glass, fill with soda water and serve.

Royal Muscadine

Raspberry Syrup	480 ml	16 oz
Grape Juice Syrup	480 ml	16 oz
Raspberry Vinegar	60 ml	2 oz

Mix. Pour 2 oz into a mineral water glass, fill with soda water and serve.

Royal Roysterer

Orange Syrup	450 ml	15 oz
Gentian Bitters	30 ml	1 oz
Extinct Acid Phosphate	30 ml	1 oz

Serve 1 to 1½ oz of syrup, shaken with an egg and served in an 8 oz glass topped with seltzer.

Senior

Strawberry Syrup	180 ml	6 oz
Pineapple Syrup	180 ml	6 oz
Cherry Syrup	180 ml	6 oz
Acid Phosphate	30 ml	1 oz

Serve 1½ oz in an 8 oz glass with soda water.

Sherry Phosphate

Sherry Wine	480 ml	16 oz
Simple Syrup	360 ml	12 oz
Wild Cherry Syrup	60 ml	2 oz
Vanilla Syrup	60 ml	2 oz
Acid Phosphates	60 ml	2 oz

Draw 6 oz of soda into an 8 oz glass and then add 2 oz of syrup. Stir gently with a spoon.

Sprague's Special

Pineapple Syrup	240 ml	8 oz
Strawberry Syrup	210 ml	7 oz
Acid Phosphate	30 ml	1 oz

Serve 1 to 1½ oz of syrup, shaken with an egg, ½ oz of sweet cream and a dash of Angostura bitters and served in an 8 oz glass filled with soda water. Garnish with a dusting of nutmeg.

Sweet Clover

Tea syrup	180 ml	6 oz
Maple syrup	90 ml	3 oz
Acid Phosphates	1½ tsp	
Soda syrup	600 ml	20 oz

Colour green with any suitable green colour.
Serve "solid" in 8 oz glass like a "phosphate"

Tokay Phosphate

Tokay Wine	450 ml	15 oz
Simple Syrup	450 ml	15 oz
Amazon Flavouring	30 ml	1 oz
Acid Phosphates	60 ml	2 oz

Draw 6 oz of soda into an 8 oz glass and then
add 2 oz of syrup. Stir gently with a spoon.

True New Yorker

Lemon Syrup	300 ml	10 oz
Catawba Syrup	300 ml	10 oz
Extinct Acid Phosphate	30 ml	1 oz

Serve 1 to 1½ oz of syrup, shaken with an egg
and served in an 8 oz glass topped with seltzer.

Wild Cherry Phosphate

Wild Cherry Extract	30 ml	1 oz
Simple Syrup	1 L	1 qt
Fruit Acid	2 tsp	
Acid Phosphate	½ tsp	

Mix and serve as a solid drink in an 8 ounce
glass. Add the Phosphate last.

Wine Lemonade

Wine Essence	15 ml	½ oz
Lemon Syrup	480 ml	16 oz
Simple Syrup	420 ml	12 oz
Citric Acid Solution	15 ml	½ oz
Caramel Colour	sufficient	
Soda Foam	sufficient	

Mix. Wine Essence is also known as Cognac Oil.

World's Fair Egg Phosphate

Lemon Syrup	240 ml	8 oz
Black Cherry Syrup	240 ml	8 oz
Vanilla Syrup	240 ml	8 oz
Syrup of Roses	240 ml	8 oz
French Champagne	60 ml	2 oz
Acid Phosphate	60 ml	2 oz
Whole Eggs	16	

To serve, place 2 ounces in an 8-ounce glass, and
fill with carbonated water, coarse stream.

Lactart Syrups

Ambrosia Lactart

Raspberry Syrup	270 ml	9 oz
Vanilla Syrup	270 ml	9 oz
Strawberry Syrup	90 ml	3 oz
Muscatel	45 ml	1½ oz

Mix. Dispense 45 ml (1½ oz) of syrup in an 300 ml (10 oz) glass, add 1 teaspoon of Lactart and 30 ml (1 oz) of sweet cream. Fill with soda.

Apricot Lactart

Apricot Syrup	480 ml	16 oz
Peach Syrup	120 ml	4 oz
Orgeat Syrup	90 ml	3 oz
Lactart	45 ml	1½ oz

Mix. Serve 45 ml (1½ oz) of syrup and 30 ml (1 oz) of cream in a 10 oz glass. Fill with soda.

Banana Lactart

Banana Syrup	480 ml	16 oz
Lemon Syrup	120 ml	4 oz
Orange Wine	90 ml	3 oz
Lactart	60 ml	2 oz

Mix. Serve 45 ml (1½ oz) of syrup and 30 ml (1 oz) of cream in a 10 oz glass. Fill with soda.

Blackberry Lactart

Blackberry Syrup	480 ml	16 oz
Black Cherry Syrup	120 ml	4 oz
Blackberry Wine	90 ml	3 oz
Lactart	45 ml	1½ oz

Mix. Dispense 45 ml (1½ oz) of syrup in an 300 ml (10 oz) glass, add 1 teaspoon of Lactart and 30 ml (1 oz) of sweet cream. Fill with soda.

Champagne Lactart

Rhine Wine	360 ml	12 oz
French Cognac	30 ml	1 oz
Sherry Wine	30 ml	1 oz
Simple Syrup	300 ml	10 oz
Lactart	60 ml	2 oz

Mix. Serve 45 ml (1½ oz) of syrup and 30 ml (1 oz) of cream in a 10 oz glass. Fill with soda.

Cherry Lactart

Black Cherry Syrup	480 ml	16 oz
Orgeat Syrup	120 ml	4 oz
Lemon Syrup	45 ml	1½ oz
Red Orange Syrup	30 ml	1 oz
Cinnamon Syrup	30 ml	1 oz
Lactart	60 ml	2 oz

Mix. Serve 45 ml (1½ oz) of syrup and 30 ml (1 oz) of cream in a 10 oz glass. Fill with soda.

Chocolate Lactart

Chocolate Syrup	600 ml	20 oz
Vanilla Syrup	120 ml	4 oz
Cinnamon Syrup	15 ml	½ oz
Lactart	45 ml	1½ oz

Dispense 1½ ounces with 1 ounce of cream and 8 or 10 ounces of carbonated water.

Cranberry Lactart

Cranberry Syrup	480 ml	16 oz
Lemon Syrup	120 ml	4 oz
Orange Wine	90 ml	3 oz
Lactart	60 ml	2 oz

Mix. Serve 45 ml (1½ oz) of syrup and 30 ml (1 oz) of cream in a 10 oz glass. Fill with soda.

Currant Lactart

Black Currant Syrup	480 ml	16 oz
Black Raspberry Syrup	120 ml	4 oz
Apple Juice	120 ml	4 oz
Lactart	60 ml	2 oz

Mix. Serve 45 ml (1½ oz) of syrup and 30 ml (1 oz) of cream in a 10 oz glass. Fill with soda.

Imperial Tea Lactart

Hyson Tea Syrup	180 ml	6 oz
Frech Cognac Syrup	90 ml	3 oz
Claret Syrup	90 ml	3 oz
Essence of Cinnamon		¼ tsp
Essence of Clove		¼ tsp
Simple Syrup	300 ml	10 oz
Lactart	45 ml	1½ oz

Mix. Serve 45 ml (1½ oz) of syrup and 30 ml (1 oz) of cream in a 10 oz glass. Fill with soda.

Lemon Lactart

Lemon Syrup	480 ml	16 oz
Pineapple Syrup	120 ml	4 oz
Catawba Wine	90 ml	3 oz
Lactart	45 ml	1½ oz

Mix. Serve 45 ml (1½ oz) of syrup and 30 ml (1 oz) of cream in a 10 oz glass. Fill with soda.

Lemon Lactic

Lemon Syrup	480 ml	16 oz
Lactic Acid	10 ml	⅓ oz
Fruit Acid		1 tsp
Curcuma colouring		15 drops
Simple Syrup	480 ml	16 oz

Mix. Serve 45 ml (1½ oz) of syrup and 30 ml (1 oz) of cream in a 10 oz glass. Fill with soda.

Maple Lactart

Maple Syrup	480 ml	16 oz
Champagne Syrup	210 ml	7 oz
Lactart	75 ml	2½ oz

Mix. Serve 45 ml (1½ oz) of syrup and 30 ml (1 oz) of cream in a 10 oz glass. Fill with soda.

Nectarine Lactart

Syrup of Vanilla	300 ml	10 oz
Champagne Syrup	210 ml	7 oz
Pineapple Syrup	90 ml	3 oz
Lemon Syrup	90 ml	3 oz
Lactart	60 ml	2 oz

Mix. Serve 45 ml (1½ oz) of syrup and 30 ml (1 oz) of cream in a 10 oz glass. Fill with soda.

Orange Lactart

Red Orange Syrup	480 ml	16 oz
Pineapple Syrup	120 ml	4 oz
Muscatel	90 ml	3 oz
Lactart	60 ml	2 oz

Mix. Serve 45 ml (1½ oz) of syrup and 30 ml (1 oz) of cream in a 10 oz glass. Fill with soda.

Orgeat Lactart

Vanilla Syrup	300 ml	10 oz
Simple Syrup	150 ml	5 oz
Cream Syrup	150 ml	5 oz
Sherry Wine	120 ml	4 oz
Lactart	45 ml	1½ oz
Essence of Noyeau		¼-½ tsp

Mix. Dispense 45 ml (1½ oz) of syrup in an 300 ml (10 oz) glass, add 1 teaspoon of Lactart and 30 ml (1 oz) of sweet cream. Fill with soda.

Peach Lactart

Peach Syrup	390 ml	13 oz
Apricot Syrup	120 ml	4 oz
Orgeat Syrup	90 ml	3 oz
Sherry Wine	90 ml	3 oz
Lactart	60 ml	2 oz

Mix. Serve 45 ml (1½ oz) of syrup and 30 ml (1 oz) of cream in a 10 oz glass. Fill with soda.

Pear Lactart

Pear Syrup	480 ml	16 oz
Champagne Syrup	90 ml	3 oz
Rhine Wine	90 ml	3 oz
Lactart	60 ml	2 oz

Mix. Serve 45 ml (1½ oz) of syrup and 30 ml (1 oz) of cream in a 10 oz glass. Fill with soda.

Pineapple Lactart

Pineapple Syrup	330 ml	11 oz
Vanilla Syrup	90 ml	3 oz
Orange Flower Syrup	90 ml	3 oz
Champagne Syrup	90 ml	3 oz
Rhine Wine	90 ml	3 oz
Lactart	45 ml	1½ oz

Mix. Serve 45 ml (1½ oz) of syrup and 30 ml (1 oz) of cream in a 10 oz glass. Fill with soda.

Raspberry Lactart

Raspberry Syrup	480 ml	16 oz
Muscatel	90 ml	3 oz
Pineapple Syrup	60 ml	2 oz
Lemon Syrup	45 ml	1½ oz
Lactart	60 ml	2 oz

Mix. Serve 45 ml (1½ oz) of syrup and 30 ml (1 oz) of cream in a 10 oz glass. Fill with soda.

Rose Lactart

Syrup of Roses	330 ml	11 oz
Vanilla Syrup	180 ml	6 oz
Red Orange Syrup	90 ml	3 oz
Muscatel	90 ml	3 oz
Lactart	60 ml	2 oz

Mix. Serve 45 ml (1½ oz) of syrup and 30 ml (1 oz) of cream in a 10 oz glass. Fill with soda.

Sherbet Lactart

Pineapple Syrup	330 ml	11 oz
Vanilla Syrup	210 ml	7 oz
Red Orange Syrup	90 ml	3 oz
Orange Flower Syrup	45 ml	1½ oz
Sherry Wine	45 ml	1½ oz
Lactart	60 ml	2 oz

Mix. Serve 45 ml (1½ oz) of syrup and 30 ml (1 oz) of cream in a 10 oz glass. Fill with soda.

Strawberry Lactart

Strawberry Syrup	480 ml	16 oz
Catawba Wine	90 ml	3 oz
Raspberry Syrup	45 ml	1½ oz
Vanilla Syrup	45 ml	1½ oz
Lactart	60 ml	2 oz

Mix. Serve 45 ml (1½ oz) of syrup and 30 ml (1 oz) of cream in a 10 oz glass. Fill with soda.

Vanilla Lactart

Vanilla Syrup	690 ml	23 oz
Lactart	60 ml	3 oz

Mix. Dispense 45 ml (1½ oz) of syrup in an 300 ml (10 oz) glass, add 1 teaspoon of Lactart and 30 ml (1 oz) of sweet cream. Fill with soda.

Fancy Drinks

Ambrosia Syrup

Pineapple juice	75 ml	2½ oz
Plum extract	15 ml	½ oz
Quince extract	15 ml	½ oz
Sol. of citric acid	30 ml	1 oz
Soda foam	60 ml	2 oz
Soda syrup	1 L	1 qt
Yellow colouring	colour light yellow	

Serve like other soda syrups, in 12-ounce glasses, with or without ice cream.

Bowler's Favourite

Wild Grape Syrup	240 ml	8 oz
Strawberry Syrup	480 ml	16 oz
Kola Extract	15 ml	½ oz
Acid Phosphate	15 ml	½ oz
Simple Syrup	2 L	2 qt
Soda Foam		sufficient

Mix and bottle for use.

Aromatic Syrup of Blackberry

Rubus Root Bark	60 ml	2 oz
Cinnamon, powder	7.5 g	¼ oz
Nutmeg, powder	7.5 g	¼ oz
Cloves, powder	4 g	1 tsp
Allspice, powder	4 g	1 tsp
Sugar	300 g	10 oz
Alcohol 20%	180 ml	6 oz
Blackberry Juice, sufficient quantity		

Reduce the Rubus Root and Aromatics to a coarse powder and percolate with alcohol until 4 oz are obtained. To this add 6 oz of blackberry juice, and dissolve the sugar by agitation. Add Blackberry Juice to make sixteen 16 oz.

Alhambra Syrup

Creme de Mandrin	120 ml	4 oz
Claret Wine	360 ml	12 oz
Simple Syrup, to make	960 ml	32 oz

Mix and bottle. Serve solid with ice.

Calisaya Syrup

Cinchona Bark	7.5 g	¼ oz
Gentian Root	20 g	⅔ oz
Orange Peel	90 g	3 oz
Cochineal	4 g	1 tsp
Caraway Seed	2 g	½ tsp
Alcohol 40%	480 ml	16 oz
Quinine Sulphate	0.5 g	⅛ tsp
Oil of Rose		1 drop
Simple Syrup, to make	4 L	1 gal

Reduce the solids to a coarse powder. Extract by percolation using the alcohol. Add remaining ingredients to the percolate.

Serve 30 ml to 45 ml (1 oz to 1½ oz) in an 240 ml (8 ounce) glass, "solid".

Cinisaya

Cinchona Tincture	90 ml	3 oz
Vanilla Extract	30 ml	1 oz
Orange Essence	1½ tsp	
Alcohol 90%	90 ml	3 oz
Water	180 ml	6 oz
Simple Syrup	90 ml	3 oz
Lemon Syrup, to make	1 L	1 qt

Mix the first five ingredients and filter. Wash the filter with a little water. Add the remaining ingredients to the liquid and colour red. Serve "solid" in an 8 oz glass.

Coca Champagne

Champagne Syrup	3.3 L	3⅓ qt
Coca Wine	480 ml	16 oz
Caramel Colouring	30 ml	1 oz
Tartaric Acid	30 ml	1 oz

Combine and bottle. Serve 30 ml (1 oz) in an 240 ml (8 ounce) glass, "solid".

Coca Tonique

Fluid Extract of Kola	15 ml	½ oz
Wine of Coca	180 ml	6 oz
Sherry Wine	60 ml	2 oz
Blackberry Brandy	30 ml	1 oz
Lime Juice	30 ml	1 oz
Raspberry Juice	120 ml	4 oz
Simple Syrup	1 L	1 qt

Serve "solid" in an 8 ounce glass, with a small amount of crushed ice.

Coca-Cola Recipe
John Reed, Pharmacist

Sugar	13.5kg	30 lbs
Water	7.5 L	2 gal
Lime Juice	1 L	1 qt
Citrate of Caffeine	120 g	4 oz
Citric Acid	60 g	2 oz
Extract of Vanilla	30 ml	1 oz
Fluid Extract of Kola	22 ml	¾ oz
Fluid Extract of Coca	22 ml	¾ oz

Combine the extracts and set aside. Take 1 L (1 quart) of water and dissolve the lime juice, caffeine and citric acid, set aside. Dissolve the sugar in the remainder of the water to make a syrup, use a gentle heat. When cool add the other two solutions with thorough mixing. Colour with caramel. This is said to be an early version of Coca-Cola.

Cream Soda
(Dr. Chase's Recipes 1881)

Sugar	1.8 kg	4 lbs
Water	1.5 L	1½ qt
Gum Arabic	30 g	1 oz
Nutmegs, ground	3	
Egg Whites	10	
Oil of Lemon	20 drops	

Combine all ingredients and bring to a simmer for 20 to 30 minutes. Serve 2 ounces "solid".

Cream Soda II
(New York Times 1894)

White Sugar	900 g		2 lbs
Tartaric Acid	60 g		2 oz
Wintergreen Oil	15 ml		½ oz
Water	1.5 L		1½ qt
Egg Whites		3	
Flour		½ cup	
Lemon Juice		1 lemon	

Use 2 to 3 tablespoons of syrup in a glass and fill with soda water.

Diamond Syrup

Vanilla Syrup	120 ml		4 oz
Pineapple Syrup	120 ml		4 oz
Lemon Syrup	120 ml		4 oz
Honey	15 ml		½ oz
Fruit Acid		¼ tsp	
Egg		1	
Gum Foam		1 tsp	
Extinct Acid Phosphate		2 tsp	

Combine all of the ingredients and serve 30 ml to 45 ml (1 to 1½oz) in a 240 ml (8 oz) glass.

Elderberry Mead

Elderberry Juice	480 ml	16 oz
Simple Syrup	1440 ml	1½ qt
French Rose Water	240 ml	8 oz
Cinnamon Water	240 ml	8 oz
Mead Extract	120 ml	4 oz
Fruit Acid Solution	15 ml	½ oz
Water	2.4 L	2½ qt

Use in any recipe that calls for mead syrup.

French Rose Cordial

Alcohol	480 ml	16 oz
Simple Syrup	480 ml	16 oz
White Bordeaux Wine	240 ml	8 oz
Essence of Rose	15 ml	½ oz

Mix and colour red with cochineal.

Gilt Edge

Creme de Mandrin	240 ml	8 oz
Strawberry Syrup	240 ml	8 oz
Orange Syrup	240 ml	8 oz
Banana Syrup	360 ml	8 oz
Simple Syrup, to make	2 L	32 oz

Mix and serve 1 to 1½ oz in a 10 oz glass. Fill the glass nearly full, leaving room to float an ounce of sweet cream on top. Dust with nutmeg.

Ginger Bouquet

Soluble Extract of ginger	45 ml		1½ oz
Solution of citric acid		1½ tsp	
Extract of sarsaparilla		1½ tsp	
Extract of vanilla		1½ tsp	
Soda syrup, to make		1 L	1 qt
Caramel, enough to colour			

Serve this as a "solid" drink in 8-ounce glasses.

Herculine Tonic

Spirit of orange	30 ml	1 oz
Tincture of vanilla	30 ml	1 oz
Tincture of citrochloride	30 ml	1 oz
Acid Phosphate	60 ml	2 oz
Soda syrup, to make	2 L	2 qt
Caramel, enough to colour light brown.		

Serve solid in an 8 oz glass.

Hot Tom

Hot Tom Extract	60 ml	2 oz
Simple Syrup	3.8 L	4 qt
Caramel Colouring	15 ml	½ oz
Foam Syrup	7.5 ml	¼ oz
Citric Acid	60 g	2 oz

Serve "solid" in 8-ounce glasses, drawing 1 or 1½ ounces of this syrup and filling the glass.

Independence Tonic.

Coffee syrup	240 ml	8 oz
Elixir of coca	120 ml	4 oz
Tincture of cinchona	60 ml	2 oz
Madeira wine	60 ml	2 oz
Raspberry syrup	480 ml	16 oz

Serve "solid" in 8-ounce glasses, drawing 1 or 1½ ounces of this syrup and filling the glass.

Honey Dew

Brandy	30 ml	1 oz
Catawba Wine	60 ml	2 oz
Clove Extract	7.5 ml	¼ oz
Strawberry Juice	60 ml	2 oz
Blood Orange	30 ml	1 oz
Pineapple Juice	60 ml	2 oz
Rose Water	15 ml	½ oz
Mace Extract		¾ tsp
Gum Foam	30 ml	1 oz
Simple Syrup	4 L	4 qt

Mix the clove and mace extract with the brandy. Mix all of the other ingredients with the simple syrup and mix thoroughly. Add the brandy mixture and mix again. Serve "solid" in 8-ounce glasses, drawing 1 or 1½ ounces of this syrup and filling the glass.

Hyde Park Tally-Ho

Punch Syrup	60 ml	2 oz
Ice Cream		2 lumps

Mix the syrup and one lump of ice cream, pour into an 8 oz glass, top with soda and ice cream.

Kola Celery Tonic

Raspberry juice	30 ml	1 oz
Fluid extract of kola		¾ tsp
Tincture of celery seed		3 tsp
Solution of citric acid		2 tsp
Soda syrup, to make	1 L	1 qt

Serve "solid" in 8 oz glass, using 1 oz of syrup.

Kola Champagne

Champagne Syrup	1440 ml	1½ qt
Kola Wine	180 ml	6 oz
Citric Acid	15 ml	½ oz
Caramel Colouring	15 ml	½ oz
Vanilla Extract		1 tsp

Serve "solid" in 8 oz glass, using 1 oz of syrup.

Kola Coca Cordial

Wine of Kola	180 ml	6 oz
French Cognac	180 ml	6 oz
Simple Syrup	1440 ml	1½ qt
Wine of Coca	60 ml	2 oz
Vanilla Extract	15 ml	½ oz
Rose Extract	15 ml	½ oz
Cinnamon Extract	15 ml	½ oz

Serve "solid" in 8 oz glass, using 1 oz of syrup.

Kola Syrup

Claret wine	360 ml	12 oz
Raspberry juice	45 ml	1½ oz
Acid Phosphates	120 ml	4 oz
Solution of citric acid	60 ml	2 oz
Soda syrup, to make	1.9 L	2 qt
Fluid extract of kola		1½ tsp
Solution of carmine, to colour deep red.		

Serve "solid" in 8 oz glass, using 1 oz of syrup.

Kolasaya

Blood orange syrup	480 ml	16 oz
Raspberry syrup	240 ml	8 oz
Wine of kola	120 ml	4 oz
Elixir of calisaya	120 ml	4 oz

Mix well and filter. In serving, draw 2 ounces of this syrup in a 12 ounce glass, add cracked or shaved ice, and fill with the coarse stream of carbonated water. Top off with some fresh raspberries or a piece of orange.

Mikado Nectar

Red Bordeaux Syrup	1 L		1 qt
Souchong Tea	120 g		4 oz
Hot Water	480 ml		16 oz
Sugar	900 g		2 lbs
Jamaican Rum (Overproof)	90 ml		3 oz
Pineapple Extract		1 tsp	
Cinnamon Extract		1 tsp	

Infuse the tea for 4 hours in a closed vessel. Strain and dissolve the sugar, heat if necessary. Add the remaining ingredients, and bottle.

Moselle Syrup

Lemon Juice	30 ml	1 oz
Vanilla Extract	2 tsp	
Orange Essence	½ tsp	
Absinthe Essence	½ tsp	
Angostura Bitters	1 tsp	
Soda Foam	sufficient	
Caramel Colouring	sufficient	
Syrup, to make	1 L	1 qt

Serve "solid" in 8-ounce glasses, drawing 1 or 1½ ounces of this syrup and filling the glass.

Mountain Dew
Saxe's New Guide (1895)

Brandy	120 ml	4 oz
Nutmeg Extract	1½ tsp	
Vanilla Extract	1½ tsp	
Fruit Acid	1 tsp	
Gum Foam	1½ tsp	
Simple Syrup	480 ml	16 oz
Phospho-Guarana	120 ml	4 oz

Mix and colour to suit.

Combine all of the ingredients and serve 30 ml to 45 ml (1 to 1½ oz) in a 240 ml (8 oz) glass. Mountain Dew is slang for moonshine.

Moxie Syrup

Wintergreen Extract	22 ml	¾ oz
Gentian Extract	22 ml	¾ oz
Syrup of Sarsaparilla	90 ml	3 oz
Caramel Colour	15 ml	½ oz
Alcohol (90%)	30 ml	1 oz
Simple Syrup	1 L	1 qt

Dissolve the oils in the alcohol and then combine the other ingredients. Mix thoroughly and bottle.

Napa Soda

Blood Orange Syrup	30 ml	1 oz
Lime Juice	1 tsp	

Serve solid in an 8 oz glass.

Nectarine Mead Syrup

Mead Extract	25 ml	¾ oz
Raspberry Juice	45 ml	1½ oz
Orange Juice	90 ml	3 oz
Orange Flower Water	15 ml	½ oz
Rose Water	120 ml	4 oz
Almond Essence	¾ tsp	
Citric Acid Solution	½ tsp	
Simple Syrup, to make	1 L	32 oz

Serve "solid" in 8 oz glass, using 1 oz of syrup.

Nerve Tonic Syrup

Syrup of Sarsaparilla	120 ml	4 oz
Ginger Syrup	60 ml	2 oz
Gentian Tincture	60 ml	2 oz
Extinct Acid Phosphate	60 ml	2 oz
Simple Syrup	1 L	1 qt
Caramel	to colour	

Combine all of the ingredients and serve 30 ml to 45 ml (1 to 1½ oz) in a 240 ml (8 oz) glass. Serve "solid".

New Orleans Mead

Tonka Beans	60 g	2 oz
Cloves	210 g	7 oz
Cinnamon	210 g	7 oz
Ginger	210 g	7 oz
Nutmeg	210 g	7 oz
Allspice	240 g	8 oz
Mace	60 g	2 oz
Sassafras Bark	900 g	2 lbs
Honey	8 L	2 gal
Simple Syrup	80 L	20 gal
Water	12 L	3 gal

Bruise the spices in a mortar, placing in a cloth bag. Immerse all in the syrup, and boil for 12 hours, no longer. Then take 2 pounds of sassafras bark, add 3 gallons of water, and boil slowly until reduced to 2 gallons; 8 ounces of allspice may be added to advantage. After the juices are sufficiently boiled, add the decoction of sassafras and 2 gallons of honey. Put 5 quarts of the syrup thus made into a suitable fountain, add enough water to make 10 gallons, and charge to 100 pounds pressure.

Oxford Cordial

Elixir of Calisaya	120 ml	4 oz
Claret Wine	120 ml	4 oz
Citric Acid Solution	1½ tsp	
Water	240 ml	8 oz
Simple Syrup	1 L	1 qt

Combine all of the ingredients and serve 30 ml to 45 ml (1 to 1½ oz) in an 8 oz glass. Serve "solid".

Peach Blow

Peach Juice	90 ml	3 oz
Raspberry Juice	180 ml	6 oz
Lemon Juice	180 ml	6 oz
Holland Gin	45 ml	1½ oz
Syrup	750 ml	26 oz
Red Colouring	sufficient	
Soda Foam	sufficient	

Combine all of the ingredients and serve 30 ml to 45 ml (1 to 1½ oz) solid in an 8 oz glass.

Punch Syrup

California Brandy	120 ml	4 oz
New England Rum	120 ml	4 oz
Vanilla Extract	1½ tsp	
Citric Acid Solution	1 tsp	
Simple Syrup	2 L	2 qt

Combine all of the ingredients and serve 1 to 1½ oz "solid" in an 8 oz glass.

Wild Cherry Syrup

Red Cherry Juice	240 ml	8 oz
Syrup of Wild Cherry	240 ml	8 oz
Oil of Bitter Almonds	6 drops	
Alcohol	1 tbsp	
Diluted Phosphoric Acid	1 tbsp	
Tincture of Cudbear	1 tbsp	
Caramel	¾ tsp	
Simple Syrup, to make	2 L	2 qt

Dissolve the oil in the alcohol and add the other ingredients. Combine all of the ingredients and serve 1 to 1½ oz in an 8 oz glass. Serve "solid".

World's Fair Fruit Champagne

Champagne Syrup	200 ml	6¾ oz
Black Cherry Juice	240 ml	8 oz
Raspberry Juice	240 ml	8 oz
Red Currant Juice	120 ml	4 oz
Citric Acid Solution	60 ml	2 oz
Essence of Lemon	15 ml	½ oz
Vanilla Extract	1½ tsp	
Foam Syrup	15 ml	½ oz

Use 45 ml (1½ oz) of syrup in a 240 ml (8 oz) glass.

World's Fair Root Beer

Root Beer Extract	30 ml	1 oz
Simple Syrup	1 L	1 qt
Caramel Colouring	2 tsp	
Fruit Acid Solution	1 tsp	

Use 45 ml (1½ oz) of syrup in a 240 ml (8 oz) glass.

Punch Recipes

Angelica Milk Punch

Simple Syrup	300 ml	10 oz
Vanilla Syrup	120 ml	4 oz
Sweet Cream	180 ml	6 oz
Angelica Wine	90 ml	3 oz
French Cognac	90 ml	3 oz
Arac de Goa	90 ml	3 oz
Egg Yolks	3	

Serve 1½ to 2 of syrup in an 8 oz glass of cold or hot soda water, drawing soda first.

Banana Punch

White Bordeaux Wine	180 ml	6 oz
Sweet Catawba Wine	90 ml	3 oz
French Cognac	60 ml	2 oz
Batavia Arrack	60 ml	2 oz
Banana Juice	240 ml	8 oz
Lime Juice	60 ml	2 oz
Simple Syrup	270 ml	9 oz
Banana Essence	1 tsp	
Caramel Colouring	1 tsp	

Serve 1½ to 2 of syrup in an 8 oz glass of cold or hot soda water, drawing soda first. Stir.

Burgundy Milk Punch

Simple Syrup	300 ml	10 oz
Vanilla Syrup	120 ml	4 oz
Sweet Cream	180 ml	6 oz
Burgundy	180 ml	6 oz
French Cognac	90 ml	3 oz
New England Rum	90 ml	3 oz

Serve 1½ to 2 of syrup in an 8 oz glass of cold or hot soda water, drawing soda first. Stir.

Catawba Milk Punch

Simple Syrup	300 ml	10 oz
Vanilla Syrup	90 ml	3 oz
Sweet Cream	150 ml	5 oz
Domestic Champagne	150 ml	5 oz
Catawba Wine	90 ml	3 oz
French Cognac	60 ml	2 oz
Arac de Goa	60 ml	2 oz
Egg Yolks	3	

Serve 1½ to 2 of syrup in an 8 oz glass of cold or hot soda water, drawing soda first. Stir.

Champagne Punch

French Champagne	180 ml	6 oz
Jamaican Rum	180 ml	6 oz
Simple Syrup	600 ml	20 oz
Fruit Acid		1½ tsp

Serve 1½ to 2 of syrup in an 8 oz glass of cold or hot soda water, drawing soda first. Stir.

Claret Milk Punch

Simple Syrup	300 ml	10 oz
Vanilla Syrup	120 ml	4 oz
Sweet Cream	150 ml	5 oz
Claret	120 ml	4 oz
Catawba	90 ml	3 oz
French Cognac	60 ml	2 oz
Jamaica Rum	60 ml	2 oz
Egg Yolks	3	

Serve 1½ to 2 of syrup in an 8 oz glass of cold or hot soda water, drawing soda first. Stir.

Eldorado Punch

Muscatel	180 ml	6 oz
Arrack	180 ml	6 oz
Jamaica Rum	90 ml	3 oz
Orange Wine	90 ml	3 oz
Simple Syrup	480 ml	16 oz
Lemon Extract		2 tsp
Fruit Acid		2 tsp

Serve 1½ to 2 of syrup in an 8 oz glass of cold or hot soda water, drawing soda first. Stir.

Frontignac Milk Punch

Simple Syrup	300 ml	10 oz
Vanilla Syrup	120 ml	4 oz
Sweet Cream	180 ml	6 oz
Frontignac	180 ml	6 oz
French Cognac	60 ml	2 oz
Jamaica Rum	60 ml	2 oz
Egg Yolks	3	

Serve 1½ to 2 of syrup in an 8 oz glass of cold or hot soda water, drawing soda first. Stir.

Haut-Sauterne Milk Punch

Simple Syrup	300 ml	10 oz
Vanilla Syrup	120 ml	4 oz
Sweet Cream	150 ml	5 oz
Haut-Sauterne	150 ml	5 oz
French Champagne	60 ml	2 oz
French Cognac	60 ml	2 oz
Arac de Goa	60 ml	2 oz
Egg Yolks	3	

Serve 1½ to 2 of syrup in an 8 oz glass of cold or hot soda water, drawing soda first. Stir.

Jamaican Rum Punch

Jamaican Rum	300 ml	10 oz
Simple Syrup	600 ml	20 oz
Lemon Extract		2 tsp
Fruit Acid		2 tsp

Serve 1½ to 2 of syrup in an 8 oz glass of cold or hot soda water, drawing soda first. Stir.

Lime Punch

White Bordeaux Wine	240 ml	8 oz
Sweet Catawba Wine	180 ml	6 oz
French Cognac	90 ml	3 oz
Jamaica Rum	90 ml	3 oz
Lime Juice	120 ml	4 oz
Soluble Lime Essence	60 ml	2 oz
Saffron Colouring		1 tsp

Serve 1½ to 2 of syrup in an 8 oz glass of cold or hot soda water, drawing soda first. Stir.

Madeira Milk Punch

Simple Syrup	300 ml	10 oz
Vanilla Syrup	120 ml	4 oz
Sweet Cream	150 ml	5 oz
Madeira	120 ml	4 oz
Oporto Port	90 ml	3 oz
French Cognac	60 ml	2 oz
Jamaica Rum	60 ml	2 oz
Egg Yolks	3	

Serve 1½ to 2 of syrup in an 8 oz glass of cold or hot soda water, drawing soda first. Stir.

Malaga Milk Punch

Simple Syrup	300 ml	10 oz
Vanilla Syrup	120 ml	4 oz
Sweet Cream	180 ml	6 oz
Malaga	180 ml	6 oz
Arac de Goa	90 ml	3 oz
Egg Yolks	3	

Serve 1½ to 2 of syrup in an 8 oz glass of cold or hot soda water, drawing soda first. Stir.

Marsala Milk Punch

Simple Syrup	300 ml	10 oz
Vanilla Syrup	120 ml	4 oz
Sweet Cream	150 ml	5 oz
Marsala	150 ml	5 oz
Alicante	60 ml	2 oz
French Cognac	60 ml	2 oz
New England Rum	60 ml	2 oz
Egg Yolks	3	

Serve 1½ to 2 of syrup in an 8 oz glass of cold or hot soda water, drawing soda first. Stir.

Moselle Milk Punch

Simple Syrup	300 ml	10 oz
Vanilla Syrup	120 ml	4 oz
Sweet Cream	120 ml	4 oz
Moselle	150 ml	5 oz
French Champagne	60 ml	2 oz
French Cognac	90 ml	3 oz
Arac de Goa	60 ml	2 oz
Egg Yolks	3	

Serve 1½ to 2 of syrup in an 8 oz glass of cold or hot soda water, drawing soda first. Stir.

Muscat Lunel Milk Punch

Simple Syrup	300 ml	10 oz
Vanilla Syrup	120 ml	4 oz
Sweet Cream	150 ml	5 oz
Muscat Lunel	120 ml	4 oz
French Cognac	90 ml	3 oz
Arac de Goa	90 ml	3 oz
Egg Yolks	3	

Serve 1½ to 2 of syrup in an 8 oz glass of cold or hot soda water, drawing soda first. Stir.

Oporto Port Milk Punch

Simple Syrup	300 ml	10 oz
Vanilla Syrup	120 ml	4 oz
Sweet Cream	150 ml	5 oz
Oporto Port	150 ml	5 oz
French Cognac	90 ml	3 oz
Arac de Goa	90 ml	3 oz
Egg Yolks	3	

Serve 1½ to 2 of syrup in an 8 oz glass of cold or hot soda water, drawing soda first. Stir.

Sherry Milk Punch

Simple Syrup	300 ml	10 oz
Vanilla Syrup	120 ml	4 oz
Sweet Cream	150 ml	5 oz
Sherry	120 ml	4 oz
Madeira	90 ml	3 oz
French Cognac	60 ml	2 oz
Jamaica Rum	60 ml	2 oz
Egg Yolks	3	

Serve 1½ to 2 of syrup in an 8 oz glass of cold or hot soda water, drawing soda first. Stir.

139

Tivoli Punch

Lemon Syrup	360 ml	12 oz
Simple Syrup	360 ml	12 oz
Jamaican Rum	120 ml	4 oz
Red Bordeaux Wine	120 ml	4 oz

Serve 1½ to 2 of syrup in an 8 oz glass of cold or hot soda water, drawing soda first. Stir.

Tokay Milk Punch

Simple Syrup	300 ml	10 oz
Vanilla Syrup	120 ml	4 oz
Sweet Cream	180 ml	6 oz
Tokay	180 ml	6 oz
French Cognac	60 ml	2 oz
Arac de Goa	60 ml	2 oz
Egg Yolks	3	

Serve 1½ to 2 of syrup in an 8 oz glass of cold or hot soda water, drawing soda first. Stir.

Victoria Punch

Red Orange Syrup	120 ml	4 oz
Orange Flower Syrup	120 ml	4 oz
Muscatel	120 ml	4 oz
Jamaican Rum	180 ml	6 oz
Simple Syrup	420 ml	14 oz

Serve 1½ to 2 of syrup in an 8 oz glass of cold or hot soda water, drawing soda first. Stir.

World's Fair Punch

Raspberry Syrup	180 ml	6 oz
Lemon Syrup	120 ml	4 oz
Champagne	90 ml	3 oz
Muscatel	90 ml	3 oz
Jamaican Rum	120 ml	4 oz
Cinnamon Extract	½ tsp	
Fruit Acid	1 tsp	
Simple Syrup	360 ml	12 oz

Serve 1½ to 2 of syrup in an 8 oz glass of cold or hot soda water, drawing soda first. Stir.

Xeres Milk Punch

Simple Syrup	270 ml	9 oz
Vanilla Syrup	120 ml	4 oz
Sweet Cream	150 ml	5 oz
Xeres	90 ml	3 oz
French Champagne	90 ml	3 oz
French Cognac	90 ml	3 oz
Arac de Goa	90 ml	3 oz
Egg Yolks	3	

Serve 1½ to 2 of syrup in an 8 oz glass of cold or hot soda water, drawing soda first. Stir.

Soda Recipes

Almond Sponge

Orgeat Syrup	30 ml		1 oz
Strawberry Syrup	15 ml		½ oz
Ice Cream		2 tbsp	
Milk		to fill	

Shake and strain into a 12 oz glass, fill with carbonated water, coarse stream, top with whipped cream and powdered nutmeg.

April Blossom

Pineapple Syrup	30 ml		1 oz
Catawba Wine (Dry)	15 ml		½ oz
Lime Juice	15 ml		½ oz
Raspberry Syrup	15 ml		½ oz
Cracked Ice		½ glassful	
Lemon Juice		½ tsp	

Using a 12 ounce soda glass, add everything but ice, add soda until ¾ full (stirring with spoon while adding soda). Add ice to finish and garnish with lemon or lime.

Blaze Du Barry

Lemon Syrup	15 ml		½ oz
Lemon juice		¾ tsp	
Angostura Bitters		¾ tsp	
Fine Sugar		1 tsp	

Carbonated water, coarse stream, enough to fill ¾ of a 12 oz glass. Stir in ingredients with a teaspoon of powdered sugar.

Brunswick Cooler

Lemon syrup	15 ml		½ oz
Orange syrup	15 ml		½ oz
Cherry syrup	15 ml		½ oz
Cracked ice		⅓ glassful	

Add carbonated water, coarse stream, to nearly fill a 12-ounce glass, "finish" with the fine stream and dress the drink with pineapple and cherry.

Burgundy Punch

Burgundy Wine	60 ml	2 oz
Syrup of Orange	30 ml	1 oz

Fill a 12 oz glass with crushed ice and draw a coarse stream of soda water to fill the glass. Decorate with slices of pineapple and orange. (T.P. Taylor & Co. Louisville, Ky.)

Capitol

Blood Orange Syrup	30 ml	1 oz
Grape Juice	15 ml	½ oz
Sherry Syrup	15 ml	½ oz
Angostura Bitters		2 dashes

Mix in a 12-ounce glass, shake vigorously, fill with carbonated water, coarse stream, and serve with straws. This formula makes a fine bitters and a delicious egg drink with soda or milk.

Cherry Cocktail

Cherry Juice	30 ml	1 oz
Lemon Juice		1½ tsp
Angostura Bitters		½ tsp
Sugar		1 tsp
Ice		⅓ glassful

Combine in an 8 oz glass and draw 2 oz of soda water, stir, and then fill with the fine stream. Garnish with a cherry and lemon twist.

Chicago

Raspberry Syrup	15 ml	½ oz
Pineapple Syrup	30 ml	1 oz
Grape Juice	30 ml	1 oz
Lemon Juice		1½ tsp
Lime Juice		1 tsp

Place in a 12 oz glass half filled with shaved ice, then fill ⅞ with carbonated water and stir thoroughly. Garnish with a cherry and mint.

Cubanade

Orange syrup	30 ml	1 oz
Grape juice	15 ml	½ oz
Lemon juice	30 ml	1 oz
Extract of ginger		2-3 drops

Put into a 12 oz glass, fill ⅞ with the coarse stream, and "finish" with the fine stream.

Dorian Cream

Orange Syrup	22 ml	¾ oz
Maple Syrup	22 ml	¾ oz
Plain Cream	60 ml	1 oz
Shaved Ice		⅓ glassful

Place in a suitable glass, fill with carbonated water, sprinkle powdered nutmeg on top and serve with straws and crackers.

Festival Fizz

Rose Syrup	15 ml	½ oz
Pineapple Syrup	30 ml	1 oz
Lemon Juice		1 tsp
Angostura Bitters		1 dash
Shaved Ice		Sufficient

Place in glass, fill with carbonated water, top off with slice of orange and cherry and serve with spoon and straws.

Fire Extinguisher

Blood Orange Syrup	30 ml	1 oz
Raspberry Syrup	15 ml	½ oz
Lemon Juice		1 tsp
Shaved Ice		½ glassful

Add several ounces of carbonated water, stir well, strain into an 8-ounce glass, and fill the latter with plain soda water, coarse stream.

Frosted Chocolate

Chocolate syrup	45 ml	1½ oz
Carbonated water	180 ml	6 oz
Shaved ice	½ glassful	

Mix in a 12 oz glass, and fill with the fine stream.

Frosted Fruit

Catawba Syrup	45 ml	1½ oz
Pure Milk	30 ml	1 oz
Ice Cream	1 tbsp	
Extract of Vanilla	1 dash	
Crushed Strawberry	1 tsp	
Crushed Pineapple	1 tsp	
Crushed Raspberry	1 tsp	
Shaved Ice	½ glassful	

Shake well, then add carbonated water.

Granola

Orange syrup	30 ml	1 oz
Grape juice	15 ml	½ oz
Lemon Juice	½ lemon	
Cracked Ice	½ glassful	

Mix in a 12 oz glass, fill with the coarse stream, and "finish" with the fine stream.

Grape-Ade

Lemon syrup	30 ml	1 oz
Grape juice	15 ml	½ oz

Serve "solid" in an 8 oz glass, filling with the coarse stream of soda water and stirring.

Grape Cooler

Grape juice	30 ml	1 oz
Orange syrup	45 ml	1½ oz
Lemon syrup	2 tsp	
Extinct Acid Phosphate	1 tsp	
Cracked ice	⅓ glassful	

Mix in a 12 oz glass, filled with the coarse stream of carbonated water, stir with a spoon, add a slice of pineapple, and serve with straws.

Grape Lemonade

Grape syrup	15 ml	½ oz
Lemon syrup	15 ml	½ oz
Acid Phosphates	dash	

Put into a 8 oz glass, fill ⅞ with the coarse stream, and "finish" with the fine stream.

Kentucky Cooler

Fill a 10 oz glass with crushed ice. Muddle four sprigs of fresh mint and fill with soda. Add a splash of blood orange syrup and a finishing sprig of mint, slice of pineapple and cherry.

Ladies' Choice

Raspberry syrup	60 ml	2 oz
Peach ice cream	2 tbsp	

Serve in 12-ounce glasses as a "soda".

Lime Juice Fizz, Hot

Lime juice	30 ml	1 oz
Sugar, powder	2 tsp	
White of egg	1	

Mix in an 8-ounce mug, fill the latter with hot water, and add some whipped cream.

Lime Slip

Pineapple syrup	60 ml	2 oz
Lime juice	15 ml	½ oz

Put into a 12 oz glass, fill ⅞ with the coarse stream, and "finish" with the fine stream.

Maid Marion

Pineapple Juice	15 ml	½ oz
Lemon Juice	1 tsp	
Raspberry Vinegar	1 tsp	

Shake and strain into a 12 oz glass ¾ full of shaved ice. Fill glass nearly full with carbonated water (coarse stream) and garnish with a strawberry and a slice of fresh orange.

Manhattan Cream

Pineapple syrup	20 ml	¾ oz
Vanilla syrup	20 ml	¾ oz
Ice cream	60 ml	2 oz
Egg	1	
Shaved or cracked ice	⅓ glassful	

Shake and strain into a 12 oz glass, fill with the coarse stream and "finish" with the fine stream.

Maple Frostbite

Maple Syrup	30 ml	1 oz
Vanilla Syrup	15 ml	½ oz
Shaved Ice	½ glassful	

Rub the rim of a tall frappé glass with a piece of orange and dip the rim of the glass into powdered sugar. Shake the syrup and ice, pour into the frappé glass, and fill to about half an inch of the top with plain soda. Add a slice of orange.

May Bells

Klub Soda	30 ml	1 oz
Ginger Wine	15 ml	½ oz
Lime Juice	1½ tsp	

Serve solid in a 8 ounce glass.

Menthe Fresher

Almond Cream Syrup	60 ml	2 oz
Mint Sprigs	2	
Ice	½ glassful	
Sugar	1 tsp	

Crush fresh mint leaves with small amount of granulated sugar; add ice; and syrup. Shake, strain and fill with carbonated water.

Mint Cooler

| Mint Syrup | 30 ml | 1 oz |
| Vanilla Syrup | 15 ml | ½ oz |

Pack an 8 ounce glass with ice, add the syrup and top with soda water. Garnish with mint.

Mint Freeze

Muddle several sprigs of in a mixing glass; add

Grape Juice	30 ml	1 oz
Black Raspberry Syrup	15 ml	½ oz
Claret Syrup	15 ml	½ oz
Ginger Syrup	15 ml	½ oz
Lemon Juice	½ lemon	
Shaved or cracked ice	½ glassful	

Fill the glass with soda water and stir; strain into a 12 oz glass with the crushed ice. Garnish with pineapple, cherry, and a sprig of mint.

Mountain Mist

Mountain Mist Syrup	30 ml	1 oz
Lemon Juice	1½ tsp	
Angostura Bitters	2 dash	

Serve solid in an 8 ounce glass. Sprinkle with a little powdered sugar and drink while effervescing.

Newport Bitters

Cherry Syrup	15 ml	½ oz
Orange Syrup	15 ml	½ oz
Lemon Syrup	15 ml	½ oz
Orange Bitters	2-3 dashes	
Cracked Ice	½ glassful	

Add syrups and bitters, fill the glass with carbonated water, mix thoroughly and decorate with a slice of orange and a cherry. Serve with straws.

Oriental Fizz

Strawberry syrup	30 ml	1 oz
Orange syrup	30 ml	1 oz
Juice of one-half lemon.		
Cracked ice	⅓ glassful	

Mix in a 12 oz glass, fill with the coarse stream of soda water, stir with a spoon.

Over the Waves

Lemon syrup	45 ml	1½ oz
Grape juice	30 ml	1 oz
Egg White	1	
Extinct Acid Phosphate	½ tsp	
Cracked ice	⅓ glassful	

Shake in a shaker or glass and shaker, strain into a 12-ounce glass, nearly fill the latter with the coarse stream of carbonated water, and "finish" with the fine stream.

Pan-American Lemonade.

Orange syrup	30 ml	1 oz
Lemon syrup	30 ml	1 oz
Sugar, powdered	1 tsp	
Extinct Acid Phosphate	1 tsp	
Cracked Ice	½ glassful	

Fill the glass with the coarse stream of carbonated water, add two slices of orange, and serve.

Pepto-Beef (Hot)

Beef Bouillon	1 tsp	
Crystal Pepsin	⅛ tsp	
Warm Water	240 ml	8 oz

Dissolve the pepsin in the warm water, then add the beef bouillon. Add to one cup of hot water. Serve with pepper and salt.

Pepto-Lime

Lime Juice	15 ml	½ oz
Lemon Syrup	15 ml	½ oz
Essence of Pepsin	¾ tsp	

Stir while adding hot water.

Pineapple Frappe

Crushed pineapple	60 ml	2 oz
Extinct Acid Phosphate	1 tsp	
Cracked Ice	½ glassful	

Mix in a 12 oz glass, fill the glass with soda water, stir, and strain into an 8 oz glass.

Pineapple Lemonade

Pineapple syrup	60 ml	2 oz
Lemon Juice	1 Lemon	
Carbonated water, to fill a 12-ounce glass.		

Mix well, dress with fruit, and serve with straws.

Pineapple Paulette

Pineapple syrup	45 ml	1½ oz
Ice cream	60 ml	2 oz
Cream	45 ml	1½ oz
Cracked ice	⅓ glassful	

Combine and shake, strain into a 12-ounce glass add carbonated water, coarse stream, to nearly fill the glass, and "finish" with the fine stream.

Pineapple Punch

Pineapple juice	60 ml	2 oz
Sugar, powdered	1 tsp	
Shaved ice	⅓ glassful	

Mix with a spoon, add 3 ounces of the coarse stream of soda water, add a little more shaved ice and a spoonful of crushed pineapple on top. Fill the glass with shaved ice, add a slice of pineapple, and serve with a spoon and straws.

Pineapple Snow

Pineapple syrup	30 ml	1 oz
Sugar, powder	1 tsp	
Cracked or shaved ice	½ glassful	

Add some carbonated water, stir in a shaker, strain into an 8 oz glass, fill the latter with the coarse stream of carbonated water, stir again, add a slice of pineapple and serve with straws.

Raspberry Royal

Raspberry syrup	45 ml	1½ oz
Raspberry vinegar	15 ml	½ oz
Cracked ice	⅓ glassful	

Mix in a 12 oz glass, nearly fill the latter with the coarse stream of carbonated water, and "finish" with the fine stream. Serve with straws.

Raspho

Raspberry syrup	20 ml	¾ oz
Orange syrup	40 ml	1¼ oz
Tincture of ginger	1 dash	
Solution of acid phosphates	1 dash	

Mix in 12-ounce glasses, using some shaved ice and the coarse stream of carbonated water.

Razzle-Dazzle

Pineapple Syrup	15 ml	½ oz
Lemon Juice	1 tsp	
Raspberry Vinegar	¾ tsp	
Sugar	1 tsp	

Add syrup and fill ⅔ full of cracked ice. Put mixing spoon in glass and turn on coarse stream of soda water. Fill ⅞ full and stir, adding more cracked ice. Garnish with a teaspoonful of crushed raspberry and a small piece of orange. Serve in thin soda glasses with straws.

Resolution Fizz

Cherry Syrup	45 ml	1½ oz
Lemon Juice	15 ml	½ oz

Pour into a mixing glass ½ full of cracked ice, stir well, strain into an 8 oz fancy glass filled ⅓ full of fine ice, add a little sodium bicarbonate on the end of a spoon, stir well, add a cherry.

Root Beer

New Orleans Mead	30 ml	1 oz
Angostura Bitters	1 dash	

Mix in an 8 ounce glass, using some shaved ice and the coarse stream of carbonated water.

Ruby Smash

Cherry Malt Syrup	60 ml	2 oz
Lemon Juice	½ Lemon	
Lactart	2 dashes	
Cracked Ice	½ glassful	

Shake well, then fill with carbonated water.

Sea Breeze Thirst Quencher

Mint Syrup	60 ml	1 oz
Orange Syrup	15 ml	½ oz
Bitters	2 dashes	
Shaved Ice	½ glass	

Garnish with a thin slice of pineapple, creme de menthe, cherry and sprig of mint.

Spring Punch

Strawberry Syrup	15 ml	½ oz
Orange Syrup	15 ml	½ oz
Pineapple Syrup	15 ml	½ oz
Lemon Juice	2 dashes	
Shaved Ice	⅓ glassful	

Place ice in glass, draw on the syrups and fill with carbonated water. Trim with slice of pineapple and two strawberries. Serve with straws.

Third Degree

Sweet Cherry Juice	30 ml	1 oz
Lemon Juice	1 tsp	
Angostura Bitters	1 dash	
Powdered Sugar	1 tsp	
Shaved Ice	½ glassful	

Add syrups and 2 oz of carbonated water to a mixing glass, strain into a glass, add a cherry and small slice of lemon peel.

Turkish Sherbet

Crushed peach	15 ml	½ oz
Nectar syrup	15 ml	½ oz
Orange syrup	15 ml	½ oz
Extinct Acid Phosphate	1 tsp	

Fill a 12 oz glass with shaved ice, stir in the above syrup's, garnish with a slice of pineapple, orange and a cherry. Serve with a straw.

Vanilla Puff (Hot)

Vanilla syrup	30 ml	1 oz
Cream	30 ml	1 oz
Egg White	1	

Shake well, strain in an 8-ounce mug, fill latter with hot water, and add whipped cream.

Vino-Lemo

Claret Syrup	60 ml	2 oz
Lemon, juice of	1	
shaved ice	¼ glassful	

Shake well, fill a 10 ounce glass ⅞ with carbonated water, stir, and add one slice of lemon and enough carbonated water to fill the glass.

Violade

Violet syrup	30 ml	1 oz
Lemon syrup	30 ml	1 oz

Fill with soda water, stir with a spoon, pour into another glass half filled with shaved ice, add two slices each of lemon and orange, add serve with straws.

White Plush

Catawba Syrup	30 ml	1 oz
Egg White	1	
Cracked Ice	½ glassful	
Milk	to fill	

Combine and shake vigorously. Strain into 12 oz glass and serve with a whipped cream.

Wild Limeade

Strawberry Juice	15 ml	½ oz
Lime Juice	½ lime	
Sugar	2 tsp	
Wintergreen Essence	2 dashes	

Shake with ice, strain and add soda water.

World's Fair

Lemon Juice	15 ml	½ oz
Checkerberry Syrup	45 ml	1½ oz
Angostura Bitters	3 dashes	
Shaved Ice	⅔ glassful	

Shake and fill glass with ginger ale.

Yabarra Chocolate

Orange Syrup	15 ml	½ oz
Chocolate Syrup	30 ml	1 oz
Cream	60 ml	2 oz
Cracked Ice	½ glassful	

Fill the glass with milk, shake and strain.

HOT DECK
COCKTAIL
1½ oz Canadian Whisky
½ oz Sweet Vermouth
2 dashes Jamaica Ginger
Stir with ice and strain
into cocktail glass.

www.extinctchemical.com

Phosphate Recipes

Angostura Phosphate

Soda Water	210 ml	7 oz
Lemon Syrup	30 ml	1 oz
Angostura Bitters	1 tsp	
Extinct Acid Phosphate	½ tsp	

Mix in an 8 ounce glass and serve "solid".

Amazon Phosphate

Rose Syrup	15 ml	½ oz
Vanilla Syrup	15 ml	½ oz
Amazon Bitters	3 dashes	

Mix in an 8 ounce glass and serve "solid".

Arctic Phosphate

Strawberry Syrup	15 ml	½ oz
Pineapple Syrup	15 ml	½ oz
Vanilla Syrup	15 ml	½ oz
Orange Syrup	15 ml	½ oz
Acid Phosphate	3 dashes	

Mix in an 8 ounce glass and serve "solid".

Bospho

Raspberry Syrup	20 ml	¾ oz
Orange Syrup	20 ml	¾ oz
Lemon Syrup	30 ml	1 oz
Lime Syrup	8 ml	¼ oz
Acid Phosphate	1 dash	
Cracked Ice	½ glassful	

Fill a 12 ounce glass ½ full with soda water and add syrup to finish. Add ice and stir thoroughly.

Celery White Cap

Celery Syrup	15 ml	½ oz
Orange Syrup	15 ml	½ oz
Lemon Syrup	15 ml	½ oz
Acid Phosphate	1 dash	
White of Egg	1	
Cracked Ice	⅓ glassful	

Shake the egg with the syrup, using one lump of ice. Fill a 10 ounce glass ½ full with soda water and pour the contents of the shaker into the glass. Add ice and stir thoroughly.

Central Park

Pineapple Syrup	30 ml	1 oz
Red Orange Syrup	30 ml	1 oz
Acid Phosphate		6 dashes

Mix in an 8 ounce glass and serve "solid".

Cherade

Cherry Syrup	22 ml	¾ oz
Orange Syrup	22 ml	¾ oz
Extinct Acid Phosphate	1 tsp	

Serve "solid" in an 8 ounce glass.

Cherry

| Wild Cherry Syrup | 30 ml | 1 oz |
| Extinct Acid Phosphate | | 4 dashes |

Fill glass with carbonated water, using coarse stream; stir well with spoon.

Cherry Root

Cherry Syrup	30 ml	1 oz
Root Beer Syrup	120 ml	4 oz
Extinct Acid Phosphate	1 tsp	

Draw syrup in 10-ounce glass and fill half full with carbonated water, fine stream, then draw in charged root beer and dash of phosphate.

Cherry Sour

Cherry Syrup	30 ml	1 oz
Simple Syrup	15 ml	½ oz
Juice of Lime	1	
Acid Phosphate	1 dash	
Shaved Ice	½ glassful	

Mix well, fill with carbonated water and top with Maraschino cherry.

Chocolate Phosphate

| Chocolate syrup | 30 ml | 1 oz |
| Acid Phosphate | 1 tsp | |

Ice and soda in 8 oz glass. No nutmeg.

Citric Phosphate (Hot)

Lemon Syrup	45 ml	1½ oz
Citric Phosphate	1 tsp	
Whole Egg	1	

Mix well in shaker, transfer to a mug and fill with simmering water.

Clarine

Claret Syrup	15 ml	½ oz
Catawba Syrup	15 ml	½ oz
Acid Phosphate	1 tsp	

Serve like other phosphate drinks.

Fakir Freezer

Claret Syrup	30 ml	1 oz
Catawba Syrup	30 ml	1 oz
Lemon Juice	1 dash	
Orange Juice	3 dashes	
Acid Phosphate	1 dash	
Cracked Ice	½ glassful	

Serve "solid" in an 8 oz glass.

Fraternity

Champagne Phosphate	45 ml	1½ oz
Lime Syrup	30 ml	1 oz
Lemon Syrup	15 ml	½ oz
Shaved Ice	⅓ glassful	

Mix in a 14-ounce lemonade glass and decorate with pineapple or cherries.

Hiawatha

Cherry Syrup	15 ml	½ oz
Orange Syrup	15 ml	½ oz
Pineapple Syrup	30 ml	1 oz
Phosphate	6 dashes	
Cracked Ice	⅓ glassful	

Serve "solid" in an 8 oz glass.

July Bracer

Raspberry Vinegar	15 ml	½ oz
Catawba Syrup	30 ml	1 oz
Simple Syrup	15 ml	½ oz
Acid Phosphate	1 tsp	

Serve solid in an 8 ounce glass.

Lemonade American Citizen

Orange Syrup	30 ml	1 oz
Lemon Syrup	30 ml	1 oz
Powdered Sugar	1 tsp	
Acid Phosphate	1 dash	
Shaved Ice	⅓ glassful	

Add slice of orange and run two straws.

Maryland Mint

Creme de Menthe	15 ml	½ oz
Ginger Syrup	45 ml	1½ oz
Acid Phosphate	1 dash	

Serve in an 8 oz glass, with cracked ice. Garnish with a mint sprig.

Mexican Rebel

Strawberry Syrup	30 ml	1 oz
Orange Syrup	30 ml	1 oz

Add a dash of phosphate and tincture of capsicum. Quarter fill glass with shaved ice.

Nipponese

Orange Syrup	15 ml	½ oz
Ginger Syrup	15 ml	½ oz
Grape Syrup	15 ml	½ oz
Pineapple Syrup	15 ml	½ oz
Acid Phosphate	2 dashes	
Fresh Mint Leaves	4	
Shaved Ice	½ glassful	

Press leaves against the sides of the glass, fill glass with soda water (coarse stream) and serve.

Orange Phosphate, Saxe's

Blood Orange Syrup	45 ml	1½ oz
Acid Phosphate	1 tsp	

Serve solid in an 8 oz glass

Parisian Blaze (Hot)

Champagne Syrup	30 ml	1 oz
Sweet Mint Syrup	15 ml	½ oz
Acid Phosphate	3 dashes	

Fill with hot water and add a slice of lemon, and a sprig of mint.

Royal Phosphate

Lemon Syrup	30 ml	1 oz
Raspberry Syrup	15 ml	½ oz
Acid Phosphate	4 dashes	
Whole Egg	1	

Combine in a shaker and add two tablespoons of shaved ice. Shake well. Strain into an 8 oz glass and fill with carbonated water.

Scorchers' Delight

Vanilla Syrup	45 ml	1½ oz
Tincture of Cardamon	3 dashes	
Acid Phosphate	5 dashes	
Shaved Ice	½ glassful	

Add carbonated water, stir, strain and serve.

Siberian Flip

Orange Syrup	30 ml	1 oz
Pineapple Syrup	30 ml	1 oz
Extinct Acid Phosphate	1 tsp	
Angostura Bitters	3 drops	
Shaved Ice	⅓ glassful	

Combine and shake well, pour into a 12 oz glass and fill with a coarse stream of soda water.

Simple Egg Phosphate

Lemon Syrup	45 ml	1½ oz
Water	60 ml	2 oz
Phosphate Solution	1 tsp	
Whole Egg	1	
Ice Cubes	2-3	

Mix well by shaking vigorously; strain into a tumbler and fill with carbonated water

Sunlight

Orange Syrup	15 ml	½ oz
Lemon Syrup	2 dashes	
Prepared Raspberry	1 dash	
Powdered Sugar	1 tbsp	
Acid Phosphate	1 tsp	
Fine Ice	½ glassful	

Fill with carbonated water and stir well; strain into a mineral glass and serve.

Sunshine

Pineapple Syrup	30 ml	1 oz
Raspberry Syrup	½ tsp	
Lemon Juice	1 tsp	
Acid Phosphate	2 dashes	

Place in an 8 oz glass and fill with soda water.

Thirst Quencher

Raspberry Syrup	60 ml	2 oz
Extinct Acid Phosphate	¾ tsp	
Water	240 ml	8 oz
Lemon Juice	½ lemon	
Shaved Ice	⅓ glassful	

Mix well by agitating in a shaker; strain and add enough water to fill a 12-ounce glass.

Tonique Fizz

Sugar	3 tsp
Abbott's Bitters	3 dashes
Lime Juice	4 dashes
Acid Phosphate	8 dashes
Egg White	1
Fine Ice	½ glassful

Shake well, pour into 12-ounce bell top glass and fill with vichy in short dashes to make fizz.

Trio-Ade

Orange, juice of		1	
Grape Juice	15 ml		½ oz
Raspberry Syrup	15 ml		½ oz
Lemon Juice		½ tsp	
Sugar		1 tsp	
Shaved Ice		½ glassful	

Mix. Half fill the glass with carbonated water, coarse stream, stir, strain into a mineral water glass and fill with fine stream.

Us Fellers

Orange Syrup	60 ml	2 oz
Grape Juice	30 ml	1 oz
Acid Phosphates	3 dashes	
Shaved Ice	⅓ glassful	

Shake, fill with carbonated water, and strain and serve in a 10 oz glass.

Egg Drinks

Best Bracer

Mint Syrup	30 ml	1 oz
Lemon Syrup	15 ml	½ oz
Pineapple Syrup	30 ml	1 oz
Whole Egg	1	
Acid Phosphate	2 dashes	

Add carbonated water, shake and strain into a 12-ounce glass.

Bimbo Flip

Strawberry syrup	45 ml	1½ oz
Ginger syrup	30 ml	1 oz
Lime juice	2 tsp	
Whole Egg	1	

Shake the egg with a single lump of ice until frothy, add the remaining incredients and shake to combine. Serve in a 12 oz glass, nearly filling with the coarse soda stream and finishing with the fine stream.

Bonnie Belle

Pineapple	22 ml	¾ oz
Vanilla Syrup	22 ml	¾ oz
Ice Cream	1 scoop	
Cracked Ice	⅓ glassful	
Whole Egg	1	

Shake, strain, toss and serve.

Carnation Flip

Pineapple Syrup	30 ml	1 oz
Strawberry Syrup	30 ml	1 oz
Cream	120 ml	4 oz
Ice cream	1 tbsp	
Whole Egg	1	
Cracked ice	⅓ glassful	

Shake and strain into a 12 oz glass, fill the latter with the coarse stream of carbonated water and sprinkle on some powdered nutmeg.

Cherry Bounce

Cherry Ripe Syrup	60 ml	2 oz
Cream	15 ml	½ oz
Whole Egg	1	
Angostura Bitters	2 dashes	

Make like an egg phosphate

Chocolate Egg Shake

Chocolate Syrup	60 ml	2 oz
Whole Egg	1	
Cracked Ice		⅓ glassful
Milk, enough to nearly fill glass		

Draw the syrup into the glass, add the egg, cracked ice and shake. Fill the shaker about one-third full of milk and shake again. Finally add the balance of the milk to fill the shaker about two-thirds full. Shake well and strain into a glass. Garnish with nutmeg or cinnamon.

Chocolate Leghorn

Chocolate Syrup	30 ml	1 oz
Vanilla Syrup	15 ml	½ oz
Whole Egg	1	
Crushed Ice		⅓ glassful

Prepare like other egg drinks. Serve in a 12 oz glass. Top with nutmeg.

Chocolate Punch

Chocolate syrup	60 ml	2 oz
Whole Egg	1	
Cracked ice		⅓ glassful
Milk, enough to fill a 12-ounce glass.		

Shake and strain into a 12 oz glass, fill with soda water, top with whipped cream.

Chicago Egg Shake

Into a 12 oz glass draw

Strawberry syrup	30 ml	1 oz
Raspberry Syrup	15 ml	½ oz
Pineapple Syrup	15 ml	½ oz
Sweet Cream	45 ml	1½ oz
Whole Egg	1	

Shake as you would other egg drinks.

Egg-a-la-Mode

Orange syrup	15 ml	½ oz
Peach syrup	15 ml	½ oz
Pineapple syrup	15 ml	½ oz
Lemon syrup	15 ml	½ oz
Whole Egg	1	
Cracked ice		⅓ glassful

Shake and strain into a 12 oz glass, fill with the coarse stream and "finish" with the fine stream.

Egg Birch

Birch Syrup	45 ml	1½ oz
Whole Egg	1	

Place in shaker, fill with milk, shake, and strain into a 12-ounce glass.

Egg Calisaya

Lemon Syrup	30 ml	1 oz
Elixir of Calisaya	15 ml	½ oz
Cracked Ice	60 ml	2 oz
Whole Egg	1	

Shake as per directions for egg drinks. Strain into a 12 oz glass, filling ¾ full with a coarse stream, and then finishing with the fine stream.

Egg Cream

Cream	30 ml	1 oz
Simple Syrup	90 ml	2 oz
Vanilla Extract	2ml	⅓ tsp
Egg Yolk	1	

Combine egg yolk and cream and mix until smooth. Add the syrup and vanilla. Served like a plain soda in a 12 oz glass. Garnish with nutmeg.

Egg Fizz

Lemon, juice of	1
Egg White	1
Powdered Sugar	4 tsp
Sweet Cream	2 tsp

Combine and shake well, strain into a 12-ounce glass. Fill with the coarse stream of carbonated water, and "finish" with the fine stream.

Egg Soda

Lemon syrup	15 ml	½ oz
Vanilla syrup	15 ml	½ oz
Cream	30 ml	1 oz
Whole Egg	1	
Ice Cubes	2-3	

Combine and shake vigorously, strain into a 12 oz glass, fill the latter ¾ with the coarse stream of soda water, and "finish" with the fine stream.

Egg Phosphate

Lemon Syrup	60 ml	2 oz
Extinct Acid Phosphate	1 tsp	
Whole Egg	1	
Ice Cubes	2-3	

Shake and strain into 12 oz glass and fill with carbonated water. Grate nutmeg on top.

Egg Phosphate (Special)

Lemon Syrup	60 ml	2 oz
Acid Phosphate	3 dashes	
Ice Cream	1 scoop	
Whole Egg	1	

Combine lemon, acid phosphate, egg and ice cream and shake until combined. Pour into 12 oz glass and fill with carbonated water.

Fantasma Nog

Wild cherry syrup	45 ml	1½ oz
Ice cream	1 tbsp	
Acid Phosphate	2 dashes	
Whole Egg	1	
Shaved or cracked ice	¼ glassful	

Shake, strain, and serve in a thin soda glass with grated nutmeg.

Floral Cream

Rose Syrup	15 ml	½ oz
Violet Syrup	15 ml	½ oz
Cream	120 ml	4 oz
Orange Flower Water	1 tsp	
Egg White	1	

Mix. Violet syrup and rose syrup are best adapted for this composition, the cream being named accordingly.

Golden Buck

Orange syrup	60 ml	2 oz
Extinct Acid Phosphate	1 tsp	
Egg Yolk	1	
Cracked ice	⅓ glassful	

Shake and strain into a 12 oz glass, fill the glass ⅞ with the coarse stream of carbonated water, and "finish" with the fine stream.

Golden Fizz

Don't Care Syrup	30 ml	1 oz
Ginger Wine	15 ml	½ oz
Simple Syrup	15 ml	½ oz
Acid Phosphate	1 tsp	
Whole Egg	1	
Shaved Ice	¼ glassful	

Shake, strain into a thin 10 ounce soda glass and garnish with grated nutmeg.

Good Samaritan

Nectar Syrup	40 ml	1¼ oz
Milk	¼ glassful	
Whole Egg	1	
Cracked Ice	¼ glassful	

Shake, strain, and serve in a thin soda glass with grated nutmeg.

Heap Of Comfort

Hock Syrup	30 ml	1 oz
Malted Milk	1 tsp	
Clam Bouillon	15 ml	½ oz
Whole Egg	1	
Acid Phosphate	1 dash	

Into a 12 oz glass ¼ full of cracked ice, add first 4 components . Shake well, strain, add acid phosphate, and fill with soda water. Pour from shaker to tumbler, top off with nutmeg.

Hawahan Chocolate Shake

Chocolate Syrup	45 ml	1½ oz
Pineapple Syrup	15 ml	½ oz
Egg, separated	1	

Separate an egg; beat the white with ½ oz of chocolate syrup, and the yolk with ½ oz of pineapple syrup; beat the two mixtures well together and then shake with 1 oz of chocolate syrup and a scoop of vanilla ice cream. Pour into a 12 oz glass and fill with soda water, fine stream.

Little Red Hen

Raspberry Vinegar	15 ml	½ oz
Raspberry Syrup	60 ml	2 oz
Whole Egg	1	
Shaved Ice	¼ glassful	

Mix and transfer to a 12-ounce glass, fill with carbonated water, strain and serve with straws.

Lunar Blend

Cherry Syrup	30 ml	1 oz
Lemon Syrup	15 ml	½ oz
Sweet Cream	30 ml	1 oz
Egg, separated	1	

Take two mixing glasses, break an egg, putting the yolk in one glass, the white into the other; into the glass with the yolk add the cherry syrup and some cracked ice, shake, add small quantity carbonated water and strain into a 12 oz glass. Into the other mixing glass add sweet cream and beat with bar spoon until well whipped, then add the lemon syrup, and transfer it into a shaker and add carbonated water, fine stream only and float on top of the yolk and cherry syrup.

Marshmallow Egg Shake

Marshmallow Syrup	30 ml	1 oz
Ice Cream	30 ml	1 oz
Whole Egg	1	

Shake and strain into a 12 oz glass, nearly filling the latter with carbonated water, coarse stream, and "finish" with the fine stream. The use of milk improves this shake.

Navy Egg Shake

Strawberry Syrup	60 ml	2 oz
Sweet Cream	45 ml	1½ oz
Whole Eggs	2	
Ginger Syrup	1 tsp	
Cracked Ice	¼ glassful	

Shake and fill with soda water, using fine stream. Strain into a 14 oz glass and serve.

New Orleans Punch

Don't Care Syrup	45 ml	1½ oz
Jamaican Rum	2 tsp	
Whole Egg	1	
Milk	to fill	
Cracked Ice	¼ glassful	

Shake and strain, fill with soda, garnish with nutmeg.

Niagara

Pineapple Syrup	60 ml	2 oz
Plain Water Ice	60 ml	2 oz
Egg White	1	

Beat the white of an egg and add the above mixture in a 12-ounce glass, mix with a spoon, and fill the glass with carbonated water, fine stream.

Old Kentucky

Don't Care Syrup	30 ml	1 oz
Champagne Phosphate	30 ml	1 oz
Sweet Cream	30 ml	1 oz
Whole Egg	1	
Shaved Ice	½ glassful	

Shake and strain, fill glass with soda water.

Oloroso

Pistachio Syrup	30 ml	1 oz
Egg Cream Syrup	30 ml	1 oz
Sweet Cream	15 ml	½ oz
Aromatic Tincture	¼ tsp	

Mix in soda mug and fill with hot water, stirring well. Top off with cinnamon.

Parisian Flip

Orange Syrup	30 ml	1 oz
Pineapple Syrup	30 ml	1 oz
Sol. Phosphates	1 dash	
Angostura Bitters	2 dashes	
Whole Egg	1	
Shaved Ice	½ glassful	

Mix thoroughly by pouring from shaker to glass. Fill glass with soda water and strain.

Phroso

Ginger Syrup	30 ml	1 oz
Lemon Syrup	30 ml	1 oz
Angostura Bitters	1 dash	
Extinct Acid Phosphate	1 tsp	
Whole Egg	1	
Cracked Ice	¼ glassful	

Shake and strain, add soda water, fine stream, and serve with nutmeg and straw.

Piff Paff Puff

Chocolate Syrup	45 ml	1½ oz
Sweet Cream	60 ml	2 oz
Egg White	1	

Place egg white in a glass, sweet cream and whip well. Then add chocolate syrup, and shake. Fill with soda water, pour into a 12 oz glass and serve.

Pike's Peak

Orgeat Syrup	30 ml	1 oz
Cream	60 ml	2 oz
Egg White	1	
Shaved Ice	⅓ glassful	

Shake well, strain and fill a 12 oz glass with coarse and fine streams of carbonated water, about equal proportions.

Republic Egg Shake

Raspberry Syrup	30 ml	1 oz
Sweet Milk	60 ml	2 oz
Malted Milk	1 tsp	
Angostura Bitters	1 dash	
Whole Egg	1	
Cracked Ice	¼ glassful	

Shake well, strain, add fine stream carbonated water to fill 12-ounce glass; finish with whipped cream; serve with straws.

Royal Cabinet

A Chicago Drink

Orange Syrup	30 ml	1 oz
Catawba Syrup	15 ml	½ oz
Sweet Cream	15 ml	½ oz
Whole Egg	1	

Serve like other egg drinks. This was a very popular drink in Chicago around 1892.

Royal Flip

Vanilla Syrup	22 ml	¾ oz
Pineapple Syrup	22 ml	¾ oz
Raspberry Syrup	22 ml	¾ oz
Whole Egg	1	
Ice Cream	1 scoop	
Cracked Ice	¼ glassful	

Prepare like other egg drinks. Serve in a 12 oz glass, starting with the coarse stream and then finishing with the fine stream.

Sizzler Shake

Sarsaparilla Syrup	60 ml	2 oz
Angostura Bitters	¾ tsp	
Whole Egg	1	
Shaved Ice	¼ glassful	

Prepare and serve as other egg shakes.

Samaritan Punch

Nectar syrup	60 ml	2 oz
Milk	¾ glassful	
Cracked Ice	¼ glassful	
Whole Egg	1	

Shake and strain into a 12 oz glass, garnish with grated nutmeg.

Scientific Egg Shake

Pineapple Syrup	15 ml	½ oz
Lemon Syrup	15 ml	½ oz
Orange Syrup	15 ml	½ oz
Plain Cream	60 ml	2 oz
Whole Egg	1	
Cracked Ice	¼ glassful	

Shake, strain, toss and serve in a 12-ounce glass, filling with fine and coarse streams.

Snow Flurries

Vanilla Syrup	22 ml	¾ oz
Pineapple Syrup	22 ml	¾ oz
Ice Cream	1 scoop	
Whole Egg	1	
Cracked Ice	¼ glassful	

Break the egg into the glass, add the other ingredients, shake, strain and toss, adding the carbonated water last.

Snow Top

Orgeat syrup	30 ml	1 oz
Plain Cream	60 ml	2 oz
Egg White	1	
Shaved Ice	½ glassful	

Prepare like other egg drinks.

Square Meal

Chocolate syrup	60 ml	2 oz
Ice cream	1 tbsp	
Whole Egg	1	
Milk, enough to fill a shaker		

Shake well, strain into a 12-ounce glass, and sprinkle on some grated nutmeg.

Strawberry Egg Shake

Strawberry Syrup	60 ml	2 oz
Plain Cream	60 ml	2 oz
Whole Egg	1	

Shake well with ice. Strain into a 10 ounce glass and fill with the fine stream.

Temptress Egg Shake

Catawba Syrup	30 ml	1 oz
Egg White	1	
Shaved Ice	½ glassful	

Fill with milk and shake thoroughly. Top off with whipped cream and serve with a spoon.

True New Yorker

Lemon Syrup	30 ml	1 oz
Catawba Syrup	30 ml	1 oz
Acid Phosphate	2 dashes	
Whole Egg	1	

Shake and fill glass with carbonated water. Pour between shaker and glass. Strain into 10-ounce glass, add nutmeg and serve.

Vinola Flip

Sherbert Syrup	30 ml	1 oz
Lemon Syrup	30 ml	1 oz
Plain Cream	30 ml	1 oz
Ice Cream	1 tbsp	
Whole Egg	1	
Nutmeg	dash	

Shake all together, strain into a 12 oz glass and fill with a coarse stream of carbonated water.

Washingtonian Egg Shake

Grape Juice	60 ml	2 oz
Powdered Sugar	10 g	2 tsp
Plain Water	60 ml	2 oz
Whole Egg	2	
Lemon Juice	½ lemon	
Shaved Ice	½ glassful	

Combine and shake vigorously. Prepare a large goblet as follows: In bottom of glass put pieces of ice, one tablespoonful of pineapple sherbet. Over this pour a ladle full of grated pineapple, then strain the contents of shaker over top. Garnish with fruit and serve with a spoon and straw.

White Velvet

Pineapple Syrup	30 ml	1 oz
Orange Syrup	15 ml	½ oz
Colonial Punch Syrup	15 ml	½ oz
Egg White	1	
Cracked Ice	½ glassful	

Shake, strain, toss and serve.

Zozia Fizz

Zozia Syrup	60 ml	2 oz
Sweet Cream	15 ml	½ oz
Whole Egg	1	
Cracked Ice	¼ glassful	

Prepare like other egg drinks. Garnish with a sprinkle of nutmeg.

EXTINCT
ACID PHOSPHATE
"Rediscovering Lost Ingredients"
www.extinctchemical.com

DAWNS BREAK COCKTAIL
1½ oz G'Vine Nouaison
½ oz Lillet Blanc
Dash of Bitters
Egg White
Stir and strain with ice then
add 3 drops Acid Phosphate.

Malts & Milkshakes

Alicante Milk Punch

Vanilla Syrup	15 ml	½ oz
Simple Syrup	30 ml	1 oz
Sweet Cream	30 ml	1 oz
Alicante Wine	30 ml	1 oz
Cognac	15 ml	½ oz
Egg Yolk	1	

Shake the eggs and cream, using one lump of ice. Incorporate the remaining ingredients and mix. Pour into a 12 oz glass and fill with soda.

Alhambra Shake

Strawberry Syrup	15 ml	½ oz
Vanilla Syrup	15ml	½ oz
Milk, rich	120 ml	4 oz
Whole Egg	1	
Acid Phosphate	3 dashes	
Malted Milk Powder	1 tsp	

Mix and shake vigorously. Pour into an 10 oz glass and fill with soda water. Dust with nutmeg.

Boston Special Shake

Vanilla Syrup	15 ml	½ oz
Strawberry Syrup	15 ml	½ oz
Acid Phosphate	3 dashes	
Malted Milk	1-2 tsp	
Whole Egg	1	
Milk	to fill	

Combine all the ingredients in a shaker with a couple of lumps of ice. Shake and strain into a 10 oz glass and fill with soda water. Garnish with a dusting of nutmeg and a strawberry.

Buffalo

Chocolate Syrup	15 ml	½ oz
Maple Syrup	15 ml	½ oz
Vanilla Ice Cream	½ tbsp	
Plain Cream	30 ml	1 oz

Shake with ice. Pour into a frappé glass, garnish with whipped cream and a cherry.

California Cream

Vanilla Syrup	45 ml	1½ oz
Orange Concentrate	45 ml	1½ oz
Sweet Cream	30 ml	1 oz
Shaved Ice		½ glassful

Mix well and fill with carbonated water. Add a spoonful of ice cream to finish.

Campus Shake

Raspberry Syrup	60 ml	2 oz
Orange Syrup		1½ tsp
Whole Egg		1
Ice Shavings	60 ml	2 oz
Milk, to fill		12 oz

Shake well, strain, fill the glass with soda, fine stream, and sprinkle grated nutmeg on top.

Canadensis Shake

Almond Syrup	15 ml	½ oz
Raspberry Syrup	30 ml	1 oz
Whole Egg		1
Milk to fill glass		
Cracked Ice		¼ glassful

Shake, strain, toss and serve.

Chocolate Aviation

Chocolate Syrup	45 ml	1½ oz
Sweet Cream		1½ tsp
Whole Egg		1

Mix together in a shaker, add hot water, and mix by pouring back and forth several times from shaker to mug. Strain into a mug and serve with whipped cream.

Clam Milkshake

Clam Juice	45 ml	1½ oz
Milk	60 ml	2 oz
Soda Water	150 ml	5 oz

Add a pinch of salt and a little white pepper to each glass; shake well.

Coffee Maltose

Coffee syrup	45 ml	1½ oz
Plain Cream	45 ml	1½ oz
Malted milk		1 tsp
Whole Egg		1
Shaved Ice		½ glassful

Shake and strain into a 12-ounce glass, nearly fill the latter with the coarse stream of carbonated water, and "finish" with the fine stream.

Coffee, Philadelphia Style

Coffee Syrup	30 ml	1 oz
Vanilla Syrup	15 ml	½ oz
Sweet Cream	15 ml	½ oz
Milk	90 ml	3 oz
Cracked Ice		½ glassful

Serve in a 12-ounce glass. Add sufficient milk to fill glass and pour from shaker to glass.

Colonial

Rose Syrup	22 ml	¾ oz
Pineapple Syrup	15 ml	½ oz
Orange Syrup	15 ml	½ oz
Sweet Cream	120 ml	4 oz
Cracked Ice		½ glassful

Shake well, strain, fill the glass with soda, fine stream, and dress with whipped cream.

Commander In Chief

Strawberry Syrup	15 ml	½ oz
Pineapple Syrup	15 ml	½ oz
Vanilla Syrup	15 ml	½ oz
Milk		to fill
Shaved Ice		½ glassful

Shake well, add soda water, fine stream, and pour from tumbler to shaker several times. Serve in a 12-ounce glass, with straws.

Cream a la Orleans

Sweet Cream	60 ml	2 oz
Chocolate Syrup	30 ml	1 oz
Orange Syrup	15 ml	½ oz

Fill ¼ of the mixing glass with ice and add cream, syrups and milk to fill. Shake well and strain into bell-shaped glass. Serve with straws.

Creme-de-Swift

Vanilla syrup	15 ml	½ oz
Strawberry syrup	30 ml	1 oz
Cracked Ice		¼ glassful
Milk		to fill

Shake, strain, and top with whipped cream.

Cream Cordial

Rose syrup	15 ml	½ oz
Pineapple syrup	15 ml	½ oz
Vanilla syrup	15 ml	½ oz
Orange syrup	15 ml	½ oz
Sweet Cream	30 ml	1 oz
Cracked ice		½ glassful

Shake and strain into a 12-ounce glass, nearly fill the glass with the coarse stream of carbonated water and "finish" with the fine stream.

Cream Pineapple

Crushed pineapple	45 ml	1½ oz
Cream	60 ml	2 oz
Crushed ice		½ glassful

Shake together, strain into a 12-ounce glass, add carbonated water, coarse stream, to nearly fill the latter, and "finish" with the fine stream.

Cream Root Beer

Root Beer	45 ml	1½ oz
Sweet Cream	90 ml	3 oz
Cracked Ice		¼ glass

Shake and strain, fill glass with soda water.

Czar of Russia Shake

Vanilla Syrup	30 ml	1 oz
Red Orange Syrup	30 ml	1 oz
Ice Cream	60 ml	2 oz
Shaved Ice		½ glass

Shake, strain into a 10 oz glass, nearly fill the latter with the coarse stream of carbonated water, and "finish" with the fine stream.

Daisy Cream

Raspberry Syrup	30 ml	1 oz
Orange Flower Syrup	15 ml	½ oz
Sweet Cream	60 ml	2 oz
Vanilla Ice Cream		2 tbsp
Milk		to fill

Shake vigorously, pour into a tall glass, fill with milk and top with whipped cream and lemon zest.

Diplomatic

Grape Juice	60 ml	2 oz
Sweet Cream	60 ml	2 oz
Ice Cream	30 ml	1 oz
Abbott's Bitters		3 dashes

Shake thoroughly, strain, pour back into shaker and add carbonated water to fill glass; "throw" as in mixing egg drinks. Garnish with nutmeg.

Egg Malted Milk

Vanilla Syrup	60 ml	2 oz
Plain Cream	90 ml	3 oz
Malted Milk		1 tbsp
Whole Egg		1
Milk		to fill

Put syrup in mixing glass, adding the malted milk last. Shake well with ice, use fine stream only, and serve in bell glass. Use very little ice.

Egg Malted Milk (Chocolate)

Chocolate Syrup	30 ml	1 oz
Plain Cream	1 tbsp	
Malted Milk	1-2 tsp	
Ice Cream	1 scoop	
Egg	1	

Shake in glass quarter filled with ice, strain, toss and serve. Garnish with a dusting of nutmeg.

Findlay's Fruit Milk

Claret Syrup	30 ml	1 oz
Sweet Cream	60 ml	2 oz
Mixed Fruits	90 ml	3 oz
Sufficient Cracked Ice		

Fill the glass with milk and shake well. Pour into serving glass.

Frosted Fruit

Catawba Syrup	45 ml	1½ oz
Sweet Milk	30 ml	1 oz
Extract of Vanilla	1 dash	
Crushed Strawberry	1 tsp	
Crushed Raspberry	1 tsp	
Crushed Pineapple	1 tsp	
Ice Cream	1 tbsp	
Shaved Ice	½ glassful	

Shake well, add carbonated water.

Fruit Malt

Malt extract, thick	180 ml	6 oz
Raspberry syrup	60 ml	2 oz
Cinnamon syrup	60 ml	2 oz
Rose syrup	60 ml	2 oz
Orange flower water	60 ml	2 oz
Orange syrup		12 oz

Serve as a "soda" drink with foam in 12 oz glass.

Glad We're Here

Strawberry Syrup	22 ml	¾ oz
Pineapple Syrup	22 ml	¾ oz
Sweet Cream	30 ml	1 oz
Angostura Bitters	1 dash	

Add a small quantity of ice, shake well, put into a 12-ounce glass, add a little carbonated water, fine stream, and enough ice cream to fill glass. Garnish with sliced pineapple and a cherry.

Golfer's Delight

Plain Cream	120 ml	4 oz
Malted Milk	30 ml	1 oz
Coffee Syrup	22 ml	¾ oz
Grape Juice	6 dashes	

Shake in an 8 ozglass ¼ filled with ice, strain, toss and serve. Garnish with a dusting of nutmeg.

Hamilton, The

Simple Syrup	45ml	1½ oz
Malted Milk Powder	2 tsp	
Lemon, juice of	1	
Ice Cream	1 spoon	

Shake with ice and pour into a tall 10 oz glass and fill with soda water.

Irish Lace Cream

Strawberry Syrup	22 ml	¾ oz
Pineapple Syrup	22 ml	¾ oz
Sweet Cream	30 ml	1 oz
Angostura Bitters	2 dashes	

Add a small quantity of ice cream, shake well, put in a 12-ounce glass, add carbonated water, fine stream, and enough ice cream to fill the glass. Garnish with pineapple and a cherry.

Japanese Milk

Almond Syrup	60 ml	2 oz
Cream	60 ml	2 oz
Strawberry Syrup	60 ml	2 oz

Fill glass nearly full of milk and shake. Add small portion of pistachio ice cream.

Jones' Special Hot Punch

Grape Juice	30 ml	1 oz
Lemon Juice	15 ml	½ oz
Sugar	2 tsp	
Egg Yolk	1	

Mix vigorously while filling mug with hot water. Top off with whipped cream and nutmeg.

Key West

Vanilla Syrup	15 ml	½ oz
Strawberry Syrup	15 ml	½ oz
Orgeat Syrup	1½ tsp	

Serve in a 10 oz glass, fill with milk.

Lambrakis Hot Lunch

Coca Cola Syrup	15 ml	½ oz
Chocolate Syrup	15 ml	½ oz
Plain Cream	60 ml	2 oz
Malted Milk	3 tsp	

Shake well, transfer into a 12 oz glass and fill with hot water. Can he made with an egg.

Lunarette

Grape Syrup	30 ml	1 oz
Vanilla Syrup	15 ml	½ oz
Ice Cream	2 tbsp	
Whole Egg	1	

Shake with ice, strain, fill with milk, and serve.

Malted Coffee

Sweet Cream	30 ml	1 oz
Malted Milk	2 tbsp	
Coffee Extract	1 tsp	

Stir briskly while adding hot water.

Malted Milk

Add to several teaspoonsful cream in a mug two tablespoonfuls malted milk and make a paste. Then add hot milk to fill, gradually stirring while doing this. Season with salt and pepper, or with celery salt and serve with soda crackers.

Malted Milk Bracer

Orange Syrup	15 ml	½ oz
Sweet Cream	30 ml	1 oz
Malted Milk	1 tbsp	
Hot Milk	240 ml	8 oz

Mix for about five seconds in an electric mixer and pour into a 12-ounce glass; then top with whipped cream and nutmeg.

Malted Milk Coffee

Malted Milk	1-3 tsp
Coffee	to fill
Sugar to sweeten as desired	

Mix the malted milk with coffee and vigorously stir. Add the sugar and serve hot.

Maple Pine

Maple Syrup	30 ml	1 oz
Pineapple Syrup	30 ml	1 oz
Ice Cream	1 scoop	
Shaved Ice	½ glassful	

Mix in a 10 oz glass with a spoon, fill glass with soda water, mix again and top off with pineapple.

Merry Widow

Grape Syrup	30 ml	1 oz
Orgeat Syrup	30 ml	1 oz
Sweet Cream	30 ml	1 oz
Whole Egg		1

Shake and strain, fill glass with milk.

Old Fashioned Milk

Vanilla Syrup	30 ml	1 oz
Milk		to fill
Cracked Ice		¼ glassful

Shake in an 8 oz glass ¼ filled with ice, strain, toss and serve. Garnish with a dusting of nutmeg.

Orange Milkshake

Buttermilk	125 ml	½ cup
Orange Juice	125 ml	½ cup
Sugar		1 tsp
Salt		dash

Shake thoroughly and serve in chilled glass.

Orgeat Cream

Orgeat Syrup	60 ml	2 oz
Sweet Cream	120 ml	4 oz
Fresh Milk	120 ml	4 oz
Ice Cream		1 tbsp
Maraschino Cherry		1

Shake well and serve in a 10 oz glass.

Peach Milk

Peach Syrup	30 ml	1 oz
Grape Juice	15 ml	½ oz
Pineapple Syrup	15 ml	½ oz
Shaved Ice		½ glassful

Fill the glass with milk, shake well and serve.

Persian

Catawba Syrup	45 ml	1½ oz
Milk	30 ml	1 oz
Vanilla Extract		1 dash
Vanilla Ice Cream		1 tbsp
Crushed Strawberry		1 tsp
Crushed Raspberry		1 tsp
Crushed Pineapple		1 tsp
Shaved Ice		½ glassful

Shake well, then fill glass with soda water.

Pineapple Shake

Vanilla Syrup	30 ml	1 oz
Pineapple Syrup	30 ml	1 oz
Milk		to fill
Shaved Ice		½ glassful

Shake in an 8 oz glass ¼ filled with ice, strain, toss and serve. Garnish with a dusting of nutmeg.

Princeton Tiger

Orgeat Syrup	60 ml	2 oz
Fresh Milk	240 ml	8 oz
Fresh Cream	15 ml	½ oz
Egg Yolk		1
Shaved Ice		½ glassful

Combine and shake. Serve in a 12 oz glass.

Royal Shake With Egg

Break one egg in mixing glass and add:

Catawba Syrup	30 ml	1 oz
Vanilla Syrup	30 ml	1 oz
Strawberry Syrup	15 ml	½ oz
Plain Cream	60 ml	2 oz

Shake with ice; use milk and serve in bell glass.

Safety First Milk Shake

Chocolate Syrup	30 ml	1 oz
Sweet Cream	60 ml	2 oz
Banana, mashed	1	
Ice Cream	1 tbsp	
Milk	to fill	

Mix thoroughly, add ice cream, and enough milk to nearly fill a 12 oz glass; mix thoroughly, and strain into another 12-ounce glass. Garnish with whipped cream and a cherry.

Sea Breeze

Whole Egg	1	
Vanilla Syrup	30 ml	1 oz
Orange Syrup	30 ml	1 oz
Grape Juice	15 ml	½ oz
Bitters	2 dashes	
Shaved Ice	½ glassful	

Fill the glass nearly full of milk, shake well, grate a little nutmeg on the top, add a little soda water (fine stream), and serve a straw.

Snowdrift Shake

Catawba Syrup	30 ml	1 oz
Egg White	1	
Shaved Ice	½ glassful	

Shake well, strain into a 12-ounce glass and serve with whipped cream and a spoon.

Spicy Shake

Mint Syrup	30 ml	1 oz
Wintergreen Syrup	30 ml	1 oz
Sweet Cream	30 ml	1 oz
Soft Ice Cream	1 scoop	

Shake well, use fine stream carbonated water, serve in regular frappé style.

Sunset Cooler

Strawberry Syrup	60 ml	2 oz
Sweet Cream	60 ml	2 oz
Strawberries, crushed	1 tbsp	

Place in a glass an 8 oz glass and fill with soda.

Superlative Shake

Catawba Syrup	45 ml	1½ oz
Pure Milk	30 ml	1 oz
Vanilla syrup	15 ml	½ oz
Crushed Fruits	3 tsp	
Ice Cream	1 tsp	
Shaved Ice	½ glassful	

Shake well, then add enough carbonated water, fine stream, to fill glass. Serve with spoon.

Tropical Cream Shake

Strawberry Syrup	22 ml	¾ oz
Pineapple Syrup	22 ml	¾ oz
Sweet Cream	30 ml	1 oz
Angostura Bitters	2 dashes	

Shake and strain, transfer to a 12 oz glass, add soda water, fine stream, and ice cream to fill the glass. Garnish with pineapple and cherry.

White Mountain

Orange Syrup	60 ml	2 oz
Sweet Cream	90 ml	3 oz
Egg White	1	
Shaved Ice	½ glassful	

Shake well, strain into a 12-ounce glass and fill with milk.

Mineral Water Salts

Apollinaris Water

Sodium Bicarbonate	60 g	2 oz
Sodium Sulphate	30 g	1 oz
Sodium Chloride	23 g	¾ oz
Magnesium Carbonate	20 g	⅛ oz
Calcium Carbonate	2 g	½ tsp
Water, sufficient	50 L	12 gal

Mix and charge the keg.

Badoit
(St. Galmier - Loire, France)

Sodium Bicarbonate	12.6 g	3 tsp
Potassium Bicarbonate	0.5 g	⅛ tsp
Calcium Bicarbonate	22.3 g	⅔ oz
Magnesium Bicarbonate	14.6 g	½ oz
Sodium Sulphate	3.0 g	⅔ tsp
Calcium Sulphate	1.8 g	½ tsp
Aluminium Silicate	3.1 g	⅔ tsp
Magnesium Chloride	11.6 g	3 tsp
Water, sufficient	19 L	5 gal

Mix and charge in the usual manner.

Bethesda Water

Sodium Carbonate	3.2 g	¾ tsp
Sodium Sulphate	1.0 g	¼ tsp
Sodium Chloride	0.26 g	$\frac{1}{16}$ tsp
Potassium Sulphate	0.13 g	$\frac{1}{32}$ tsp
Calcium Carbonate	4.0 g	1 tsp
Magnesium Carbonate	4.4 g	1⅛ tsp
Water	19 L	5 gal

Mix and charge in the usual manner.

Carlsbad Water

Sodium Sulphate	9.7 g	½ tsp
Sodium Bicarbonate	6.8 g	1¾ tsp
Sodium Chloride	1.9 g	½ tsp
Potassium Sulphate	0.25 g	$\frac{1}{16}$ tsp
Water	19 L	5 gal

Mix, filter and charge in the usual manner.

This mixture closely represents Carlsbad Sprudel water in essential constituents.

Crab Orchard Water
(Spring located in Kentucky)

Magnesium Sulphate	71 g	2⅓ oz
Sodium Sulphate	49 g	1⅝ oz
Potassium Sulphate	19 g	⅔ oz
Sodium Chloride	52 g	1¾ oz
Water, sufficient	19 L	5 gal

Mix and charge in the usual manner.

Hathorn Water
(Medicinal)

Sodium Carbonate	640 g	22 oz
Sodium Chloride	70 g	2⅓ oz
Sodium Bromide	0.45 g	⅛ tsp
Potassium Chloride	3.25 g	¾ tsp
Calcium Chloride	45 g	1½ oz
Magnesium Chloride	45 g	1½ oz
Water	19 L	5 gal

Hunyadi Water
(Medicinal)

Magnesium Sulphate	33.5 g	1⅛ oz
Sodium Sulphate	33.8 g	1⅛ oz
Potassium Sulphate	0.2 g	1/16 tsp
Sodium Chloride	2.5 g	⅝ tsp
Sodium Bicarbonate	1.0 g	½ tsp
Water	19 L	5 gal

Mix and charge in the usual manner.

Kessel Water

Sodium Chloride	32 g	1 oz
Sodium Bicarbonate	5 g	1¼ tsp
Magnesium Sulphate	15 g	½ oz
Calcium Sulphate	6 g	1½ tsp
Potassium Sulphate	1 g	¼ tsp
Water	19 L	5 gal

Mix and charge in the usual manner.

Perrier

Calcium Carbonate	6.0 g	1½ tsp
Calcium Sulphate	1.0 g	¼ tsp
Sodium Chloride	0.6 g	⅛ tsp
Silica	0.5 g	⅛ tsp

Mix and charge in the usual manner.

Saratoga Water

Sodium Chloride	45 g	1½ oz
Sodium Sulphate	38 g	1¼ oz
Sodium Bicarbonate	30 g	1 oz
Magnesium Carbonate	30 g	1 oz
Water	19 L	5 gal

Mix and charge in the usual manner.

Selters (Seltzer) Water

Sodium Bicarbonate	115 g	4 oz
Sodium Chloride	85 g	3 oz
Calcium Chloride, dry	15 g	½ oz
Magnesium Chloride	15 g	½ oz
Water, sufficient	40 L	10 gal

Dissolve the magnesium and calcium salts in 8 oz (240 ml) of water and then add it to the sodium salts dissolved in a pint of water. Mix.

Vichy Water

Sodium Bicarbonate	300 g	10 oz
Sodium Phosphate	15 g	½ oz
Sodium Chloride	7.5 g	¼ oz
Potassium Bicarbonate	16 g	½ oz
Magnesium Sulphate	30 g	1 oz
Calcium Chloride	16 g	½ oz
Water, sufficient	40 L	10 gal

Combine the first five ingredients and dissolve in 1 L (1 qt) of water. Pass through a fine sieve and rub through, using more water if necessary.

Dissolve the calcium chloride in 120 ml (4 oz) of water and add it to the other solution. Add more water to make 2 L (2 qt), shake and then add this to a 40 L (10 gallon) soda tank.

Bitters & Medicinal

Amazon Bitters

Sweet orange peel	90 g	3 oz
Red cinchona	60 g	2 oz
Yellow cinchona	60 g	2 oz
Red saunders	30 g	1 oz
Calamus	20 g	¾ oz
Cassia buds	1 tsp	
Cinnamon bark	1 tsp	
Cloves	1 tsp	
Nutmeg	1 tsp	
Alcohol 75%	480 ml	16 oz

Mix the solids, reduce to fine powder, and extract by slow percolation with the alcohol. To prepare the bitters, mix 1 ounce of this extract with 15 ounces of 40% alcohol.

For "soda" purposes a more desirable formula is made as follows:

Amazon Bitter Extract	13 oz
Rose Essence	2 oz
Vanilla Extract	1 oz

Mix and bottle.

American, Eau

Oil of mace,		drops 1
Oil of cloves		drops 1
Oil of cinnamon		drops 1
Oil of rosemary, pure		drops 2
Oil of lavender flowers		drops 2
Oil of neroli petal		drops 3
Sugar	180 g	9 oz
Alcohol (90%)	480 ml	16 oz

Dissolve the oils in the alcohol and the sugar in some water and combine. Add water to make one gallon and colour a rose tint.

Angelica Ratafia

Angelica Seed	33 g
Angelica Root	11 g
Bitter Almond	11 g
Sugar	900 g
Alcohol 90%	1.7 L

Bruise the first 3 ingredients and macerate in the alcohol for 7 days, shaking occassionaly. Filter the extract. Dissolve the sugar in the water to make a syrup and then combine the 2 liquids.

Angostura Bitters

Calisaya bark	60 g	2 oz
Tonka	45 g	1½ oz
Red Saunders	15 g	½ oz
Bitter orange peel	15 g	½ oz
Cardamom	15 g	½ oz
Ceylon cinnamon	15 g	½ oz
Galangal	7.5 g	¼ oz
Gentian	7.5 g	¼ oz
Zedoary	7.5 g	¼ oz
Angelica root	2 g	½ tsp
Cloves	2 g	½ tsp
Ginger	2 g	½ tsp
Alcohol	2.4 L	80 oz
Water	1 L	32 oz
Caramel	120 ml	4 oz
Malaga Wine	360 ml	12 oz

Reduce the solids to coarse powder. Macerate for 14 days in the alcohol and water. Combine the extract, caramel and wine and bottle.

Benedictine

This liqueur contains a large number of aromatic substances, all in very small amount, so that the flavour of no one is pronounced. To produce it the following Extract may be employed:

Myrrh, contused	0.8 g	¼ tsp
Cardamom, no shells	0.8 g	¼ tsp
Mace, bruised	0.8 g	¼ tsp
Extract of aloes	3.2 g	¾ tsp
Ginger, Jamaica, bruised	8 g	1½ tsp
Galanga, bruised	8 g	1½ tsp
Bitter orange peel, cut	8 g	1½ tsp
Water, distilled	60 ml	2 oz
Alcohol, deodorized	150 ml	5 oz

Macerate for 7 days, agitating frequently, express and filter. Prepare also the following mixture:

Oil of rosemary	1 drop
Juniper, fresh	1 drop
Carciamom	2 drops

Hyssop		3 drops
Angelica root		5 drops
Sassafras		6 drops
Yarrow		8 drops
Bitter Almond Oil		10 drops
Cascarilla		12 drops
Anise		12 drops
Ginger		12 drops
Galanga		24 drops
Wormwood, French		30 drops
Bitter Orange Oil, fresh		86 drops
Lemon Oil, fresh		36 drops
Vanillin	0.065 g	½ grain
Coumarin	0.065 g	½ grain
Ammonia Water		15 drops
Acetic Ether	90 ml	3 oz
Spirit of Nitrous Ether	165 ml	5½ oz
Extract of licorice, pure	15 ml	½ oz
Caramel	15 ml	½ oz
Water	60 ml	2 oz
Alcohol	60 ml	2 oz

Dissolve the caramel in the mixed alcohol and water, add the remaining ingredients of the mixture, incorporate the whole with the preceding filtrate, macerate the whole for 7 days, agitating occasionally, filter and wash the filter with 70% alcohol to make the filtrate measure 16 ounces. The latter separates on standing, and must be shaken before use.

To prepare the liqueur, use

Extract	75 ml	2½ oz
Alcohol, deodorized	1.5 L	50 oz
Sugar	1.56 kg	52 oz
Distilled Water, to make	3.8 L	1 gal

Dissolve the Extract in the alcohol, the sugar in the water, mix the two solutions and filter clear.

To make a good liqueur, it is recommended to store the Extract for at least 2 years, and the liqueur for not less than 1 year.

Berlin Bitters

Cinchona powder	30 g		1 oz
Bitter orange peel	30 g		1 oz
Calamus powder	30 g		1 oz
Gentian powder	30 g		1 oz
Columbo powder	30 g		1 oz
Rhubarb powder		1½ tsp	
Cinnamon powder		¾ tsp	
Cloves, powder		1 tsp	
Alcohol, Water, to make	480 ml		16 oz

Mix the solids, and extract by slow percolation, with 70% alcohol.

To make the bitters, mix 1 ounce of this extract with 15 oz of 40% alcohol. To make Berline Wine Bitters, replace the alcohol and water with sweet catawba or sherry wine.

Bischof or Bishop Extract
(Tinctura Episcopalis)

Bitter Orange Peel	90 g	3 oz
Orange berries	45 g	1½ oz
Cassia bark	4 g	1 tsp
Cloves	4 g	1 tsp
Oil of Bitter Orange	drops 40	
Oil of Lemon	drops 10	
Alcohol, deodorized	480 ml	16 oz
Water, distilled	480 ml	16 oz

Reduce the solids to coarse powder, macerate with the alcohol and water for 8 days, then express. In the liquid obtained, dissolve the two oils and filter clear if necessary. Curacao orange peel should be preferred for the above.

Bischof Liqueur may be prepared by adding 15 ml (½ oz) of extract and 75 g (2½ oz) of sugar to a bottle of red wine.

The beverage Cardinal Liqueur may be prepared by adding 20 drops of this Extract and 45 g (1½ oz) of sugar to a bottle of white wine.

Blackberry, Elixir of

Blackberry Root	30 g	1 oz
Galls	30 g	1 oz
Cinnamon Saigon	30 g	1 oz
Cloves	15 g	½ oz
Mace	15 g	½ oz
Ginger	15 g	½ oz
Blackberry Juice	720 ml	18 ozs
Simple Syrup	720 ml	18 ozs
Brandy 40%	480 ml	16 oz

Reduce the solids to a moderately coarse powder and moisten it with good brandy. Percolate it with the alcohol until one pint of extract is obtained. To this add the blackberry juice and simple syrup, mix thoroughly.

Other flavours can also be used, such as vanilla extract, orange oil, etc. The brandy can also be replaced with whisky, preferably not scotch.

If the colour of the mixture is not dark enough it may be tinctured with sufficient caramel.

Boker's Bitters

A concentrated preparation, or Boker's Bitters Extract, may be made as follows:

Bitter orange peel	45 g	1½ oz
Quassia	30 g	1 oz
Calamus	30 g	1 oz
Catechu	15 g	½ oz
Cardamom	10 g	⅓ oz
Alcohol 90%	300 ml	10 oz
Water	180 ml	6 oz

Mix the solids, reduce to fine powder, and extract by slow percolation with a mixture of the alcohol and water.

To prepare the bitters, mix 30 ml (1 oz) of this extract with 540 ml (18 oz) of water and 360 ml (12 oz) of alcohol.

Boonekamp's Bitters

Orange berries	150 g	5 oz
Gentian	90 g	3 oz
Bitter orange peel	45 g	1½ oz
Cascarilla	45 g	1½ oz
Cinnamon bark	40 g	1¼ oz
Turmeric	22 g	¾ oz
Cloves	22 g	¾ oz
Rhubarb	10 g	⅓ oz
Wormwood	10 g	⅓ oz
Saffron	4 g	⅛ oz
Oil of anise	1 tsp	
Sugar	360 g	12 oz
Alcohol 30%	3.8 L	1 gal

Reduce the solids to a coarse powder, mix all the ingredients and macerate for 7 days, agitating occasionally. Filter and bottle.

Carmelite Spirit
(Karmeliter Geist.)

Oil of Bitter Orange	drops 15
Oil of Melissa	drops 6
Oil of coriander	drops 6
Oil of lemon,	drops 8
Oil of mace.	drops 3
Sugar	360 g	12 oz
Alcohol 90%	1.9 L	½ gal
Distilled Water, to make	3.8 L	1 gal

Dissolve the oils in the alcohol, the sugar in the water, mix the two liquids, and filter.

Chypre, Eau de

Oil of Lemon, fresh	3 drops
Oil of Bergamot	2 drops
Oil of Cassia	1 drop
Oil of Neroli, petal	1 drop
Ambergris, 10%	1 drop
Alcohol 90%	480 ml	16 oz
Simple Syrup	1 L	32 oz

Dissolve in alcohol and let stand for 7 days. Combine with simple syrup and bottle.

Cinchona Elixir

Calisaya Bark	240 g	8 oz
Sweet Orange Peel	240 g	8 oz
Cinnamon Bark	60 g	2 oz
Vanilla Bean	45 g	1½ oz
Cardamom Seeds	30 g	1 oz
Cloves	15 g	½ oz
Nutmeg	15 g	½ oz
Sugar	1100 g	2½ lbs
Alcohol 90%	1.1 L	38 oz
Water, to make	3.8 L	1 gal

Grind the calisaya, cinnamon, cloves, cardamom and nutmeg to a course powder. Mix one pint of alcohol with 8 oz of water. Moisten the powder with ½ a pint of the alcohol-water mixture and macerate for 48 hours. Strain and reserve the liquid and solids. Transfer the solids to a percolator, pack firmly, and pour the remain alcohol-water mixture on it. Cork and set aside for another 48 hours before percolating.

Finely chop the orange peel and vanilla and put them in a vessel with the remainder of the alcohol (22oz). Macerate for 48 to 72 hours. Strain and reserve both the solids and liquid.

Begin percolating the solids from step 1, adding water to the solids once liquid has disappeared from the surface of the percolator. Continue adding water until 4 pints has passed through. Filter the liquid through a muslin strainer.

Empty the percolator and place the vanilla and orange peel into it. Pour the calisaya percolate through and add water until 4 pints have passed. Combine all the extracts and dissolve the sugar, without heat. Add water and bottle.

Clove Cordial

Oil of Cloves	30 drops	
Oil of Cinnamon (true)	6 drops	
Oil of Mace	3 drops	
Sugar	720 g	24 oz
Alcohol	1.5 L	50 oz

Dissolve the oils in the alcohol, the sugar in the water, mix the two solutions and add water to make 4L (1 gallon). Colour with caramel.

Coca, Elixir of

Fluid Extract of Coca	60 ml	2 oz
Simple elixir	420 ml	14 oz
Alcohol 90%	15 ml	½ oz
Magnesium Carbonate, a sufficient quantity		

Mix the coca in a mortar with magnesium carbonate to form a cream. Add the Simple Elixir, stirring well, and filter. Lastly, add the alcohol.

Coffee Ratafia

Ground Coffee	330 g	11 oz
Alcohol 90%	2 L	2 qt
Sugar	900 g	2 lb

Macerate the coffee with the alcohol for 7 days, agitating occasionaly. Strain and filter then mix the sugar with water and mix the two liquids. Dilute with water to make 4 L (1 gallon).

Columbat, Elixir

Oil of Juniper	12 drops	
Oil of Lemon	9 drops	
Oil of Angelica	6 drops	
Oil of Cassia	6 drops	
Sugar	720 g	24 oz
Alcohol 90%	1.7 L	56 oz

Dissolve the oils in the alcohol, the sugar in water and mix the solutions, add water to make 4L (1 gallon). Colour a rose tint and filter clear.

Cordiale, Eau

Oil of Lemon	15 drops	
Oil of Sweet Fennel	6 drops	
Oil of Cardamom	6 drops	
Oil of Cloves	3 drops	
Sugar	840 g	28 oz
Alcohol	1.7 L	56 oz

Dissolve the oils in the alcohol and sugar in the water, add water to make 4 L (1 gallon). Combine the solutions and filter.

Daffy's Elixir
(Elixir Of Health)

Senna	120 g	4 oz
Guaiac wood	60 g	2 oz
Elecampane root,	60 g	2 oz
Anise seed	60 g	2 oz
Caraway seed	60 g	2 oz
Coriander seed	60 g	2 oz
Licorice root	60 g	2 oz
Raisins	240 g	8 oz
Alcohol 40%	3 L	2 qt

Reduce the drugs to a coarse powder, and mix them with the diluted alcohol. Add the raisins, chopped fine, to the mixture and macerate 14 days, shaking daily; then filter and bottle.

Damiana Bitters

Damiana	30 g	1 oz
Angostura	15 g	½ oz
Bitter orange peel	15 g	½ oz
Canada snake root	15 g	½ oz
Lemon peel	7.5 g	¼ oz
Cardamom	3.9 g	1 tsp
Cloves	3.9 g	1 tsp
Coriander	1.9 g	½ tsp

Grind the spices and extract by percolation with a mixture of 10 oz alcohol and 6 oz of water.

Dandelion, Elixir Of
(Compound Elixir Of Taraxacum)

Dandelion Extract	30 ml	1 oz
Wild-Cherry Bark Extract	30 ml	1 oz
Gentian Extract	1 tsp	
Bitter Orange Peel Extract	2 tsp	
Cinnamon Extract	1 tsp	
Licorice Extract	1 tsp	
Anise, powder	¼ tsp	
Caraway, powder	¼ tsp	
Coriander, powder	¼ tsp	
Simple Elixir	420 ml	14 oz
Magnesium Carbonate, a sufficient quantity		

Triturate the extracts and powdered drugs in a mortar with carbonate of magnesium in amount sufficient to form a creamy mixture, then gradually add the simple elixir, stirring well, and cover the mixture and permit it to macerate an hour, then filter it.

This elixir was devised by Prof. P. C. Candidus, of Mobile, and the formula was presented at the meeting of the American Pharmaceutical Association, 1869. Prof. Candidus stated that this elixir completely masks the bitter taste of sulphate of quinine, and he recommended it as a vehicle for administering that substance. Since one of the ingredients is licorice (see Elixir of Glycyrrhizin), we may suppose that glycyrrhizin aids in overcoming the bitterness.

Fennel Aquavit

Oil of Fennel, sweet	15 drops	
Oil of Anise	6 drops	
Oil of Caraway	3 drops	
Oil of Coriander	3 drops	
Sugar	360 g	12 oz
Alcohol 90%	1.8 L	60 oz

Dissolve the oils in the alcohol, the sugar in the water, mix the two solutions and add water to make 4L (1 gallon).

Gentian, Elixir of

Extract of Gentian	1¼ tsp	
Aromatic Spirit	2½ tsp	
Vanilla Extract	2 tsp	
Simple Syrup	30 ml	1 oz
Aromatic Elixir, to make	480 ml	16 oz

Dissolve the Extract of Gentian in 2 oz of Aromatic Elixir then add the simple syrup, Aromatic Spirit, vanilla and enough Aromatic Elixir to make 16 oz. Filter if necessary. Use one teaspoon per drink.

Glyoyrrhiza, Elixir of
(Aromatic Elixir of Liquorice)

Glycyrrhiza Extract	60 ml	2 oz
Oil of Cloves	6 drops	
Oil of Cinnamon Ceylon	6 drops	
Oil of Nutmeg	4 drops	
Oil of Fennel	12 drops	
Purified Talcum	1½ tbsp	
Aromatic Elixir, to make	480 ml	16 oz

Mix the oils with the purified talcum powder. Add the Glycyrrhiza extract and 14 oz of Aromatic Elixir. Filter and add enough Aromatic Elixir to make sixteen 16 ounces.

Greek Bitters

Lemon Oil	80 drops	
Wormwood Oil	48 drops	
Angelica Oil	40 drops	
Calamus Oil	40 drops	
Mace Oil	24 drops	
Clove Oil	24 drops	
Bitter Almond Oil	24 drops	
Cardamon Oil	12 drops	
Sugar	3 kg	6½ lbs
Water	6 L	1½ gal
Alcohol 90%	7 L	1¾ gal

Mix the oils in the alcohol and dissolve the sugar in the water. Mix, and colour brown.

Guarana, Elixir of

Fluid Extract of Guarana	90 ml	3 oz
Aromatic Elixir	90 ml	3 oz
Compound Elixir of Taraxacum	300 ml	10 oz

Mix and allow to stand for forty eight hours, filter and bottle.

Hamburg Bitters

Cinnamon	15 ml	½ oz
Cassia buds	15 ml	½ oz
Quassia	10 g	⅓ oz
Gentian	10 g	⅓ oz
Bitter orange peel	10 g	⅓ oz
Agaric	6.5 g	1¼ tsp
Cardamom	3 g	¾ tsp
Grains of paradise	2 g	½ tsp
Acetic ether*	8 ml	¼ oz
Diluted alcohol	3.8 L	1 gal

Grind the spices into a coarse powder, add to the liquids and macerate for 7 days, agitate occasionally, express and filter.

Hop Cordial

The following is a palatable preparation not inferior to the so-called Hop Bitters:

Hops	52 g	1¾ oz
Dandelion	52 g	1¾ oz
Gentian	52 g	1¾ oz
Chamomile	52 g	1¾ oz
Orange peel, sweet	52 g	1¾ oz
Alcohol, deodorized	1.6L	54 oz
Water, distilled	1.9 L	64 oz
Simple syrup	360 ml	12 oz

Reduce the solids to coarse powder, percolate slowly with the mixture of alcohol and water. Once the liquid is obtained filter if required and add the cold simple syrup.

Juniper Liqueur

Oil of juniper		48 drops
Oil of Coriander		3 drops
Sugar	660 g	22 oz
Alcohol	1.7 L	56 oz
Distilled Water, to make	3.8 L	1 gal

Dissolve the oil in the alcohol, the sugar in the water, mix the two solutions and filter clear.

Kola Liqueur

Kola nuts, roasted	100 ml	3½ oz
Vanilla extract	45 ml	1½ oz
Arrack, true	45 ml	1½ oz
Sugar	1.7 kg	56 oz
Cochineal powder	1 g	¼ tsp
Alcohol	1.44 L	48 oz
Water	1.44 L	48 oz

Macerate the kola and cochineal with the alcohol for 7 days, agitate occasionally. Strain, add the arrack, vanilla and the sugar dissolved in the water, filter clear and bottle.

Krambambuli Liqueur
(Magdebtirg)

Oil of Lemon		drops 9
Oil of Lavender		drops 6
Oil of Melissa		drops 3
Oil of Mace		drops 3
Oil of Wormwood		drops 3
Oil of Cubeb		drops 3
Oil of Sage		drops 3
Oil of Sweet marjoram		drops 3
Oil of Cardamom		drops 3
Sugar	720 g	24 oz
Alcohol (90%)	1.9 L	½ gal
Water, to make	3.8 L	1 gal

Dissolve the oils in the alcohol, the sugar in the water, mix the two solutions, colour red with black cherry juice and filter clear.

Lavender, Compound Tincture

Oil of Lavender	6ml	1½ tsp
Oil of Rosemary	10 drops	
Cinnamon	10 g	⅓ oz
Nutmeg	10 g	⅓ oz
Red Sanders	20 g	⅔ oz
Alcohol 90%	1 L	1 qt

Macerate the cinnamon, nutmeg and red sanders in the spirit for 7 days. Strain and add the oils. Use ½ to 1 teaspoon per 8 ounce glass.

Leroy's Vomito-Purgative Elixir

Fluid Extract of Senna	45 ml	1½ oz
Tartar Emetic	¼ tsp	
White Wine	480 ml	16 oz

Mix the senna in a mortar with magnesium carbonate to form a cream, add the wine, stir, and filter. Dissolve the tartar emetic in the filtrate.

Malt Bitters

Sweet orange peel	60 g	2 oz
Bitter orange peel	60 g	2 oz
Red cinchona	30 g	1 oz
Angostura bark	30 g	1 oz
Cardamom	30 g	1 oz
Cinnamon bark	30 g	1 oz
Cognac	1.4 L	1½ qt
Malt extract, liquid	1.4 L	1½ qt
Water	1.0 L	1 qt

Grind and and percolate the drugs with the cognac and water. Add the malt extract

Nutmeg Creme

Oil of Nutmeg	8 drops	
Sugar	540 g	18 oz
Alcohol 90%	510 ml	17 oz
Water, to make	1.0 L	1 qt

Dissolve the oils in the alcohol and the sugar in the water. Mix the two and colour red.

Oleo Balsamic Mixture
(Hoffmann's Balsam of Life)

Oil of Lavender		¼ tsp
Oil of Thyme		¼ tsp
Oil Of Lemon		¼ tsp
Oil of Mace		¼ tsp
Oil of Orange Flowers		¼ tsp
Oil of Cloves		¼ tsp
Oil of Cinnamon		¼ tsp
Balsam of Peru 80		¾ tsp
Alcohol 90%	450 ml	15 oz

Dissolve the oils and the Balsam of Peru in the alcohol and let the solution stand for a few days and then filter. Use ¼ to ½ teaspoon in a soda or glass of wine.

Orange Bitter, Elixir of

Orange Peel	105 g	3½ oz
Absinthium	30 g	1 oz
Menyanthes leaves	30 g	1 oz
Cascarilla	30 g	1 oz
Cinnamon Cassia	30 g	1 oz
Gentian	22 g	¾ oz
Carbonate of Potassium	5 g	1 tsp
Sherry Wine, to make	480 ml	16 oz

Mix the coarsely ground solids with potassium carbonate. Moisten with sherry and macerate for 24 hours. Place in a percolator and extract with the sherry until 16 oz are obtained.

Orange Bitters

Sweet Orange Zest	120 g	2 oz
Lemon Zest	60 g	1 oz
Gentian	60 g	1 oz
Cascarilla	60 g	1 oz
Alcohol 25%	2 L	2 qt

Macerate the solids in ½ of the alcohol for one week. Strain and reserve the liquid. Pack the solids into a percolator and pass the remaining alcohol through. Combine the liquids and bottle.

Paradise Water

Oil of Lemon	12 drops	
Oil of Angelica Root	6 drops	
Oil of Calamus	3 drops	
Oil of Aniseed	3 drops	
Oil of Cardamom	3 drops	
Oil of Coriander	3 drops	
Sugar	840 g	28 oz
Alcohol 90%	1.6 L	52 oz

Dissolve the oils in the alcohol, the sugar in water and mix the solutions, add water to make 4L (1 gallon). Colour a green and filter clear. Historically leaves of silver were added to the liqueur.

Peach Bitters (American)

Peach Kernels	90 g	3 oz
Angostura Bark	40 g	1⅓ oz
Pale Brandy (57%)	1.25 L	42 oz
Sugar	300 g	10 oz
Peach Juice	630 ml	21 oz

Grind the solids and macerate in the alcohol for 14 days. Boil and filter the peach juice and dissolve the sugar. Strain, express and filter the alcohol extract and combine the liquids.

Peruvian Bitters
(Calisaya or Cinchona Bitters)

Cinchona bark	240 g	8 oz
Bitter orange peel	60 g	2 oz
Cinnamon bark	15 g	½ oz
Galangal		1 tsp
Cloves		1 tsp
Vanilla		1 tsp
Alcohol 70%	480 ml	16 oz

Extract by slow percolation with alcohol. To make the bitters, mix 1 part of this extract with 6 parts of alcohol and 9 parts of water.

Spanish Bitters

Orris root	30 g	1 oz
Calamus	30 g	1 oz
Polypody	15 g	½ oz
Bitter orange peel	15 g	½ oz
German chamomile	7.5 g	¼ oz
Coriander	7.5 g	¼ oz
Centaury	4 g	1 tsp
Alcohol	300 ml	10 oz
Water,	180 ml	6 oz

Extract by percolation with a mixture of alcohol and water. To prepare the bitters, mix 1 part of extract with 6 parts of alcohol and 9 parts of water.

Stomach Elixir

Tormentilla Root	30 ml	1 oz
Pimpinella Root	30 ml	1 oz
Oil of Peppermint	drops 12	
Oil of Wormwood	drops 4	
Simple Syrup	120 ml	4 oz
Alcohol 90%	840 ml	28 oz

Mix the first three ingredients, reduce to coarse powder, extract by percolation with alcohol to obtain 750 ml (25 oz) of liquid; to the latter add the oils dissolved in 90 ml (3 oz) of alcohol, and the syrup; colour brown and, if necessary, filter.

Stoughton Bitters
Codex Medicamentarius of 1818 - Tinctura Amara

Wormwood	90 g	3 oz
Bitter orange peel	90 g	3 oz
Gentian	90 g	3 oz
Rhubarb	60 g	2 oz
Cascarilla	15 g	½ oz
Aloes, socotrine	15 g	½ oz
Diluted alcohol	3.8 L	1 gal

Reduce the solids to powder and extract with the liquid, either by maceration or percolation.

Swedish Bitters
(Elixir of Long Life)

Aloes	6 g	1½ tsp
Agaric	6 g	1½ tsp
Rhubarb	6 g	1½ tsp
Gentian	6 g	1½ tsp
Zedoary	6 g	1½ tsp
Galangal	6 g	1½ tsp
Ginger	6 g	1½ tsp
Myrrh	6 g	1½ tsp
Saffron	6 g	1½ tsp
Theriac	12 g	3 tsp
Sugar	90 g	3 oz
Dilute Alcohol, to make	1 L	1 qt

Mix the first nine powdered ingredients, extract by percolation with the diluted alcohol to obtain 840 ml (28 oz) of product; to the latter add the sugar and theriac previously well mixed, agitate occasionally until the sugar is dissolved, and filter.

A simple alternate recipe:

Tincture of Gentian	1½ oz
Tincture of Aloes & Myrrh	3 oz
Tincture of Rhubarb	3 oz
Alcohol 60%	7½ oz

Swiss Alpine Bitters
Concentrated Preparation

Wild Cherry Bark	30 g	1 oz
Cinchona Bark	30 g	1 oz
Bitter Orange Peel	15 g	½ oz
Sweet Orange Peel	15 g	½ oz
Cardamom	7.5 g	¼ oz
Caraway	7.5 g	¼ oz
Cinnamon	3.25 g	¾ tsp
Cloves	3.25 g	¾ tsp
Nutmeg	3.25 g	¾ tsp
Alcohol, 75%	480 ml	16 oz

Grind the solids, and extract by percolation with alcohol. The bitters may be prepared by mixing 30 ml (1 oz) of the extract with 450 ml (15 oz) of 40% alcohol.

Union Bitters

Gentian	120 g	4 oz
Peruvian Bark	60 g	2 oz
Roman Chamomile	30 g	1 oz
Quassia Bark	15 g	½ oz
Orange Peel	15 g	½ oz
Alcohol 50%	4 L	1 gal

Reduce the ingredients to a course powder. Macerate in alcohol for 14 days, express and filter.

Vermouth

Oil of Wormwood		24 drops
Oil of Calamus		6 drops
Oil of Cinnamon		1 drop
Oil of Cloves		1 drop
Sugar	700 g	24 oz
Alcohol 90%	1.7 L	56 oz
Water, to make	3.8 L	1 gal

Dissolve the oils and spirit in the alcohol, the sugar in the water, mix, colour green with chlorophyll or tincture of grass, and filter clear.

This recipe is sometimes prepared with only oil of Wormwood, which is increased to 30 drops.

Vermouth II
(Wormwood Liqueur)

Oil of Wormwood		drops 6
Oil of Angelica Root		drops 2
Oil of Galanga		drops 2
Oil of Bitter Almonds		drops 2
Spirit of Nitrous Ether	6 ml	1½ tsp
Alcohol, deodorized	1.8 L	60 oz
Water, distilled	1.5 L	50 oz
Sugar	900 g	2 lbs

Dissolve the oils and spirit in the alcohol, the sugar in the water, mix, colour green with chlorophyll or tincture of grass, and filter clear.

Walnut Brandy

Vanilla	0.5 g	⅛ tsp
Aniseed	1 g	¼ tsp
German chamomile	2 g	½ tsp
Cloves	5 g	1¼ tsp
Cardamom	5 g	1¼ tsp
Cinnamon	5 g	1¼ tsp
Calamus	8 g	2 tsp
Linden, flowers	8 g	2 tsp
Sweet orange peel	12 g	3 tsp
Lemon peel	12 g	3 tsp
Coriander	12 g	3 tsp
Cognac, best	60 ml	2 oz
Rum, Jamaica	60 ml	2 oz
Alcohol	810 ml	27 oz
Water	810 ml	27 oz
Walnuts, dried	150 g	5 oz

The walnuts used for the above should be collected before the outer peel has hardened, and through which a pin or needle can be pass easily. Dry in a cool, ventilated, location until they have turned a dark, almost black, in colour. Crushed them and add the remaining coarsely ground solids and liquids. Macerate for 8 weeks, agitating occasionally; strain and filter.

Wild Cherry Bitters

Wild cherry bark	300 g	10 oz
Mitchella	75 g	2½ oz
Juniper Berries	30 g	1 oz
Prickly Ash Bark	15 g	½ oz
Sugar	600 g	20 oz
Alcohol 40%	3.4 L	7 pints

Mix the first four coarsely ground ingredients and extract by maceration with the alcohol for one week. Strain and dissolve the sugar.

Wild Cherry Bitters II

Wild cherry bark	300 g	10 oz
Sweet orange peel	60 g	2 oz
Cinchona	45 g	1½ oz
Cardamom	30 g	1 oz
Hazelwort	15 g	½ oz
Diluted alcohol	3.0 L	3 qt
Honey	600 ml	20 oz
Simple syrup	480 ml	16 oz
Water, to make	3.8 L	1 gal

Reduce the solids to coarse powder, extract with the diluted alcohol by maceration or percolation, add the remaining liquids, and filter.

Wormwood Bitters

Orange berries	75 g	2½ oz
Gentian	45 g	1½ oz
Wormwood	22 g	¾ oz
Cinnamon	15 g	½ oz
Galangal	10 g	2½ tsp
Ginger	10 g	2½ tsp
Angelica root	6 g	1½ tsp
Cloves	3 g	¾ tsp
Oil of cinnamon		30 drops
Oil of lemon		25 drops
Oil of anise		20 drops
Whiskey or diluted alcohol	3.8 L	1 gal

Mix the solids, reduce to coarse powder, mix the whole, macerate for 7 days, agitating occasionally, express and filter clear.

Wormwood Creme

Oil of Wormwood		24 drops
Oil of Cassia		8 drops
Oil of Cloves		8 drops
Sugar	1350 g	3 lb
Alcohol 90%	1.7 L	56 oz

Dissolve the oil in the alchol and mix the sugar with some water. Combine the two liquids and dilute with water to make 4 L (1 gallon). Colour green. Filter if required.

Art of Drink
www.artofdrink.com

Bibliography

1. The Standard Manual of Soda and Other Beverages (1897)
   by Emil Hiss

2. Saxe's new guide, or, Hints to soda water dispensers (1895)
   by De Forest Saxe

3. Uncle Sam's water wagon; 500 recipes for delicious drinks (1919)
   by Helen Watkeys Moore

4. Elixirs And Flavoring Extracts. Their History, Formulae, & Preparation (1892)
   by John Uri Lloyd

5. A Treatise on Beverages, or, The Complete Practical Bottler. (1888)
   by Charles H. Sulz

6. Unofficial Pharmacopoeia Comprising Over 700 Popular Preparations (1881)
   by P. Blakiston, 1881

7. A Compendium of Modern Pharmacy and Druggists' Formulary (1886)
   by Walter B. Kilner

8. Beverages and their Adulteration (1919)
   by Harvey W. Wiley

9. What to Drink; the Blue Book of Beverages (1920)
   by Bertha Edson Lay

10. The Dispenser's Formulary (1930)
    Published by Federated Business Publications

11. Soda fountain beverages : a practical receipt book (1917)
    Dubelle, G. H. (George H.)

12. Practical guide to candy-making and soda dispensing
    Mackie Brothers

Recipes

Index

CPSIA information can be obtained at www.ICGtesting.com
Printed in the USA
BVOW08s2012100515

399658BV00022B/254/P